COMPOSING AMB
THE EARLY MUSIC OF MO

Dedicated respectfully to all my inspiring students, past, present and future.

With thanks.

Composing Ambiguity:
The Early Music of
Morton Feldman

ALISTAIR NOBLE
Australian National University, Australia

Routledge
Taylor & Francis Group

LONDON AND NEW YORK

First Published 2013 by Ashgate Publisher

Published 2016 by Routledge
2 Park Square, Milton Park, Abingdon, Oxfordshire OX14 4RN
711 Third Avenue, New York, NY 10017, USA

First issued in paperback 2016

Routledge is an imprint of the Taylor & Francis Group, an informa business

British Library Cataloguing in Publication Data
A catalogue record for this book is available from the British Library

The Library of Congress has cataloged the printed edition as follows:
Noble, Alistair.
 Composing ambiguity : the early music of Morton Feldman / by Alistair Noble.
   p. cm.
 Includes bibliographical references and index.
 ISBN 978-1-4094-5164-8 (hardcover) 1. Feldman,
Morton, 1926-1987--Criticism and interpretation. 2. Composition (Music) I. Title.
 ML410.F2957N63 2013
 780.92--dc23

                                                                    2012035941

ISBN 13: 978-1-138-27053-4 (pbk)
ISBN 13: 978-1-4094-5164-8 (hbk)

Contents

See asterisks for follow up in bibliography

List of Figures and Tables

Figures

Tables

Acknowledgements

Colleagues at The Australian National University have been encouraging and supportive in so many ways, both personally and professionally. Their generosity with time, expertise and advice is much appreciated. Among those who have given crucial assistance at various times are Professor Sasha Grishin, Professor Adam Shoemaker, Professor Larry Sitsky, Deborah Crisp, Dr Bradley Cummings, Dr Kate Bowan, Professor Toni Makkai, Professor Joan Beaumont, Associate Professor Kylie Message, Dr Carolyn Strange, Dr Ruth Lee Martin, Jim Cotter, Carol Lilley, Professor Penny Oakes, Professor John Warhurst, Dr Ann Moffatt, Dr Kevin White, Dr Stephen Wild, Allan Walker, Marguerite Boland, Dr Jennifer Gall, Dr Rani Olafsdottir and Dr Amy Chan.

Very many other people have kindly given advice at crucial moments, or asked pertinent questions. Among these, I must mention Dore Ashton, Jan Williams, Christian Wolff, Dr Felix Meyer, Professor Keith Potter, Professor Anne Shreffler, Professor Christoph Neidhöfer, Professor Gianmario Borio, Dr Tom Hall, Dr Brett Boutwell and Dr Jennifer Iverson.

All the editorial staff at Ashgate have been so kind and helpful. Heartfelt thanks to Laura Macy and Aimée Feenan for generous encouragement and assistance in realising this project.

Archival materials have been an essential part of this research, and many people at the following institutions have been extraordinarily generous with professional expertise and time, and in facilitating access to materials:

- Paul Sacher Foundation, Basel, Switzerland;
- Music Library, SUNY Buffalo, USA;
- The Getty Research Institute, Los Angeles, USA.

Musical examples are reproduced with the permission of the publishers, C.F. Peters, and for his kind assistance I thank Mr Gene Caprioglio of their New York office. Manuscript materials are reproduced with the permission of the Paul Sacher Foundation, Basel.

The project was initially supported by an Australian Postgraduate Research Award stipend. Archival research and attendance at international conferences has been made possible by grants from The Australian National University, including a Vice-Chancellor's travel grant in 2007 and a research stipend awarded by the Paul Sacher Foundation in 2008. Of crucial importance to the research were several visits to the Paul Sacher Foundation, Basel. I am especially grateful to Dr Felix Meyer and all the staff of the Foundation for their expert assistance and encouragement, and for allowing generous access to the unique manuscript materials held in the Morton Feldman Collection.

Some of the material of Chapter 2 was explored in 'Music as Trans-site: The Strange Case of Morton Feldman's *Intermission 5*', a paper presented at *Transitions: 18th International Congress of the International Musicological Society*, Universität Zürich Musikwissenschaftliches Institut, July 2007. I discussed certain implications of the deleted section of *Piano Piece 1952* (Chapter 3) in 'Morton Feldman's other Piano Piece 1952: Positioning a Recent Manuscript Discovery', a paper presented at *Music as Local Tradition and Regional Practice: Twenty-Ninth National Conference of the Musicological Society of Australia*, The University of New England, Armidale, September 2006. The analysis of *Intermission 6* was tested as 'Morton Feldman's "Line of Becoming": Action and Improvisation in *Intermission 6*', a paper presented at the *5th Biennial International Conference on Music Since 1900*, University of York, July 2007. I am grateful to Dr Carolyn Strange and Professor John Docker for the invitation to present a paper in which I discussed Feldman's two-dimensional model: 'Morton Feldman's Picture Plane', at the *Research School of Humanities Friday Forum*, The Australian National University, 5 October 2007. The research that ultimately became Chapter 5 was first presented as 'Primitive Designs: Hearing/Analysing Morton Feldman's Graphic Scores' at *Seventh International Conference on Music Since 1900/Music Analysis Conference*, Lancaster Institute for the Contemporary Arts, Lancaster University, 28–31 July 2011.

Family and friends have given invaluable advice, encouragement and 'perspective' – and generously managed to put up with me for the past several years: much love and thanks especially to my parents, Peter, Colin, Francesca, Isabelle, Georgia, Kiko, Andrew, Weng, Sue, Catherine and Malcolm, Bronwyn and John, Nonie and Tim, Edwina and Craufurd, the Hoffmann family, Lars and Austin.

Chapter 1
Listening to Process, Playing the System

Playing Feldman's music was the beginning of the journey that finds a way station in this book. In the experience of performing his music, I found that what actually happened often took me by surprise; things that seemed uncontrolled turned out not to be, points of significance and structural importance suddenly became explicit in unexpected ways. I always came away with an overpowering feeling of the music as carefully planned, designed and constructed. I could not sense chance-derived material or structure, any randomness, not even much in the way of meditative quietness. Rather, the music felt tense and intense, compelling and uncompromising, beautiful but difficult; and this seemed to play out further in the surprisingly polarised reactions of audiences. I set out, then, to try to solve these puzzles for myself. Along the way, I quickly found that I was far from alone in wondering about Feldman's music.

The music of this New York-born composer has increased in significance during recent years, if numbers of performances, recordings, magazine articles and reviews are anything to go by. A survey of commercial recordings devoted entirely to Feldman's work illustrates this trend clearly: between 1960 and 1992 (a period of 32 years) there were only 16 albums of Feldman's work released; for the subsequent eight-year period, 1992–99, there were 34, while between 2000 and 2007, there were 41.[1] Similarly, the recent rise of online fan sites, blogs and discussions serves to document the rise of Feldman's global cult. Yet strangely, as Dora Hanninen has pointed out, the scholarly literature seems not to have kept pace with this expanding audience: 'Now, more than fifteen years after Feldman's death, one might well ask why theorists and analysts haven't produced more work on Feldman's music'.[2]

Part of the difficulty is that, while Feldman's music is often described as delicate, quiet, passive and gently intuitive,[3] it is also, in some circumstances, irritating, discomfiting, or even profoundly disturbing. Questioned about the increasing popularity of Feldman's music in the mid-1990s, Christian Wolff admitted to a degree of bemusement: 'I don't know what that means. Let's face

---

[1] For a comprehensive and regularly updated discography, refer to Chris Villars, 'Morton Feldman Discography', http://www.cnvill.net/mfdiscog.htm.

[2] Dora Hanninen, 'Feldman, Analysis, Experience', *Twentieth-century Music*, 1/2 (2004), 226.

[3] See, for example, Amy Beal, '"Time Canvases": Morton Feldman and the Painters of the New York School', in James Leggio (ed.), *Music and Modern Art* (Abingdon: Routledge, 2001), 231, 236.

it, it's an esoteric music. There's no way you're going to get a big audience for it, especially those last pieces. It's a very rarefied kind of experience'.[4] In any case, we should take care not to essentialise the character of this music, or approach it with too many easy assumptions. Catherine Hirata has expressed this eloquently:

> Why analyse the music of Morton Feldman? We might answer this question by pointing to the reasons we analyse any music. We want to develop our sensitivity to particular ways of hearing – so that we might even begin to hear more than we've ever heard before, and so that we might begin to understand what we're hearing in a way that we hadn't before.[5]

Certainly, there is much beauty in Feldman's work, expressed and apprehended on a number of levels, but there may also be a sense of loss, of ambiguity, a certain tension, and a sense of frustration or even anger concealed. Hirata, again, has written candidly of *For Frank O'Hara*, a 1970s work, 'It is easy to imagine someone not liking *For Frank O'Hara* very much. For, in some ways, its ambivalence is frustrating'.[6] Concert audiences have always been divided over Feldman's work. The art critic Dore Ashton (a long-standing friend of Feldman's) observed of a 1964 concert featuring Feldman's *Out of 'Last Pieces'*, 'everything seemed familiar to me even as half the audience noisily decamped'.[7]

In the face of this significant ambiguity, we may wonder, how is this music made? How does it work? Why was it made that way? What purpose did it, or does it, serve? As the small scholarly literature makes clear, there are no easy or obvious answers to these questions, and indeed the wider context of Feldman's work is at least as complex as the work itself. Feldman's work is informed, for example, by his sense of Jewishness (no simple thing to unravel), and in this sense we may appreciate that he belongs to that group of late-twentieth-century composers who may be powerfully described as post-Holocaust. Similarly, he is a Cold War composer (his career almost exactly matching that of the Cold War period) – indeed, the works discussed in this book date from the early part of Feldman's career and coincide with the shift in American politics marked by the election of Eisenhower in 1952.

Given this general complexity, and our lack of certainty regarding almost every aspect of Feldman's music, my primary aim in this book is to investigate

---

[4]   David Patterson, 'Cage and Beyond: An Annotated Interview with Christian Wolff', *Perspectives of New Music*, 32/2 (Summer 1994), 73.

[5]   Catherine Hirata, *Analyzing the Music of Morton Feldman* (PhD Dissertation, Columbia University, 2003), 261.

[6]   Ibid., 162.

[7]   Dore Ashton, 'Stefan Wolpe – Man of Temperament', in Austin Clarkson (ed.), *On the Music of Stefan Wolpe: Essays and Recollections* (Hillsdale, NY: Pendragon Press, 2003), 99.

the design of Morton Feldman's music of the early 1950s with regard to the organised structuring of both pitch and time. The study is founded upon the analysis of four strikingly different works: *Intermission 5*, *Piano Piece 1952*, *Intermission 6* and *Intersection 3*. In the investigation of these works, I show that, despite their differences, they have much in common in terms of the ways in which pitch material is deployed, and in the organisation of time. Not all of the evidence for this organisation is explicit in the published scores, and in some cases it may have been purposefully hidden. Examination of the sketches and early manuscripts has provided vital clues to the organisational procedures, and clarified the properties of the structures themselves. In particular, the sketchbooks contain strong evidence for Feldman's development of a two-dimensional model of musical structure (a direct analogy to the painter's canvas) that has far-reaching implications for our understanding of his ideas and methods. The importance of the visual arts to Feldman has been much discussed, but here, I suggest, we have a confirmed model that enables more direct, formal comparison than has hitherto been possible.

Beyond the central empirical analysis, this study opens out around two areas of broader discussion. Firstly, it will contribute to the ongoing investigation of Feldman's relations to the visual arts field, helping us to move beyond superficial comparison to deeper structural analogy. Secondly, the analysis will assist in mapping Feldman's position within the field of musical production of his time and place, and in so doing lead to greater understanding of the structures of that field. Given that all analysis is reductive,[8] I am not pretending to achieve any complete study; rather, I simply aim to place a few solid foundation stones for future scholars in this field to build upon.

Feldman's Two-dimensional Canvas

Among the many pages of annotations in Feldman's sketchbooks dating from early 1952 are two closely related diagrams that are of crucial importance to an understanding of his conceptual modelling of music, and his compositional practice.[9] While these are discussed in closer detail in later chapters, they are extremely important to my analysis, and warrant introduction at the outset.

The earliest of these diagrams (see Figure 1.1), with associated text, has been dated by Sebastian Claren to 1952.[10] However, the context of its place in the

---

[8]   See the discussion of this point in Robert Walser, 'Popular Music Analysis: Ten Apothegms and Four Instances', in Allan F. Moore (ed.), *Analyzing Popular Music* (Cambridge: Cambridge University Press, 2003), 25.

[9]   Paul Sacher Foundation, Basel, Morton Feldman Collection.

[10]   Sebastian Claren, *Neither: Die Musik Morton Feldmans* (Hofheim: Wolke, 2000), 578.

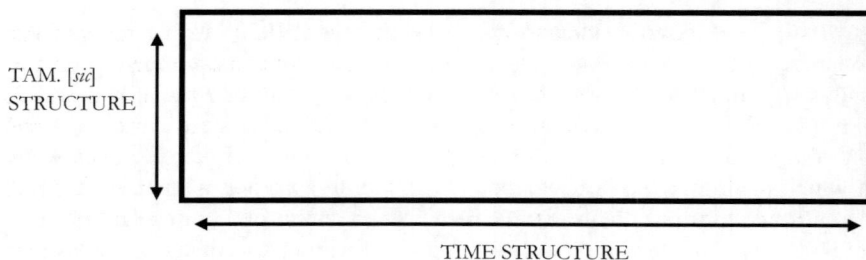

TAM. [*sic*]
STRUCTURE

TIME STRUCTURE

Figure 1.1   Diagram transcribed from Feldman's sketchbooks, *ca* 1950
Paul Sacher Foundation, Basel, Morton Feldman Collection. Used by permission.

sketchbooks (among sketches for the *Projection* series of 1950–51) suggests that it more likely dates from 1950 or 1951. The text begins with the heading 'Structure and the Structural Cell', and continues (with Feldman's characteristically flamboyant orthography), ꓶ

> STRUCTURE: If we think of music in terms of filling out a continuity, with pauses and places of rests, structure of any kind is then impossible. Structure can not be constructed in the linear fashion but must be seen in its entirety. One must then [work?] on the exact proportion. The time structure then makes it possible to create music as on a canvas or better yet not unlike the architect's four walls or the engineer's [bridge?] across a river. Structure then makes us ask what the basic materials are and what is unnecessary. Most important structure teaches us that these basic materials are in a state of complete equality. No matter how complicated a "flourish" seems to be. As we also deal with degradations of sound then immediately as we conceive a work we have also a tambre [*sic*] structure [the diagram transcribed as Figure 1.1 appears at this point in the text] I consider the basic material in a crystalized [*sic*] structural situation a purely sound experience [clothed?] by time. A sound experience divorced from harmony as well as counterpoint and melody. EX (few meas. From my *Structure 1*).[11]

It would seem that this fragmentary passage may be a sketch for either a talk or an essay, otherwise unknown. The piece referred to as *Structure 1* is unknown or lost, unless it is to be identified with the work now known as *Structures* for string quartet (traditionally dated to March 1951). It is clear that in this passage Feldman was tending to a conceptual model that is two-dimensional. This is made explicit in the diagram of timbre over time, which for Feldman is a theoretical canvas upon which he can construct musical structures in a non-linear fashion. At first glance

---

[11]   Paul Sacher Foundation, Basel, Morton Feldman Collection. In transcribing this text, I have indicated more-or-less illegible words with square brackets and question marks. I have included sentences that Feldman crossed out.

uninterestingly simple, even facile, this diagram in fact has profound implications: the model is a unified mechanism for apprehending and composing music in two dimensions, according to 'exact proportion'. Using this conceptual engine, it is evident that the composer may construct both vertical-timbral structures, and horizontal-time structures,[12] and that the flattened conceptual canvas necessarily _— it_ unifies the two. In his mind's eye, and perhaps also literally, this enabled Feldman _unifies_ to compose with the work laid out before him in its entirety, like a painting. (It is _representations_ probably no accident that Feldman's diagram is strikingly similar in proportions _of the 2_ to Jackson Pollock's large works of this period.) Crucially, this suggests an understanding of compositional structures that allows for more direct comparison with painterly structures than would otherwise be the case. If one allows that music has, for example, a third dimension of spatial depth, the direct structural comparison with painting or drawing becomes more difficult.

It should also be noted at this point that some of the terminology in this fragment resonates with echoes of the words of other composers known to Feldman at this time. In particular, the final sentence, with the phrase 'crystallized structural conception' has a strong affinity with Varèse's manner of speaking about music.[13] On the other hand, the idea of the materials of music (including silence) as existing in complete equality might well originate with Cage.[14] Despite these echoes, one senses that Feldman was, in this period of 1950–52, working to forge a conceptual model for his own music which, while touching upon and even inter-meshing with the models of his neighbours in the field at that time, nonetheless occupied its own productive space.

In another sketchbook, with material dating from late 1951 through to 1952, Feldman sketched a variant of this diagram in which the upper and lower limits of the timbre-axis were defined by the range of the piano. While Feldman's precise understanding of the term 'timbre' is not clearly defined, this demonstrates that it encompassed pitch and register. This second diagram is accompanied by a quantity of obscure text annotations, which may relate to the formulation of a graphic score, perhaps one of the *Intersection* pieces. In the midst of this text, however, one statement stands out with startling clarity: 'The happening in time is the reality. Space in music is an illusion'.

Is time in painting an illusion?

---

[12] There are perhaps two possible interpretations of Feldman's interesting distinction between pauses and rests: on the one hand this may indicate the difference between actual silence and resonating (sustained) sound; on the other, the distinction may perhaps be concerned with rests as measured, notated silence and pauses as relatively free (outside the measured space of time).

[13] See Edgard Varèse, 'Rhythm, Form, Content' [1959], in Elliott Schwartz and Barney Childs (eds), *Contemporary Composers on Contemporary Music* (New York: Holt, Rinehart and Winston, 1967), 203.

[14] See, for example, John Cage, 'Lecture on Nothing' [1949/50], in *Silence: Lectures and Writings by John Cage* (Middletown, CT: Wesleyan University Press, 1961), 109–10.

Is any form of musical notation concerned with this?

By the later part of 1951, then, it would seem that Feldman was working with a decisively two-dimensional model, and that he was concerned with the deployment of sound materials over elapsed time. While not discounting the affect of spatial depth entirely, he apparently did not identify it as a 'real' part of the compositional structure. Not only does this confirm a direct compatibility with the painter's canvas in general, it also implies (in the context of the New York art field of that time) a clear affinity with the formalist aesthetic and ideology of the flat picture plane.[15] Christian Wolff, who knew Feldman at this period, has given us one rare insight into Feldman's working practice in the early 1950s, which confirms this interpretation of the sketchbook annotations:

> Feldman used to work by putting his manuscripts up on the wall so that he could step back and look at them the way an artist looks at a picture. I'm not sure about this, but I have the feeling sometimes he might have thought of something to do "down here" and then go back "up here." It was really like a canvas rather than a linear, narrative structure.[16]

Most importantly, this insight into Feldman's thinking provides some clues for approaches to analysis. The two-dimensional model offers a theoretical basis for the analysis of the work and while, like any theoretical construct, this is not absolute or definitive, it is nonetheless tremendously helpful in constructing meaning. In terms of conventional analysis (if there can be said to be such a thing in the twenty-first century), Feldman's music does seem to offer few points of traction. However, this two-dimensional model offers a way for us to understand the deployment of musical materials in a conceptually non-linear space defined by the axes of timbre/pitch over time. Within this frame, we may begin to identify and describe the shapes, forms and structures that make up a work. Furthermore, such analysis need not exclude any of the varied sources, and is as useful for hearing a performance as it is for reading a score, thus providing (to some extent at least) a common matrix for dealing with otherwise problematically disparate materials.

Analysing Feldman

In a short essay originally written in 1988, Morton Feldman's colleague and friend Christian Wolff wrote of Feldman's *Piano Piece 1952*, 'What is there to say? The

---

[15]　See, for example, the discussion of Jackson Pollock in Clement Greenberg, '"American-Type" Painting' [1955], in Ellen Landau (ed.), *Reading Abstract Expressionism: Context and Critique* (New Haven, CT: Yale University Press, 2005), 205.

[16]　David Patterson, 'Cage and Beyond', 72.

music appears to be unanalyzable'.[17] Curiously, however, the essay continues with a perceptive analysis of certain explicit pitch-structures evident in the piece. Wolff's essay, I would suggest, is one of the most important pieces of writing on Feldman's early work in so far as it exemplifies the fundamental tensions and problems that have shaped the study of Feldman's music. Essentially the problem is this: there is a tradition of understanding Feldman's work as being unsystematic, unstructured and perhaps 'composed' by either intuitive or chance-driven methods, but this is not supported by strong evidence and seems to be contradicted by close examination of the work.

Wolff attempted to resolve this tension by suggesting that, while certain patterns and structures are patently evident in the work itself, they should not be connected to any intentionality on Feldman's part ('Strictly speaking, I'd say he had nothing in mind').[18] Recent analysis (by Steven Johnson, Thomas DeLio, Catherine Hirata and others) has shown that Feldman's music is indeed carefully organised, planned and designed, in ways that cannot be adequately explained as the product of intuitive or chance procedures. Christian Wolff's intuition that certain identifiable structures in *Piano Piece 1952* are significant has been shown to be correct (although we may no longer so easily discount Feldman's intentions). The four works discussed in this book are each saturated with evidence of highly structured design, planned in considerable detail by the composer. Furthermore, although Feldman was not a college or university-educated composer (as some of his peers were), he had spent the better part of a decade studying with two very skilled and highly regarded composers in turn: Wallingford Riegger and Stefan Wolpe. The complexity and technical sophistication of Feldman's works of the late 1940s (the *Illusions* for piano, for example) is such as to confound any notion of Feldman's naivety as a composer. Reading these pieces in 1950, even Pierre Boulez found them 'very finely developed'.[19]

Feldman himself was not afraid of analysis and openly acknowledged its usefulness. We may note, for example, that he spoke (in different contexts) of analysing Steve Reich's *Four Organs*,[20] and Wolpe's string quartet.[21] He did,

---

[17]   Christian Wolff, 'The Sound Doesn't Look Back (1995): On Morton Feldman's Piano Piece 1952', http://www.cnvill.net/mfwolff2.htm#wolff5. Originally published in Christian Wolff, *Cues: Writings and Conversations* (Köln: MusikTexte, 1998), 370–78.

[18]   Ibid.

[19]   Pierre Boulez, 'Letter from Pierre Boulez to John Cage: May 1950' in Jean-Jacques Nattiez and Robert Samuels (eds), *The Boulez–Cage Correspondence* (Cambridge: Cambridge University Press, 1993), 58.

[20]   Morton Feldman, 'Toronto Lecture: April 17th 1982', transcribed by Linda Catlin Smith, in Chris Villars (ed.), *Morton Feldman Says: Selected Interviews and Lectures 1964–1987* (London: Hyphen Press, 2006), 146–7.

[21]   Austin Clarkson, 'Conversation about Stefan Wolpe: 13 November 1980', in Chris Villars, *Morton Feldman Says*, 107.

however, sometimes speak of 'systems' negatively (although not consistently): 'In art, it is the system itself that holds out false promise, that deceives'.[22] Such statements seemed to encourage the popular belief that Feldman's music was composed un-systematically, and that the music cannot therefore be sensibly analysed. Feldman himself made little effort to discourage this romantic notion.

There are, however, a number of serious difficulties with the reasoning. Most importantly, we must take care not to conflate the term 'system' with process, method or technique. Feldman's music may not have had a clearly defined system, at least in the sense in which his generation of composers used the word (often as a euphemism for serialism, although Feldman seems usually to have had a broader definition in mind), but he certainly employed procedures, methods and techniques, however unconventional. A further problem is the confusion of composition with analysis. A work might conceivably have been composed without any known, identifiably conventional system of pitch or rhythmic organisation, but the analyst will nevertheless be able to identify forms and structures, or patterns and levels of organisation that are evidently present in the work.[23] The elucidation of these structures, regardless of how they were put together (com-posed) is one of the primary objectives of my analysis, although it is also possible to speculate, on the basis of the analysis, about the procedures employed in the composition process. Even a randomising method of composition depends entirely upon the generative procedures adopted by the composer, and Feldman himself was uncomfortable with such practice. In one of his earliest published writings, in 1958, he argued (in direct criticism of Cage's methods), 'Chance itself is the most academic procedure yet arrived at, for it defines itself as a technique immediately'.[24] Speculation about compositional procedure, however, need not necessarily be the purpose of analysis at all; compositional and analytical procedures are very different things, and they serve different ends.

Multi-layered ambiguity is a key characteristic of Feldman's music. As Mark Janello has observed, 'what happens is paradoxically both justified and uncalled for'.[25] From the relative distance of the twenty-first century, for example, it is not at all clear whether it is appropriate to understand Feldman's 1950s work as prefiguring post-modernism, or as a relic of the old, early-twentieth-century aesthetic of high modernism. These terms, of the modern and post-modern, are

---

[22]   Morton Feldman, 'Some Elementary Questions' in B.H. Friedman (ed.), *Give My Regards to Eighth Street: Collected Writings of Morton Feldman* (Cambridge, MA: Exact Change, 2000), 63–4.

[23]   In some situations, the reverse may also be true: certain types of compositional system are very difficult to reconstruct from the completed score unless clues are available concerning the nature of the system. This is one of the ways in sketches are often useful.

[24]   Morton Feldman, 'Sound, Noise, Varèse, Boulez' [1958], in B.H. Friedman (ed.), *Give My Regards to Eighth Street*, 1.

[25]   Mark Janello, *The Edge of Intelligibility: Late Works of Morton Feldman* (PhD Dissertation, University of Michigan, 2001), 40.

indeed problematic in themselves, and not at all solidly defined; I use them here in recognition of the ongoing discourse in musicology that is framed in these terms.[26] We may also note that Feldman sensed some such turning point, as evidenced by his 1967 essay 'After Modernism' – although his conclusions were, appropriately enough, ambiguous.[27]

For the most part neither tonal nor serial, Feldman's music inhabits a uniquely constructed space that Feldman (to some extent) encouraged others to believe was naively or even intuitively contrived – 'Boys, forgive me for speaking in broken music!', he once joked to a group of Princeton composers.[28] He very rarely commented upon technical aspects of compositional procedure, and then mostly in his later years.[29] Yet the more we examine the work itself, the more controlled it sounds. Even Feldman's much-discussed alternation between various forms of more-or-less conventional and graphic notations seems, in hindsight, to enact a coherent dialectic concerning the parameters of freedom and control of musical material. This is not only a personal dialectic – it is also one closely related to explicit and implicit tensions in post-war New York and the field of cultural production at large.

Questions

May one wonder, in the twenty-first century, what Feldman's music means, or meant? What might it tell us about the world in which he lived and worked? What does it tell us, as musicians, musicologists and composers, about how we came to be as we are? After all, any historicised investigation is implicitly concerned with our own present, and all analysis is inevitably historicised. In this area, our view is as yet obscured by the fact that we know so little about the music itself and how it was made, how it is structured. At this point it is useful to frame the over-arching aims of this book as questions: if Feldman had no explicit 'system', how then is the work made in terms of pitch deployment and the architecture of time? To take this a step further, we may ask: what are the compositional methods and procedures that may be deduced from the available source materials? What are the

---

[26] Debate and discussion on this issue is very much alive in the early twenty-first century. See, for example, the 17 essays by leading scholars in Karol Berger and Anthony Newcomb (eds), *Music and the Aesthetics of Modernity: Essays* (Cambridge, MA: Harvard University Press, 2005).

[27] Morton Feldman, 'After Modernism' [1967] in B.H. Friedman (ed.), *Give My Regards to Eighth Street*, 67–79.

[28] Morton Feldman, 'The Future of Local Music' [1984] in ibid., 161.

[29] For example, Cole Gagne and Tracy Caras, 'Soundpieces Interview', in Chris Villars (ed.), *Morton Feldman Says*, 87–96; and Morton Feldman, 'The Future of Local Music' [1984], in B.H. Friedman (ed.), *Give My Regards to Eighth Street*, 157–95.

implications of these methods and procedures for our understanding of Feldman's thinking and his work?

In seeking to develop answers to these closely inter-related questions, I have resisted the temptation to make a generalist study, a grand overview. There are two reasons for this: firstly, I would argue that Feldman-studies generally have not quite progressed to the point where a useful comprehensive study is possible; and, secondly, if one attempts to address the full range of source materials in some depth (sketches, scores, contextual documents and so forth), the subject is simply too vast for a single book. Instead, I seek to combat certain generalist fallacies (e.g. that Feldman's music is all quiet, that it is intuitively indeterminate, or that it cannot be analysed) with particularities. To this end, I have chosen works as analytical subjects that are in many ways astonishingly different from each other, yet have two things in common: they are all for solo piano, and they were all composed around 1952–53. These parameters themselves are a part of the establishment of a contained space of investigation, where generalisation may be (relatively) minimised in favour of the particular. The piano was Feldman's own instrument, and he composed for it prolifically. More importantly, his early reputation was built, to a large degree, upon performances of the 1950s works for piano given by David Tudor. While the chamber and orchestral works are no less important in the broader picture of Feldman's work, the present study takes the analysis of piano works as a starting point for what is intended as a contribution to a larger, ongoing discourse.[30]

Feldman's graphic scores of the early 1950s are important, not only in terms of his own development as a composer, but also as works whose wide influence extended over the next few decades. At the same time, however, they present a particular set of problems for the analyst. In pursuing my main object of identifying structures that shed light upon Feldman's management of pitch and time, it is apparent that the argument may be most explicitly built upon analysis of the more conventionally notated works. The comparison between staff-notated and graphic

---

[30]   As the instrument he played himself, the piano had special significance for Feldman – this is evident in writings, lectures and interviews throughout his career. Piano music was a most important part of his output up until the early 1960s, and again in the last decade of his life. Between 1964 and 1977, however, he produced no published work for solo piano. It is almost as though his aesthetic ideal of piano sound had eventually dropped out of the range of hearing. In purely practical terms, this reflects the fact that Tudor was performing less, and eventually not at all. This in turn relates directly to changing structures of the field of musical production, as expressed in the changing social dynamics together with the divergent interests of Feldman and Tudor (to a certain extent competitive, as Tudor devoted more of his time to composition and less to performing the works of other composers). It was not until the late 1970s, with the appearance of Roger Woodward and later Aki Takahashi, that Feldman once again had performers he trusted to realise his very personal conception of pianism, and of the sound-frame of the piano as an instrument. See also John Holzaepfel, *David Tudor and the Performance of American Experimental Music, 1950– 1959* (PhD Dissertation, City University of New York, 1994).

works of the early 1950s is, however, extremely valuable and serves to highlight some fundamental aspects of Feldman's thinking.

With works chosen from any period of Feldman's career, one might very well make a similar investigation of the structuring of pitch and time. Rather than scattered sampling, however, I decided after much consideration to focus upon one narrowly defined time period. The early 1950s were a crucial period for Feldman's development as a composer. During these years, he is known to have formed friendships with a number of important painters, writers and musicians in New York, whose various influences played a major role in the development of his artistic thinking. It was also at this period that he made the first explicit actions to establish his public presence in the field of music production in New York (to borrow Pierre Bourdieu's terminology).[31] In this process, we may begin to map his personal aims and concerns as a composer at this moment and the structures of the field in which he sought a space to operate.

Ultimately, we may collectively seek to build an understanding of Feldman's career trajectory; such an understanding, however, must be built from a deep analysis of many moments along that trajectory. This study, focusing upon the period around 1952, is a contribution to our understanding of one such point in Feldman's career and as such it informs our appreciation of his subsequent work.

Two other factors helped to narrow the focus to the period around 1952. Firstly, the works of this time have a certain iconic stature in the popular and scholarly literatures, although very few have been analysed in close detail. Secondly (and coincidentally), as I gathered primary source materials for this study, particular works drew attention to themselves through the very nature of the source materials; many of Feldman's pieces of this period have exceptionally interesting associated sketches and early versions, which provide valuable clues to key aspects of compositional structuring. In this way, it must be acknowledged that the source materials have to some extent shaped the terms of reference of this study.

Debating Feldman

Published contemporary criticism, analysis or serious discussion of Feldman's work of the 1950s was almost non-existent. Henry Cowell's article of 1952, while supportive of the efforts of Cage and his close colleagues to promote their work, offered no detailed analytical comment on Feldman's work specifically. Discussing a graphically scored work titled *Intersection #3* (actually an early version of the work now known as *Intersection 1*), Cowell simply showed that,

---

[31] Pierre Bourdieu, 'The Field of Cultural Production, or: The Economic World Reversed' [1983], in Randal Johnson (ed.), *The Field Of Cultural Production: Essays on Art and Literature* (New York: Columbia University Press, 1993), 29–73.

while the performer may choose precise pitches within broad parameters, many other aspects of the work are clearly defined.[32]

Stefan Wolpe also made passing reference to Feldman's work in his lectures of the 1950s at Yale, Black Mountain College and Darmstadt.[33] In a few instances, these brief mentions do represent valuable critical commentary, although the clarity of this critique may have been somewhat mitigated at the time by his singular delivery (refer, for example, to Milton Babbitt's reminiscence of Wolpe's 1951 Yale lecture).[34] A few of Wolpe's texts were published in the 1960s, but those most pertinent to the study of Feldman did not appear in print until more recently.[35]

John Cage was primarily interested in those aspects of Feldman's music that he understood as 'indeterminate'. Thus, his discussion of Feldman's music focused always upon the graphic scores (more specifically, the *Intersection* pieces), while recognising, like Cowell, that even then only certain clearly delineated elements of these pieces were indeterminate.[36] Wolpe, in contrast, saw the pitch notation in Feldman's graphic scores as crudely determined (by register), rather than indeterminate and he openly disapproved of this relative inaccuracy.[37] Pierre Boulez, in his letters to Cage, also disapproved of the inexactitude of Feldman's graphic notation ('Much too imprecise and too simple').[38] These criticisms may well have influenced the waning of Feldman's interest in graphic notations. He was certainly aware of problems and limitations with the graphic notation – in

---

[32]   Henry Cowell, 'Current Chronicle', *The Musical Quarterly*, 38/1 (January 1952), 131.

[33]   For a Wolpe bibliography, see Austin Clarkson (ed.), *On the Music of Stefan Wolpe: Essays and Recollections* (Hillsdale, NY: Pendragon Press, 2003), 346–7.

[34]   Milton Babbitt, 'Recollections of Stefan Wolpe', http://www.wolpe.org/page1/page10/page10.html#Milton%20Babbitt.

[35]   Among those texts which make explicit reference to Feldman's work are Stefan Wolpe, 'On New (and not-so-new) Music in America' [Darmstadt, 1956], trans. Austin Clarkson in *Journal of Music Theory* 28/1 (1984), 1–45; and 'Thoughts on Pitch and some Considerations Connected with It' [1952], *Perspectives of New Music* 17/2 (1979), 28–57.

[36]   In this context, and dating from the period with which this book is concerned, are several crucial texts: John Cage, 'Lecture on Nothing' [1949/50], in *Silence: Lectures and Writings by John Cage* (Middletown, CT: Wesleyan University Press, 1961), 109–26; 'Lecture on Something' [1950/51], in ibid., 128–45; 'Indeterminacy', in ibid., 35–40; and 'Juilliard Lecture' [1952], in *A Year From Monday* (Middletown, CT: Wesleyan University Press, 1969), 95–111.

[37]   Stefan Wolpe, 'Thoughts on Pitch', 49. Text of a talk given at Black Mountain College, August 1952.

[38]   Pierre Boulez, 'Letter from Pierre Boulez to John Cage: August 1951', in Jean-Jacques Nattiez and Robert Samuels (eds), *The Boulez–Cage Correspondence*, 103. Cage replied, 'Feldman, who has great difficulty imagining that you do not like his work, will send you a new *Intersection* on graph for piano'. See John Cage, 'Letter from John Cage to Pierre Boulez: summer 1951', in ibid., 110.

particular, he was bothered by the perception that these scores allow the performer freedom, which, he said later, was not his primary intention.[39]

The lectures and writings of Cage dating from the 1950s have been by far the most influential commentaries upon Feldman's work of this period, with several important texts appearing in print as early as 1959. That Cage played a crucial part in raising public awareness of Feldman's work cannot be doubted but, as a result, there has been a strong tendency ever since to hear Feldman as mediated by Cage's writings. Feldman himself recognised this problem, and even in the early 1950s sought to clarify his situation and maintain a certain distance from Cage (commenting after Cage's 'Lecture on Something', ostensibly about Feldman's music, 'That's not me; that's John').[40] In later years, Feldman would often acknowledge the broader debt he owed to Cage while distancing his work from any suggestion of Cage's specific influence. 'Cage was not my teacher', he once pointed out, 'if anything, I think I influenced Cage'.[41] At least some of the criticism Feldman levelled at composers like Boulez was equally applicable to Cage,[42] and it is perhaps significant that, although Feldman very often talked about his friendship with Cage, he rarely spoke specifically of Cage's music.[43]

Cage, as previously noted, apart from his personal encouragement of Feldman, had narrowly specific interests regarding Feldman's work. As a result, Cage's public discussion of Feldman's work is restricted to only a couple of pieces of the early 1950s, and it is little wonder that it was the graphic scores that seemed to him most significant. Regarding Feldman's more conventionally notated works, Cage offered little comment (beyond the provocative observation that 'Feldman's conventionally notated music is himself playing his graph music')[44] and by the late 1960s it was clear that the two friends' interests, aims and aesthetic outlook had diverged significantly. One of the most important primary-source texts documenting the relationship is the series of radio conversations recorded in 1966–67. Listening to these, it becomes evident that, by the late 1960s, Feldman and Cage, while conversing amicably, were in many ways at cross-purposes.[45] As early as 1965, some of Feldman's other friends seem to have been concerned that Cage's interpretations might be harmful to public perception of Feldman's work:

[39]   Morton Feldman, 'Liner Notes' in B.H. Friedman (ed.), *Give My Regards to Eighth Street*, 6.

[40]   Quoted in John Cage, *Silence*, 128.

[41]   Austin Clarkson, 'Conversation about Stefan Wolpe: 13 November 1980', in Chris Villars, *Morton Feldman Says*, 110.

[42]   See Morton Feldman, 'Sound, Noise, Varèse, Boulez', 1–2.

[43]   For one exception, see Morton Feldman, 'Crippled Symmetry' [1981], in B.H. Friedman (ed.), *Give My Regards to Eighth Street*, 145.

[44]   Quoted in Frank O'Hara, 'New Directions in Music: Morton Feldman' [1959], in ibid., 216.

[45]   Morton Feldman and John Cage, *Radio Happenings: Conversations – Gespräche*, trans. Gisela Gronemeyer (Köln: MusikTexte, 1993).

'A close and valued friend once became annoyed at my persistent admiration of Cage. "How can you feel this," he said, "when it's apparent that everything he stands for negates your own music?"'[46] A striking comment – and it is interesting that Feldman should choose to publish it.

Cage's views concerning Feldman's work of the 1950s cannot be ignored. On the other hand, we must also strive to understand Feldman's work in a broader context and from other perspectives. I would argue that the natural emphasis in Cage's writing on the indeterminate aspects, which he understood to some extent in terms of Zen philosophy, has too heavily influenced the secondary literature on Feldman's work until quite recently. Since the mid-1990s, however, the development of a small but vigorous analytical discourse concerning Feldman's work has rapidly revealed that the music itself is much more organised and intelligently controlled than earlier writers acknowledged.

Although several earlier essays made significant contributions to the establishment of this discourse,[47] the first major indicator of new directions in the study of Feldman's music was *The Music of Morton Feldman*, a collection of analytical essays edited by Thomas DeLio, published in 1996.[48] While the book has attracted some criticism,[49] it remains seminally important in so far as it represents a substantial body of work by varied scholars demonstrating that work from several periods of Feldman's life is indeed susceptible to analytical investigations of various kinds. Thus, *The Music of Morton Feldman* represents some of the first rigorous forensic examination of the Feldman music, clearing away some of the mythology, and tackling the music itself head-on. Most notably, the essays in this book documented and illuminated some of the levels of observable organisation in Feldman's music: his work may not have been produced by a capital-S 'System', but he certainly had systems and processes of his own ('So I can't relate or identify with any system whatsoever, not even that which I make myself').[50] These essays revealed that pieces ranging from early graphic scores to late works all show remarkable evidence of detailed, intelligent organisation on several levels.

---

[46]   Morton Feldman, 'The Anxiety of Art' in B.H. Friedman (ed.), *Give My Regards to Eighth Street*, 29.

[47]   Of particular relevance to the scope of the present study are Christian Wolff, 'The Sound Doesn't Look Back'; and Gianmario Borio, 'Morton Feldman e l'Espressionismo astratto: La costruzione di tempo e suono nelle miniature pianistiche degli anni Cinquanta e Sessanta', in *Itinerari della musica americana* (Lucca: Una Cosa Rara, 1996), 119–34, http://www.cnvill.demon.co.uk/mfborio.htm.

[48]   Thomas delio (ed.), *The Music of Morton Feldman* (Westport, CT: Greenwood Press, 1996).

[49]   See David Nicholls, 'The Music of Morton Feldman [review]', *Music and Letters*, 78/4 (November 1997), 631.

[50]   Alan Beckett, 'International Times Interview' [1966], in Chris Villars, *Morton Feldman Says*, 32.

None of the essays in *The Music of Morton Feldman* dealt with the works discussed in this present book, although two addressed works of the 1950s: John Welsh wrote about Feldman's pioneering graphic score *Projection 1* (1950),[51] and Thomas DeLio analysed *Last Pieces #3* (1959).[52] Regarding *Projection 1*, Welsh showed that, although specific pitch is 'indeterminate' (that is to say, determined by the performer), Feldman deployed the elements of timbre, density, register and silence in identifiably structured ways. Of particular relevance to the present study, Welsh found that, on several levels of structure, the piece falls into two parts, with marked changes of register and timbre just after the 2:1 partition of the duration of the work. DeLio, in his examination of *Last Pieces #3*, found that Feldman was organising material at the levels of pitch-class, of interval and of set. Among the characteristics of Feldman's deployment of these materials, DeLio showed that interval class 3 (minor 3rd) is notably favoured, and indeed used to form several crucial 'linguistic' sets (diminished triads and seventh chords in this case). Interestingly, these sets are sometimes left incomplete, as are some passages that seem otherwise to be systematically developing statements of the 12-tone aggregate – notes are withheld, in other words, contrary to the listener's expectation. DeLio also noticed that the overall architecture of the work seems to fall into two parts, not unlike *Projection 1*.

During the decade since the publication of *The Music of Morton Feldman*, a small group of scholars have continued the close reading of Feldman's work as a project of formal analysis while also seeking ways to present the results of this analysis in a manner sensitive to contemporary musicology. Marion Saxer's *Between Categories: Studien zum Komponieren Morton Feldmans von 1951 bis 1977*,[53] for example, gracefully combines discussion of selected works with analysis of Feldman's philosophical and aesthetic contexts. In this way, Saxer investigates Feldman's work and writing in relation to William James, John Dewey, Kierkegaard, Samuel Beckett and of course abstract expressionism. Ulrike Rausch has further developed this connection between Feldman (also Cage and Brown) and the New York painters of the 1950s in her study *Grenzgänge: Musik und Bildende Kunst im New York der 50er Jahre*, which discusses briefly several works of the early 1950s, including *Intermission 5*.[54]

Subjecting several works from the period in question to close reading of pitch material, Paul Undreiner's findings, in his 2009 dissertation *Pitch Structure in*

---

[51]   John Welsh, '*Projection I* (1950)', in Thomas DeLio (ed.), *The Music of Morton Feldman*, 21–35.

[52]   Thomas DeLio. '*Last Pieces* #3 (1959)', in ibid., 39–68.

[53]   Marion Saxer, *Between Categories: Studien zum Komponieren Morton Feldmans von 1951 bis 1977* (Saarbrücken: Pfau-Verlag, 1998).

[54]   Ulrike Rausch, *Grenzgänge: Musik und Bildende Kunst im New York der 50er Jahre* (Saarbrücken: Pfau-Verlag, 1999).

Morton Feldman's Compositions of 1952,[55] tend to concur with those of DeLio
in noting that Feldman was manipulating pitch materials on several levels.
More importantly, his work helps to fill a significant gap in our knowledge by
concentrating upon the level of pitch-class sets. In this way, Undreiner has shown
that Feldman's work can often be read in terms of surprisingly recurrent trichords
(e.g. 012, 016) made up of the composer's favoured interval classes.

As more of Feldman's own writings, interviews and lectures have become
available in recent years, it has become easier to link analytical observations with
the philosophical and aesthetic concerns evident in these writings. The analysis
of such texts, however, is not without its problems – not least of which is due to
the previously noted fact that Feldman rarely spoke of technical matters. He did,
however, talk a great deal about art, and the relation between his own music and
the visual arts. Jonathan Bernard argued in his essay 'Feldman's Painters' (2002)
that this may be the crucial area of investigation for the analysis of Feldman's
music.[56] Certainly, it is difficult to avoid discussion of the visual arts in any study
of Feldman. Among the several writers who have pursued this avenue of research,
Steven Johnson is singularly important. As editor of *The New York Schools of
Music and Visual Arts*,[57] Johnson curated a collection of essays that has served
as a basis for the understanding of Feldman's work in the early twenty-first
century. Although tending to favour the contextual in their analysis, these essays
nonetheless outline many of the important issues and questions concerning the work
of Feldman and also the immediate milieu. Most important of all for our present
purpose is Johnson's own contribution, 'Jasper Johns and Morton Feldman: Why
Patterns?'[58] Here, Johnson combined deeply perceptive formal analysis of both
music and visual art with a solid appreciation of contexts to provide a dramatically
new perspective upon Feldman's work, in the process shedding significant light
on our understanding of the work of Jasper Johns. This is, in many ways, a model
of recent analytical writing in combining the formal and contextual analyses of
traditional musicology while also opening a cross-disciplinary window to art
theory/history.

This is by no means the only useful approach, however. Catherine Hirata, in her
thoughtful and imaginative dissertation *Analyzing the Music of Morton Feldman*,
has made a complex and sophisticated contribution to the study of Feldman's
work.[59] Hirata's approach, like Johnson's, is a model of openness in musicological

---

[55]   Paul Stephen Undreiner, *Pitch Structure in Morton Feldman's Compositions of
1952* (PhD Dissertation, State University of New Jersey, 2009).

[56]   Jonathan Bernard, 'Feldman's Painters', in Steven Johnson (ed.), *The New York
Schools of Music and the Visual Arts* (New York: Routledge, 2002), 173–216.

[57]   Ibid.

[58]   Steven Johnson, 'Jasper Johns and Morton Feldman: Why Patterns?', in ibid.,
217–47.

[59]   Catherine Hirata, *Analyzing the Music of Morton Feldman* (PhD Dissertation,
Columbia University, 2003).

investigation, eschewing conventions of formal analysis while seeking to find new ways of engaging with the very sounds themselves. Hirata reminds us that analysis in musicology is both performative and personal, and her dissertation is remarkable for presenting a highly personalised yet informed reading of the work that is firmly positioned within the context of the wider analytical discourse.

Of particular interest is Hirata's effort to hear the works, note-by-note, in rigorous and thoughtful detail. Her dissertation is a record of extraordinarily intense, active and informed listening. In a footnote, however, Hirata does acknowledge one important contention: while some (including Hirata herself) may seek to isolate and explain more-or-less autonomous moments in Feldman's music, isolated sound events as 'the sounds of the sounds themselves',[60] it is by no means certain that we experience music in such a way:

> [Christopher] Hasty also questions, however, whether we really ever experience an autonomous moment, arguing (in part) that the experience of novelty requires not an isolation of the present from past and future, but an integration of the three.[61]

Between these two points of view, I take Hasty's side. I find that the sense of the individual sounds as parts of a great and complex, multi-dimensional web greatly overpowers the moments of glancing novelty in Feldman's music. This remains the case even if this web, as some may argue, is only partly of Feldman's design. As I show in my analysis of *Intermission 6*, for example, it is apparent that the seemingly 'random' sounds of *Intermission 6* are parts of a larger figure, however distorted or fragmented – and this indeed is how I hear it.

Subsequent to Hirata's dissertation, Dora Hanninen's substantial essay 'Feldman, Analysis, Experience'[62] presented a considered summing-up of the state of the field to *ca* 2004 before embarking upon detailed discussion of two late Feldman works. Hanninen's essay also represents a synthesis of score-based analysis with a keen appreciation of certain performative and aural points of discussion. It is this appreciation of the aural experience that perhaps offers a way of dealing with those aspects of some of Feldman's works that do resist conventional methods of analysis, such as the dislocation of notated voices in the works where Feldman instructs each performer to play in their own time.[63]

While these scholars and others have made important contributions, one might question whether the field has attained the level of a conversation or dialogue. Rather, it often seems that each writer is making relatively isolated statements,

---

[60]   Ibid., 32–3.

[61]   Ibid., 73–4 (fn). Hirata is here referring to Christopher Hasty, *Meter as Rhythm* (New York: Oxford University Press, 1997), 298.

[62]   Hanninen, 'Feldman, Analysis, Experience', 225–51.

[63]   This is a common feature of Feldman's work of the late 1950s and early 1960s (see for example the *Duration* series) but prefigured by *Intermission 6* as early as 1952.

in what amounts to a near vacuum. One indicator of the extent of this problem is that very few Feldman works have received close attention from more than one investigator.[64] Furthermore, very many of his pieces have received as yet no detailed analytical attention at all. Of the works discussed in this present book, *Intermission 6* has been mentioned by many in passing but not examined closely, *Intermission 5* has been discussed briefly by a mere handful of writers,[65] while Christian Wolff and Paul Undreiner have both examined *Piano Piece 1952*.[66]

Primary Source Writings and Sketches

One of the significant issues remaining to be dealt with thoroughly in writing on Feldman's music is that of primary source materials. Among many other problems, we have as yet no complete, accurate chronology of Feldman's works.[67] The generally accepted composition dates of many Feldman works are in fact conjectural at best, although this has rarely been acknowledged. Clearly, this makes it extremely difficult to make specific comparison or cross-reference to the musical or painterly works of his contemporaries, Feldman's personal situation at the time of composition, socio-political contexts – or even simply Feldman's other works. This is one of the factors hindering analytical study of Feldman's work, and our lack of understanding of Feldman's working procedures is a direct result. In this study, therefore, I seek to give special emphasis to the primary source materials; these include Feldman's sketches, associated annotations, writings (published and unpublished), interviews and recordings.

Preserved at the Paul Sacher Stiftung in Basel is an almost complete set of Feldman's sketchbooks of the 1950s.[68] Original sketch material survives for many works of this period, in addition to early drafts and later fair copies made for publication. In all cases, the sources for a single work differ from one another (I hesitate to say 'conflict', as this seems unnecessarily negative) – and we may thus begin to map at least some of Feldman's compositional decision-making through the various stages of composition, performance and revision for publication. For

---

[64]   Hirata and DeLio have both discussed parts of *Last Pieces* in some detail, from very different perspectives. See Catherine Hirata, *Analyzing the Music of Morton Feldman*, 31–64 and Thomas DeLio, '*Last Pieces* #3 (1959)', in Thomas DeLio (ed.), *The Music of Morton Feldman*, 39–70.

[65]   Among them Gianmario Borio, 'Morton Feldman e l'Espressionismo astratto', 119–34; Ulrike Rausch, *Grenzgänge*, 31–9; Sebastian Claren, *Neither*, 61, 187; Paul Stephen Undreiner, *Pitch Structure*, 19–28.

[66]   Christian Wolff, 'The Sound Doesn't Look Back'; Paul Stephen Undreiner, *Pitch Structure*.

[67]   Claren's 'Werkverzeichnis' is the most thorough compiled to date, but should not be considered authoritative. See Sebastian Claren, *Neither*, 547–75.

[68]   Paul Sacher Foundation, Basel, Morton Feldman Collection.

some works, there are even multiple sketches, or sketches which themselves show signs of substantial revision. Some writers have placed emphasis on Feldman's occasional suggestions that he did not make sketches, when in fact Feldman rarely spoke of such things, and then only late in life;[69] the evidence of his manuscript legacy shows that this is by no means an accurate understanding of his working practice in the 1950s. Similarly, the composer often mentioned his argument with Karlheinz Stockhausen, who could not understand Feldman's advice to 'leave the sounds alone; don't push them'.[70] One imagines that if Stockhausen had ever seen the sketch materials that we now have available, he would have felt vindicated in his suspicion that this was not an entirely truthful description of Feldman's compositional method. Feldman certainly did push the notes around, sometimes drastically (as in *Extensions 3* or *Piano Piece 1952*, for example, where the entire structure of the works was altered by the deletion of large sections). In fact, Feldman's alterations and revisions affect all aspects of the music: pitch-class, register, form, rhythm, dynamic and pedalling. That said, however, it must be acknowledged that there are great differences between Stockhausen's methods of handling musical materials (with serial procedures of permutation, for example) and Feldman's ostensibly more flexible approach.

In this study, I am not seeking any kind of 'authentic' source or interpretation; rather, my concern is with finding coherent ways to address the very complexity of the diverse source materials. Much, if not all, of the meaning of music may reside in its 'web of culture', to borrow Gary Tomlinson's phrase (itself echoing Clifford Geertz),[71] yet our apprehension of such a web (in a historicised sense) rests upon the artefacts of that culture, whether they be musical sketches, recordings, newspapers or bus tickets. Incorporation of sketches to the analyses presented here demonstrably provides insight into many aspects of the works that could not be obtained in any other way. While this insight may not be essential to our enjoyment (or dislike, for that matter) of the music, it certainly deepens and enriches that apprehension, and extends our understanding.

Examination of sketches in relation to any composer's work immediately complicates the notion of the work as an absolute entity. Anne Shreffler has noted this in relation to her study of the Webern sketches,

---

[69]   For example, Amy Beal, 'Time Canvases', 231. For one such instance, see Morton Feldman, 'Darmstadt Lecture' [1984], in Chris Villars, *Morton Feldman Says*, 202.

[70]   David Charlton and Jolyon Laycock, 'An Interview with Morton Feldman' [1966], in ibid., 28.

[71]   Gary Tomlinson, 'The Web of Culture: A Context for Musicology', *Nineteenth Century Music*, 7/3 (April 1984), 350–62.

> Rather than serving up a circular argument of validation, sketch study can open
> up a work, reducing our perception of its autonomy by making audible the
> different voices present at various stages of its meaning.[72]

In investigating and analysing sketches and other primary sources, we are forced
to come to terms with the materials themselves as evidence for a work that is
changeable to the extent even of multiplicity. Publication cannot be considered
final, as very many composers (Feldman among them) revise and alter pieces
long afterwards. In addition, third-party interventions (in the form of editing and
engraving, for example) continue this process of transformation.

Feldman's 1950s music was, for the most part, not published until the 1960s.[73]
The relationship between the published scores and the original compositions of
the 1950s is problematic – or to cast it in a more positive light, complex. In some
cases, the works made famous by David Tudor were substantially revised years
later, at the time of publication. A 1952 performance of *Piano Piece 1952*, for
example, quite likely presented a work substantially different from that we know
today, with two movements instead of one.[74]

As if this were not already difficult enough, the inclusion of a composer's
recorded performances as primary source material is similarly rewarding and
problematic at once. Clearly, recordings are of an entirely different substance to
the written score, and the extent to which they may be compared is debatable.
Recordings are certainly valuable documents of particular performances, but we
recognise that they come to us distorted not only by time but also by various human
and technological mediators (of course, our perceptions of published scores and
concert performances are equally subject to similar mediations). Oddly, we have
no conventional difficulty in discussing (or indeed commercially marketing) a CD
of a composer performing as though it were somehow in essence the same work as
that written down – even when it differs substantially, as is the case with Feldman's
Intermission 5.[75] Clearly, the matter of musical source-materials is complicated;
whatever a musical work is exactly, it is not exclusively either on the page or in the
sound. To ignore any of these varied sources in the interest of clarity or simplicity,
however, is to perpetrate a deception about the complex and subtle nature of the
music itself.

Music, as Philip Bohlman once observed, may be what we think it is – or it
may not.[76] Few would argue that the musical work exists only on the page, but

---

[72]   Anne C. Shreffler, *Webern and the Lyric Impulse: Songs and Fragments on Poems
of Georg Trakl* (Oxford: Oxford University Press, 1994), 13.

[73]   An exception: Morton Feldman, *Illusions* [c. 1948], *New Music. A Quarterly of
Modern Composition*, 23/4 (October 1951).

[74]   See Chapter 3.

[75]   See Chapter 2.

[76]   Philip Bohlman, 'Ontologies of Music', in Nicholas Cook and Mark Everist (eds),
Rethinking Music (Oxford: Oxford University Press, 1999), 17.

equally it seems inadequately defined by performance or recording. Somehow, it can be all of these – and none. As one reads a score and hears it in the mind, is this performance? As one listens to a concert performance while thinking at the same time about a hundred other things, is that Feldman? I take the position that there is such a thing as a musical work. What exactly that is, or where exactly it resides, I am not sure – but it is certainly by no means an autonomous entity. If we cannot be sure, in analysis and discussion, of apprehending the very work itself (perhaps too subtle, changeable, complex and fragile for tangible contact), then we may at least examine closely the evidences for the work's existence; these are our source materials. In my model then, the various notations and recordings are evidence for the existence of a work, and evidence for developing understandings of what the nature of that work may be, or may have been. My analysis is in no sense comprehensive – the very idea of comprehensive analysis (if by that we mean a study of everything that one can know about a work) is in any case unattainable in practice.

In this study, I am at least partly interested in Morton Feldman's decision-making as a composer, and within this construct it is possible to discuss some of the ways in which his musical work (whatever that may be exactly) took shape. In music analysis, so much concerned with matters of design and compositional process, there is a fine line to be walked between the study of a composer's thinking and the intentionalist fallacy.[77] Feldman, for example, considered 'space' in music to be illusory,[78] and this is most interesting – but it need not prevent us from discussing his work in terms of spaces that may seem quite evident to us.

While we may investigate Feldman's decision-making on the basis of primary evidence, the significance of this in relation to the work lies in our reading/hearing, not in Feldman's intent. Furthermore, one cannot pretend that this creative decision-making on Feldman's part was in any sense an autonomous activity. It is useful to think of this loosely in terms of Pierre Bourdieu's model, as outlined in 'The Field of Cultural Production'.[79] Thus, we might conceive of Feldman as an individual enacting a career trajectory within a space defined by his own disposition and habitus, as opposed to the opportunities and restrictions offered by the very structure of the field of cultural production itself. Any perceived autonomy is strictly relative. Thus, when I discuss a particular compositional

---

[77] This refers to a confusion of the meaning of a text with the author's intention. See W. Wimsatt and M. Beardsley, 'The Intentional Fallacy' [1954], in *The Verbal Icon: Studies in the Meaning of Poetry* (London: Methuen, 1970), 3–20.

[78] Sketchbook annotation, c. 1952. Paul Sacher Foundation, Basel, Morton Feldman Collection.

[79] The classic text is Pierre Bourdieu, 'The Field of Cultural Production, or: The Economic World Reversed' [1983], in Randal Johnson (ed.), *The Field Of Cultural Production*. For discussion of Bourdieu's theory in the context of musicology, see Stephen Miles, 'Critical Musicology and the Problem of Mediation', *Notes*, 2nd Series, 53/3 (March 1997), 722–50.

action (for example Feldman's decision to break apart the carefully constructed *Intermission 6*),[80] I am implicitly speaking not only of Feldman's personal action, but also his position in the field and the structure of the field. In this sense, the reader will appreciate the extent to which this book is on many levels (and of necessity) a preliminary sketch. Each and every analytical point made in the chapters that follow might itself be the subject of a much larger study, connecting Feldman's localised decision-making through the web of the field's structure and in turn its relations with adjacent or contingent fields (the economic or political, for example). While this model is useful and appropriate for the study of Feldman and his work, I am not suggesting that it is in any sense 'true' or 'real'; like all theoretical models, it is simply a frame for the investigation.

By my use of the term 'work' throughout this book, I wish to invoke a Deleuzian multiplicity rather than any sense of an autonomous, finite entity:

> Music has always sent out lines of flight, like so many "transformational multiplicities," even overturning the very codes that structure or arborify it; that is why musical form, right down to its ruptures and proliferations, is comparable to a weed, a rhizome.[81]

In this passage, Deleuze and Guattari are consciously echoing Pierre Boulez, from whom they borrow the description of music as a growing weed.[82] For Deleuze and Guattari, the relation between a work and the world is not analogic but rhizomatic: 'contrary to a deeply-rooted belief, the book is not an image of the world. It forms a rhizome with the world, there is an aparallel evolution of the book and the world'.[83] This stems in part from their desire to avoid suggestions of binary logic: mimicry, they suggest, 'is a very bad concept'. While my work is informed by such an attitude I have, for the sake of readability, retained the more conventional terms of analogy, metaphor, homology and even simply 'connection'. My use of these terms should be understood, as with my understanding of the author's decision-making, not as a simplistic suggestion of simple binary relationships but rather in terms of an implicit wider web of which the relation between two entities is only a fragmentary part, isolated for the purpose of discussion.

---

[80]   As discussed in Chapter 4.

[81]   Gilles Deleuze and Félix Guattari, *A Thousand Plateaus: Capitalism and Schizophrenia* [1980], trans. Brian Massumi (London: Continuum, 2004), 13.

[82]   Ibid., 569. Note that their understanding of the musical work and musical form is rather conservative in so far as they are largely concerned with a classically French view of the European canon of notated, composed concert works. For discussion of this curious aspect of Deleuze and Guattari's work, see Jeremy Gilbert, 'Becoming-Music: The Rhizomatic Moment of Improvisation', in Ian Buchanan and Marcel Swiboda (eds), *Deleuze and Music* (Edinburgh: Edinburgh University Press, 2004), 121. I choose, however, to read their use of the term 'form' in the broadest possible sense.

[83]   Ibid., 12.

In his own writings, interviews and lectures, Feldman was rather shy of discussing many aspects of his work in detail, a characteristic not unusual among composers. Nevertheless, close reading of his essays and interviews does, I would suggest, provide more information than perhaps even he realised. The reasons for his public reticence about technical aspects of the music may be traced back to 1950, and a powerfully significant incident involving Milton Babbitt and John Cage:

> At this first meeting I brought John a string quartet. He looked at it for a long time and then said, "How did you make this?" I thought of my constant quarrels with Wolpe, and how just a week before, after showing a composition of mine to Milton Babbitt and answering his questions as intelligently as I could, he said to me, "Morton, I don't understand a word you're saying." And so, in a very weak voice I answered John, "I don't know how I made it."[84]

It is clear that Feldman did indeed know how he understood the piece to have been made (at least in terms of the immediate procedures by which it was manufactured), but decided, in reaction to the experience with Babbitt, that it might be easier to avoid discussion of the matter. This incident, and Cage's delighted reaction rapidly became part of Feldman's personal and public mythology – by 1963 it was enshrined in print on a record cover.[85] The manner of speaking and writing that Feldman developed so successfully during the 1960s and 1970s was to a large extent a constructed safe language, the boundaries of which are often evident in interviews.[86] Throughout his career, Feldman would almost always avoid giving a direct answer to the question 'how was it made?' There is precedent for this in the public discourse of the abstract expressionist painters; as Feldman's friend Mark Rothko, for example, wrote in 1947, 'Pictures must be miraculous: the instant one is completed, the intimacy between the creation and the creator is ended. He is an outsider'.[87] Curiously, these attitudes of both Feldman and Rothko, in so far as they seem to de-emphasise the processes of composition, suggest a certain confidence in the old romantic/modernist idea of a 'finished' work, as a finite, autonomous object.

---

[84]　Morton Feldman, 'Liner Notes' [1962], in B.H. Friedman (ed.), *Give My Regards to Eighth Street*, 4.
[85]　Morton Feldman, liner notes for *Feldman/Brown* LP record (Time Records 58007/s8007, 1963). Reprinted as 'Liner Notes' [1962], in B.H. Friedman (ed.), *Give My Regards to Eighth Street*, 4.
[86]　One very explicit and well-known example is found in Heinz-Klaus Metzger's interview. Heinz-Klaus Metzger, 'Prolog: Über Jiddishkeit', in Walter Zimmermann (ed.), *Morton Feldman Essays* (Kerpen: Beginner Press, 1985), 7.
[87]　Mark Rothko, 'The Romantics Were Prompted' [1947/48], in Ellen Landau (ed.), *Reading Abstract Expressionism: Context and Critique* (New Haven, CT: Yale University Press, 2005), 141.

I would suggest, however, that Feldman's own statements concerning his music, while often admittedly oblique, are perhaps more revealing of compositional concepts and methods than superficial examination suggests. We urgently need to re-examine Feldman's words as much as his music – he may have been all along telling us what was going on, but perhaps we have not always been listening/ reading in quite the right ways. The quotation given above, for example, tells us a great deal about the mechanics of Feldman's position-taking in the field as it operated in 1950, and the positioning of Feldman's work at this time in relation to other agents in his immediate vicinity (Babbitt, Wolpe and Cage).

Having said that, it is of course clear that on some occasions, and perhaps in answer to certain lines of questioning, Feldman could be purposefully uninformative. Furthermore, in the available interviews it is surprisingly rare that Feldman was asked specific technical or procedural questions regarding composition (the interview conducted by Cole Gagne and Tracy Caras in 1980 is a notable exception).[88] We should not underestimate the extent to which interviewers, as powerful mediators of Feldman's voice, have influenced our posthumous reading of his statements.

Analytical Approach

My approach to this music rests upon three principles:

- an emphasis of the particular over the general, and of working from the particular to the general;
- the inter-linking of what might conventionally be understood as formal and contextual analyses;
- the prioritising of primary sources.

Each of the central chapters discusses first the source materials, proceeds to analysis of the musical texts, and in the final sections widens the scope to address larger themes in the light of the analysis. My analyses are based upon all available primary sources for these works, seeking to understand the significant structures of each work and, where possible, to trace some evidence for Feldman's decision-making in the process of revision.

Rather than imposing an established analytical system on the material evidence, I began by making notes of the most obviously salient, elemental features of each work, its defining characteristics as I observed them through reading, playing and listening. From this analytic surface, I worked deeper into the finer details of each work, bearing in mind as much as possible the ramifications of all the available source materials. I made constant reference to the associated

---

[88]   Cole Gagne and Tracy Caras, 'Soundpieces Interview', in Chris Villars, *Morton Feldman Says*, 87–96.

annotations in Feldman's sketchbooks, many of which (initially cryptic) became clarified in their meaning as the analysis progressed. The analysis, while in some senses empirical, is nonetheless consciously a personal hearing of the works, and in this sense performative. While much of the discussion centres upon the notated evidences, my analysis is always intended to be heard; the conclusions are drawn from this personal hearing of the works, informed by close examination of available materials. Hanninen has argued an attitude to analysis that is broadly similar to my own:

> Feldman's music resists analysis (what music doesn't?), but it does not defy analysis. To insist that it does, intrinsically, is to make two mistakes: to assume that the current repertory of tools and methodologies are all we have; and to relegate analysis to a study of notes, overlooking the gap between notes and sounds and all it might contain. Analysis is an inquiry into musical experience; the inspiration for analysis is curiosity. What is it about Feldman's music? If we can hear it, can we find ways to "think it"?[89]

My framing of the argument in first-person terms is an acknowledgement, and a reminder, of the essential subjectivity of even the most rigorous analytical reading and hearing. These are indeed 'analytical fictions' to borrow Marion Guck's famous phrase,[90] and inherently pluralistic (in the sense of Deleuze and Guattari's observation that 'the two of us wrote *Anti-Oedipus* together. Since each of us was several, there was already quite a crowd').[91]

This book is not a historiographic study, and neither is it an analysis of reception, although aspects of both are implicitly component parts of the contextual analysis. In combining formal and contextual approaches, I have sought a way of working around the ideological debates concerning formal analysis that have, over the past few decades, periodically paralysed musicology in the wider sphere. In the absence of 'the work' as a concrete object, the range of evidences for the work's existence and its distinctive (or otherwise) properties may be comfortably considered to extend far beyond the score. Study of extra-musical materials (personal letters, for example) might form part of the analysis of the work itself. Similarly, to extend this further, a close study of the socio-economic situation in New York of 1952 is perhaps as much an analysis of *Intermission 5* as a close reading of the score(s). The crucial work for the analyst, then, is in drawing the connections and illuminating 'rhizomatic' homologies.

The aims of this book, while carried out within the context of the analytical model outlined above, are relatively modest. However, the analysis presented here, and the conclusions drawn, should be understood to rest within the space of

---

[89]   Hanninen, 'Feldman, Analysis, Experience', 249–50.
[90]   Marion Guck, 'Analytical Fictions', *Music Theory Spectrum*, 16/2 (Autumn 1994), 217–30.
[91]   Gilles Deleuze and Félix Guattari, *A Thousand Plateaus*, 3.

such broader discussion. It is helpful, once again, to think of this broad model of analysis in terms drawn from Pierre Bourdieu. Through his models of complex, nested and interconnected structures (of works and fields), we may conceive of elaborate homologies between all the elements. If the structure of a work is in part homologous to the structure of the musical field, which in turn has structural homologies with other fields, we may draw direct and indirect analytical connections on many levels. Echoing Bourdieu, I must suggest that this should not be understood as a mechanistic model, but rather one that is essentially fluid.[92] The structures of the fields are in constant flux, changing in response both to outside influence and to the actions of those operating within. Thus, while the space of action available for a composer like Feldman was defined by the existing structure of the field at any given moment, his actions as composer within the defined space also restructured the field.

Under this model, it may be understood that what I have hitherto referred to as formal and contextual analyses, in the conventional sense, are to my mind one and the same. Wherever I have used these terms formal and contextual, they should be understood in this sense of a unified view. Similarly, I always use the term analysis in the broadest sense, which incorporates both aspects of the formal and contextual in conventional understanding. The model outlined briefly above, derived from Bourdieu, offers one useful theoretical framework for bringing these two areas of analysis together: that of the internal structures of musical works, and that of the historical, social and political contexts.[93]

Systems and Processes

The four analytical chapters of this book interconnect in many ways, and I present the main argument in increments for readers who wish to absorb the detail along the way. Recognising , however, that some will wish to dip into the book out of interest in a particular work, I have also tried to make each chapter an essay that may be read independently. While a certain amount of recapitulation of key points is thus necessary, I have kept this to a minimum. Chapter 2 uses a study of *Intermission 5* to unravel some of the ways in which Feldman's pitch deployment is organised, and the ways in which this is meshed with the organisation of time. Crucial to this is Feldman's understanding of the 'chromatic field' (this is a term,

---

[92]   Pierre Bourdieu, 'The Field of Cultural Production, or: The Economic World Reversed' [1983], in Randal Johnson (ed.), *The Field Of Cultural Production*, 65.

[93]   Bourdieu himself does not deny the importance of formal analysis, while remaining critical of a formalism that disallows the sociological. See, for example, Pierre Bourdieu, 'Principles for a Sociology of Cultural Works' [1986], in ibid., 189.

with obvious visual reference, used by Feldman himself),[94] or 12-tone aggregate (usually unordered), deployed across a determined space of time.

The third chapter, built around a discussion of *Piano Piece 1952*, picks up several points noted in the previous chapter and develops them further with reference to this very different work and its unpublished companion piece. Most importantly, this chapter examines Feldman's use of pitch-class repetition within and between chromatic fields and the ways in which such repetition, when applied to a pitch-class set, may give rise to recognisable motivic figures (albeit part-concealed beneath an abstract surface).

Chapter 4 demonstrates that all the types of structure identified in the other two analyses may also, rather surprisingly, be found in the flexibly scored *Intermission 6*. At the same time, I examine here some of the complex tensions between Feldman's detailed control of materials at the composition stage, and the particular freedoms he sometimes allowed performers. In this study, as with the others, examination of the sketch materials and early drafts is vitally important to understanding the internal structures of the work.

The examination of *Intersection 3*, in Chapter 5, represents something of a departure in so far is it engages with one of Feldman's grid-notated scores. We find, however, that there are remarkable consistencies of structure, material and method – in all respects comparable to those of the other works analysed. On the basis of these analyses, we may identify quite particular kinds of structure, pertaining to the organisation of both sound (instrumentation, pitch, register and timbre) and time (form, rhythm, meter, duration), which in turn serve as clear evidence that there are some clear and consistent underlying principles and aesthetic presuppositions informing Feldman's work. Despite the extravagantly varied surfaces of Feldman's works of the 1950s, there are certain consistent ideas, elements and compositional procedures.

To some extent, it may be said that one of the aspects of Feldman's work that distinguishes it from so many of his contemporaries is that it deals very much with the elemental materials of music – or to be more precise, particular elemental materials of the music of his time. Some of these elemental aspects as evident in the four works discussed here are the dynamics of loud and soft (binary extremes), of attack and decay, of the deployment of the 12-tone aggregate as an entity in itself rather than as the basis of extended development, and similarly, the deployment of subsets of the aggregate (such as chromatic tetrachords) as structural motifs. These are of course basic materials that we might find in Babbitt, Boulez or Carter (and there is thus a powerful under-current of commonality), but Feldman uses them in a distinctive manner abstracted from broader conventions of linearity and development, and thus they seem to mean something rather different in his music.

---

[94] See for example Morton Feldman, 'Toronto Lecture' [1982], in Chris Villars, *Morton Feldman Says*, 144; also Morton Feldman, 'The Future of Local Music' [1984], in B.H. Friedman (ed.), *Give My Regards to Eighth Street*, 183.

I would like, in closing, to return to Christian Wolff's comments on *Piano Piece 1952*: 'What is there to say? The music appears to be unanalyzable. I don't see any system'.[95] In this instance, he went on to outline a brief but perceptive analysis of Feldman's *Piano Piece 1952*, taking note of both audible and written structures. Wolff resisted, however, the notion that these structures were consciously manipulated by Feldman ('I see no interest as such in pitch class or interval pattern organization'),[96] yet identified a number of instances of exactly this kind of organisation.

A very interesting process is at work in attempts like Wolff's to analyse Feldman's music while theorising that the task is impossible. Feldman's contemporaries and associates were indeed curious as to how his music was made (as the very existence of Wolff's essay indicates). Yet they also had a personal interest in maintaining Feldman's mythologies to some extent (including, perhaps, notions concerning the mystery of art, art without technique, an apolitical art, or art without dialectic),[97] in so far as their own mythologies might be contingent upon Feldman's (either in parallel or opposition), or, in some cases, in presenting arguments for their own mythologies of Feldman's music. The ongoing deconstruction and analysis of this network of mythologies is certainly an important part of current work on this period.[98] John Cage, in particular, had a distinctive view of Feldman's work, much reiterated over many years, which may have had little to do with the reality of how Feldman actually worked. In this way, we can see that ideas still commonly encountered today, of Feldman's music as indeterminate, or as composed according to some Zen non-organisation of sound for sound's-sake, are essentially Cagean notions. While perhaps not altogether false, such interpretations of Feldman's work should be appropriated with caution. The views of Cage and Wolff are perhaps most safely understood as ideological interpretations of Feldman's work – and this is no negative criticism, as surely all analysis is either explicitly or implicitly ideological.

Feldman's several written attacks on systems-based music centre on the idea that the conceptual system too often became what was heard, rather than the physical sounds: 'If one hears what one composes – by that I mean not just paper music – how can one not be seduced by the sensuality of the musical sound?'[99] He often presented his arguments on the subject in a historical context, as Peter Dickinson reported in an interview-based article from 1966:

---

[95]   Christian Wolff, 'The Sound Doesn't Look Back'.

[96]   Ibid.

[97]   For a brief discussion in relation to visual arts of the post-war period, see Pam Meecham and Julie Sheldon, *Modern Art: A Critical Introduction* (London: Routledge, 2005), 187–8.

[98]   See, for example, Claus-Steffen Mahnkopf (ed.), *Mythos Cage* (Hofheim: Wolke, 1999) and Horst Bredekamp, 'John Cage and the Principle of Chance', in Karol Berger and Anthony Newcomb (eds), *Music and the Aesthetics of Modernity*, 99–107.

[99]   Morton Feldman, 'Sound, Noise, Varèse, Boulez', p. 1.

Feldman feels that Boulez ends a long tradition of composers whose main interest is in how the music is made. He deplored the so-called attitude of progress and the obsession with systems and justifications. For Feldman the work of Varèse provided an answer. In *Ionisation* (1931) the music seems to be writing itself, walking a tightrope, and above all the composer is interested in how it sounds … The past is overwhelming and Feldman's own reaction has been to refine or reject those elements that do not correspond to his own vision.[100]

From the perspective of the twenty-first century, this is a complex and confusing argument, particularly in the suggestion of Feldman's relationship with pasts both actual and imagined. If, as Feldman suggests (via Dickinson), Boulez ends a long line of tradition, who were his predecessors in that lineage? While Feldman held Boulez's teacher and mentor Messiaen in low regard, Feldman and Boulez did share several ancestors in their imagined musical genealogies: Debussy and Webern most importantly.[101]

The idea that process might be of paramount importance ('the obsession with systems and justifications') has certainly lived on in many interesting ways – Boulez may hardly be said to be the end of it. In the post-modern world, process was frequently privileged over outcome in music and art – an attitude that belongs to a tradition of thought to which Cage was an influential contributor.[102] In contrast, the notion that a composer's systems and processes should be concealed to some degree is an old one: there have been many composers who have concealed or destroyed their sketch material to enact this kind of aesthetic position.[103] Feldman claimed on one occasion, (rather disingenuously) that he did not 'keep' sketches.[104]

Is it perhaps possible that Feldman's concern was not so much with systems in themselves but with explicit systems? That he wanted us to hear the sounds rather than the mechanism of composition? Let it be noted that this does not mean that he was claiming to compose without any systems/processes, simply that he held an

---

[100]   Peter Dickinson, 'Feldman Explains Himself During His First Visit to Europe in 1966', in Chris Villars, *Morton Feldman Says*, 20.

[101]   References to Debussy and Webern in Feldman's writing, interviews and lectures are too numerous to discuss here in detail. For an early expression of Feldman's contempt for Messiaen, see Morton Feldman, 'Mr. Schuller's History Lesson' [1963], in B.H. Friedman (ed.), *Give My Regards to Eighth Street*, 10.

[102]   For one discussion, see Kristine Stiles, 'Performance', in Robert Nelson and Richard Shiff (eds), *Critical Terms for Arts Theory* (Chicago, IL: The University of Chicago Press, 2003), 85. See also John Cage, 'Composition as Process' [three lectures given at Darmstadt, 1958], in John Cage, *Silence*, 18–56.

[103]   For a discussion of this aspect of Debussy's working practice, see Roy Howat, *Debussy in Proportion: A Musical Analysis* (Cambridge: Cambridge University Press, 1983), 6.

[104]   Morton Feldman, 'Darmstadt Lecture' [1984], in Chris Villars, *Morton Feldman Says*, 202.

aesthetic position, part of a long-standing tradition, within which it was considered bad manners (and perhaps also bad business) to flaunt one's systems. Yet, Feldman himself admitted, 'For the composer the truth is always the process, the system'.[105] No doubt the apparent ambiguity of Feldman's music stems, in part, from this aesthetic position of the concealed system, akin to that aspect of early 1950s New York painting that Harold Rosenberg described as 'a discipline of vagueness'.[106] In 1982 Feldman wrote,

> Composers, of course, do not use light, but sound, which historically is fixed into systems of sorts, which adhere to varying degrees of predictability or adventurous relationships.[107]

Here, it is not only the 'system of sorts' that is crucial, but the 'varying degrees of predictability or adventurous relationships'. In this polarity lies the very essence of the technical and aesthetic ambiguity that is so characteristic of Feldman's work – and of its inbuilt, deep tensions. Additionally, while the structure and method of Feldman's composition is unconventional, it is not isolated from the work of other composers (even as diverse as Pierre Boulez and Elmer Bernstein – the latter also studied with Wolpe), nor was it produced in isolation from other arts (in particular the visual art of abstract expressionism). If, through close reading of Feldman's work, we may identify certain characteristic structures, procedures and methods, then it becomes possible to understand the work more deeply than has hitherto been possible. We may then move beyond generalist discussion and begin to examine in more detail the internal discourses of the works themselves, the trajectory of Feldman's work over time, and also make more direct and meaningful connections to the work of other composers and artists (in effect, to begin to knit Feldman's work into the contemporary world of music, art, aesthetics, society and politics). This is a project with two-way benefits: not only do we begin to understand Feldman better, but also the very specificity of this will inform our understanding of the wider culture and society he inhabited.

---

[105]   Morton Feldman, 'Conversations Without Stravinsky' [1967], in B.H. Friedman (ed.), *Give My Regards to Eighth Street*, 55.

[106]   Harold Rosenberg, 'The American Action Painters', in Ellen Landau (ed.), *Reading Abstract Expressionism: Context and Critique* (New Haven, CT: Yale University Press, 2005), 194.

[107]   Morton Feldman, 'More Light' [1982], in B.H. Friedman (ed.), *Give My Regards to Eighth Street*, 150.

Chapter 2
'to create music as if on a canvas':[1]
Intermission 5 (1952)

Art and Life

Between 1950 and 1953, Feldman composed a series of six short piano pieces titled *Intermission*. They are explicitly expressive of a state of in-between-ness and, more than this, they are indicative of Feldman's understanding of the relation between music composition and ordinary life:

> *Intermission* means between; I wrote a number of them as a part of living, that is, I did many other things during the day than just writing music. The writing of one of them never took more than two hours.[2]

There is a sense in Feldman's words of musical composition being apart, rather than simply 'a part', and this hints at the natural tensions between his pursuit of a career as a composer, the reality of dependency upon a job in the family business, and the pressures or distractions of family life. Feldman was at this time, and indeed until in his mid-forties, working in the family business for a living.[3] At this time, musical composition was an intermission with respect to his everyday life, as the hearing of it is for an audience. This is a curious reversal of the conventional meaning of an intermission: the interval of time when the audience takes a break from an artistic performance.

Feldman's sketchbook annotations show that he felt that the pressures of family and business were a hindrance to his composition despite the associated material comforts; only two pages after the original sketch of *Intermission 5*, he wrote of 'the two basic inertias that I am aware of intensely: family obligation

---

[1]   From a Feldman sketchbook of the early 1950s. Paul Sacher Foundation, Basel, Morton Feldman Collection.

[2]   Quoted in program note for a recital given by David Tudor at the University of Illinois on 22 March 1953. Tudor began the recital with Feldman's *Extensions 3* and *Intermission 5*. The Getty Research Institute, Los Angeles, David Tudor Papers; also at http://www.cnvill.net/mftitles.htm.

[3]   In the absence of a Feldman biography, Claren's chronology remains the most useful reference. Sebastian Claren, *Neither: Die Musik Morton Feldmans* (Hofheim: Wolke, 2000), 523.

and outside authority'.[4] The issue of family and business in relation to Feldman's composition work is complicated. While it is clear that in some respects he resented the impositions of family and work (to some extent the same thing for Feldman, working in a family business), these very impositions provided an income unrelated to his artistic work. To some extent, this income made him a relatively autonomous artist in the sense that it was not essential for his work to be commercially marketable.[5] On the other hand, we might wonder what price was paid, aesthetically, for this reliance upon classically *bourgeois* economic and social support.

Investigating how this tension between social and economic obligation and Feldman's composition work may be reflected in his music is complex and problematic, if we are to avoid reductionism. How, to express this in Bourdieu's terms, might we analyse the tension of structural homology between Feldman's musical production and the economic field? At a superficial level, it seems that we should not read too much passivity into Feldman's work. For Feldman, music, like art, was always a site of action, a space where 'lines of becoming'[6] might be drawn and struggled with, always imbued with anxiety and tension. This was clearly conceptualised in opposition to his perceived 'inertia' of the workaday world: 'The artist works to bring everything "about", but outside my window if it were not for a musical mind everything seems static, fixed, petrified.'[7] In Feldman's mind, the artist or composer works to make things actively alive, in contrast to the petrified inertia of the outside world. It is likely that Feldman's public hostility toward audiences in the 1950s stemmed in part from this fundamental attitude.[8] This was to some extent characteristic of the art world of New York in the 1950s, as Pam Meecham and Julie Sheldon have described,

> The post-war period saw a rise in what was termed the "first-person aesthetic", which went in tandem with a rejection of advocacy for social causes and even for a socially relevant art. The former social crusader somewhat abruptly took on the mantle of outsider. The reasons for the shift away from the artist-citizen to

---

[4]   Paul Sacher Foundation, Basel, Morton Feldman Collection.

[5]   Bourdieu has suggested that even for the most autonomous of artists there are consumers, but that in this case the consumers tend to also be competitors in the same field. Pierre Bourdieu, 'Field of Power, Literary Field and Habitus' [1986], in Randal Johnson (ed.), *The Field Of Cultural Production: Essays on Art and Literature* (New York: Columbia University Press, 1993), 169.

[6]   This phrase of Feldman's is associated with early versions of *Intermission 6* (see Chapter 4).

[7]   Paul Sacher Foundation, Basel, Morton Feldman Collection (*ca* 1952–53, annotation associated with sketches for *Extensions 4*).

[8]   Dore Ashton, 'Stefan Wolpe – Man of Temperament', in Austin Clarkson (ed.), *On the Music of Stefan Wolpe: Essays and Recollections* (Hillsdale, NY: Pendragon Press, 2003), 98.

the artist as alienated outsider in opposition to mainstream values (among whom Jackson Pollock was archetypal) can be traced to the increasing dominance of a formalist aesthetic and post-war monetary and political values.[9]

The problem of the outside world as opposed to the inner world of the artist haunted Feldman for many years (and perhaps for his entire career). He raised the issue in dialogue with Cage in their radio conversations of the late 1960s, speaking of the role he imagined for himself as 'The old-fashioned role of the artist – deep in thought'.[10] This deep thought was constantly under threat, it seems, from the outside world, exemplified in this conversation by transistor radios at the beach, 'blaring out rock'n'roll'.[11] Interestingly, in this recorded conversation, one has the sense that Cage understood exactly the psychological difficulty that Feldman was talking about, but that he had found ways to rationalise the outside world into his life as a composer. Having composed a piece for 12 radios, Cage observed 'Now whenever I hear radios – even a single one not just twelve at a time, as you must have heard on the beach, at least – I think, "Well, they're just playing my piece"'.[12] It was a joke, of course, but a serious one, and we are left with a lingering sense of the deep aesthetic difference between the two composers. For Feldman, establishing a dividing boundary between his work as an artist and everything else seems to have been a necessary function of his creative process. The state of in-between-ness with which the *Intermissions* are concerned was for Feldman not passive but active, and implicitly confrontational.[13] This perspective, or artistic-political stance, was still evident as late as 1983, when Feldman joked 'I think of the whole world as my mother-in-law. I really do.'[14]

Sources and Dating

The composition date of *Intermission 5*, as with much of Feldman's work of the 1950s, is somewhat conjectural. The work is conventionally dated to

---

[9] Pam Meecham and Julie Sheldon, *Modern Art: A Critical Introduction*, 2nd edn (London: Routledge, 2005), 174.

[10] John Cage and Morton Feldman, *Radio Happenings: Conversations – Gespräche*, trans. Gisela Gronemeyer (Köln: MusikTexte, 1993), 17.

[11] Ibid., 11.

[12] Ibid., 11–12.

[13] In this sense, one might argue that *Intermission 5* was composed as an opposition to the external, conventional world, and part of a tradition of such critique extending back through early twentieth-century modernism to the individualist romanticism of the nineteenth century.

[14] Morton Feldman, 'Johannesburg Lecture 2: Feldman on Feldman', in Chris Villars (ed.), *Morton Feldman Says: Selected Interviews and Lectures 1964–1987*, transcribed by Rüdiger Meyer (London: Hyphen Press, 2006), 176.

1952, although there is no primary evidence for this beyond the fact that it was performed by David Tudor on 10 February 1952. Similarly, the manuscripts for *Intermission 3* and *Intermission 4* are undated; *Intermission 3*, however, was performed as early as July 1951, while *Intermission 4* first appeared together with *Intermission 5* in February 1952.[15] On the basis of available evidence, we may allow that the work might have been composed at any time between the summer of 1951 and 10 February 1952.[16] *Intermission 4* and *Intermission 5* may have been produced in relatively close succession, between the later part of 1951 and the first weeks of 1952 (in addition to the documentary evidence, they share certain musical materials). These two pieces were first performed by David Tudor, together with *Intermission 3*, on 10 February 1952,[17] and the neat copy of an early version of *Intermission 5* in the Tudor papers probably dates from this time.[18] The *Intermission* pieces and perhaps *Intermission 5* in particular, quickly became a significant part of Tudor's recital repertoire.[19]

The *Intermission* pieces were not published until the early 1960s (Feldman signed a contract with Edition Peters, New York, in February 1962).[20] At some point in the process of preparing the works for publication, Feldman decided to omit *Intermission 3* and *Intermission 4* from the published series, but retained the original numbering. The published series then, consists of *Intermission 1* and *Intermission 2* published as a pair, and *Intermission 5* and *Intermission 6* published separately.

There are five written sources for *Intermission 5*:

---

[15] Sebastian Claren, *Neither*, 550, 553.

[16] The ordering of material in the sketchbooks does not help to clarify matters: the program for the 10 February 1952 concert is pasted into the sketchbook several pages before the sketch for *Intermission 5*. The sketchbook contains material dating from 1951 through to 1953, in a confused ordering that seems not to be chronological. *Intermission 5* is immediately preceded by material from *Extensions 4*, and followed by an early version of *Intermission 6*. Several subsequent pages of annotations are dated to January and March of 1952. Paul Sacher Foundation, Basel, Morton Feldman Collection.

[17] Sebastian Claren, *Neither*, 553; see also Volker Straebel, 'Notes on the Edition', in Volker Straebel (ed.), *Morton Feldman: Solo Piano Works 1950–64* (New York: Edition Peters, 2000), 59 [unnumbered].

[18] The Getty Research Institute, Los Angeles, David Tudor Papers, 980039, Box 9, 24. An early copy of the sketch at a stage before some of the revisions were made. No tempo marking.

[19] Claren mentions several performances of the *Intermission* pieces (either as a set numbered 1–5, or in smaller groups) during the early 1950s. However, there are many gaps in our knowledge of the performance of Feldman's works at this period, and the secondary sources do not always agree. Sebastian Claren, *Neither*, 525–30.

[20] Ibid., 532. Bourdieu has noted that the 'time-lag between supply and demand tends to become a structural characteristic of the restricted field of production'. Pierre Bourdieu, 'Field of Power, Literary Field and Habitus', 169.

1. The autograph manuscript sketch, held by the Paul Sacher Stiftung, Basel (undated).[21]
2. Another manuscript, David Tudor's performing score, is held by the David Tudor Archives, The Getty Centre for the History of Art and Humanities, Los Angeles (undated).[22]
3. The original autograph master-copy (ink on vellum) made for the Peters edition of 1962, now held by the Music Library, University at Buffalo, The State University of New York (dated 1952).[23]
4. The first published edition, a holographic reproduction of (3). Edition Peters, 1962.[24]
5. A second published edition, based upon (3), computer-typeset with minor corrections and new errors.[25]

No two of these scores are exactly alike, and even the most recent computer-typeset edition cannot be considered authoritative or comprehensive. The original sketch is full of interesting details that provide small clues to Feldman's working procedure. We should not necessarily assume, however, that this was the first sketch; the extant autograph may have been worked out in earlier sketches now lost or destroyed, or otherwise derived from pre-compositional material. This possibility is supported by the observation that *Intermission 4* and *Intermission 5* have several distinct structures in common, suggesting that both works were derived from similar or related material.

The various sketch materials and manuscripts are important for a study of *Intermission 5*, chiefly in so far as they show evidence of a certain amount of reworking of the material in several stages. The Tudor copy represents a version of the piece derived from the earliest form of the extant sketch, while the sketch itself was subsequently reworked – either after the first performances or immediately prior to publication (or perhaps both). Feldman, who famously claimed in response to Stockhausen's questioning, that he did not push his material around 'even a

---

[21]   Paul Sacher Foundation, Basel, Morton Feldman Collection. The sketch shows considerable evidence of reworking of pitch, enharmonic spellings and dynamics. There is no tempo marking.

[22]   The Getty Research Institute, Los Angeles, David Tudor Papers, 980039, Series 1b, Box 9, 24.

[23]   Music Library, University at Buffalo, The State University of New York, Buffalo, C.F. Peters Collection of Morton Feldman Manuscripts, 1961–69, Mus. Arc. 2.4, Box 2, 41.

[24]   Morton Feldman, *Intermission 5* (New York: Edition Peters, 1962).

[25]   Morton Feldman, '*Intermission 5*', in Volker Straebel (ed.), *Solo Piano Works 1950–64*, 3–4. All earlier sources give the top note of the opening chord as F♯/G♭, not G; the loud chord in m. 23 is also incorrect – F4 should read F♯4.

little bit',[26] is here caught in the act of making revisions of several kinds: to pitch-content, rhythm, dynamic and tempo.

To my knowledge, no recording of *Intermission 5* was ever released on LP record, but at the time of writing the work has appeared on six commercially released compact discs, the first in 1990.[27] We might reflect upon the fact that the first commercial recording of *Intermission 5* was released a full 38 years after the work was composed; it is likely that this reveals a changing perspective on Feldman's early work in the years following his death in 1987. Of the 35 Feldman works issued on LP record, there is a preponderance of graphic scores; in fact, the early 1950s period was represented almost entirely by graphic scores. None of the *Intermission* series was commercially issued.[28] In part, this reflects the fact that it was the (supposedly indeterminate) graphic scores that had caught the imagination of the various media agents seeking to market Feldman's music during this period.

Crucially important among recent releases are two recordings of the piece on a compact disc issued by Berlin label Edition RZ in 1994. This disc is made up of previously unreleased recordings made for German radio between 1956 and 1979, and includes performances of *Intermission 5* by both David Tudor and Feldman himself.[29] On the one hand, there can be no doubt that these are valuable primary source recordings. At the same time, close examination of them quickly demonstrates the difficulties and problems associated with recorded performance as musicological source material. For example, there may be a high degree of uncertainty regarding the circumstances of the recording, and the effect this may have had upon the realisation of the work. We are dealing with a source that has been mediated not only by the performer and his or her instrument but also the technology and circumstances of the recorded performance, not to mention the interventions of technicians, engineers and editors – all of which may be difficult or even impossible to document.

The earlier of the two recordings, made by Tudor in 1956,[30] displays all the flair and vitality that was characteristic of Tudor's playing. For those of us accustomed to hearing the published version of the work (which, unlike Tudor's early version,[31] is marked 'Slow'), Tudor performs in a surprisingly brisk manner,

---

[26]   Morton Feldman, 'Crippled Symmetry', in B.H. Friedman (ed.), *Give My Regards to Eighth Street: Collected Writings of Morton Feldman* (Cambridge, MA: Exact Change, 2000), 143. The story has also been told elsewhere – see for example Morton Feldman, 'Johannesburg Lecture 2', in Chris Villars (ed.), *Morton Feldman Says*, 176.

[27]   Sebastian Claren, in *Neither*, 605. For a regularly updated discography, see Chris Villars, *Morton Feldman: Discography*, http://www.cnvill.net/mfdiscog.htm.

[28]   Ibid.

[29]   *Morton Feldman*. CD (Berlin: Edition RZ 1010, 1994).

[30]   For Norddeutscher Rundfunk. See sleeve notes, ibid.

[31]   The Getty Research Institute, Los Angeles, David Tudor Papers, 980039, Box 9, 24.

and there are a few places where one senses an impatience with the long measured silences, as he cuts them slightly short. In this recording, there are several notable deviations from the published score:

- In measure 3, Tudor plays a pair of demi-semiquavers (32nd notes) rather than semiquavers (16ths): evidence that he was playing from the early copy preserved in his papers rather than one more closely related to the published version.
- In measure 24, Tudor follows the left hand E1 with an F♯1, while omitting the grace-notes in the right hand at the end of the measure (Figure 2.1). This variant is not notated in any of the extant scores, and may perhaps be considered an error.[32]

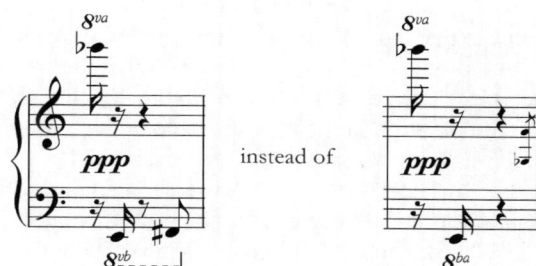

Figure 2.1   Feldman, *Intermission 5*, m. 24. David Tudor's 'wrong' note, as recorded and as written

- In the final 18 measures, Tudor consistently plays the two-measure repeated motif as though it were in 5/8 time rather than the notated 3/8 + 3/8 (Figure 2.2). In addition, Tudor plays the repetition motif only eight times instead of nine – most likely another mistake.

---

[32] Examination of the Tudor copy suggests that in performance he may have misread an F♯ belonging to the treble of the next system as belonging to the measure above; the systems are notated without spaces between (a common practice of Feldman's), and notes on ledger-lines do encroach upon neighbouring systems at several points.

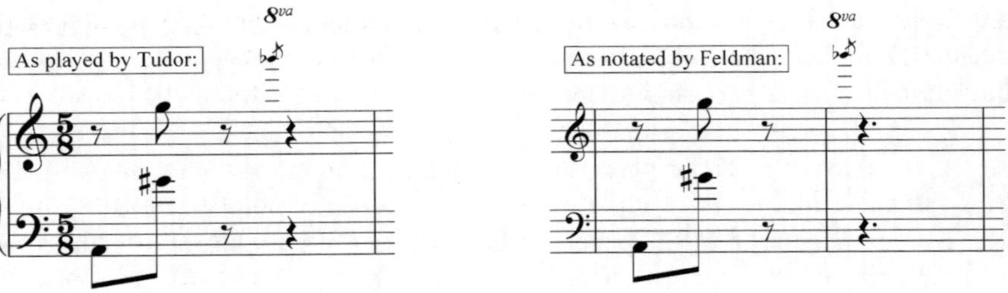

Figure 2.2   Feldman, *Intermission 5*, mm. 55–72. Tudor's rhythmic variant

There is no specific evidence for this rhythmic variant in any of the scores. It may be noted, however, that the early manuscripts (including Tudor's copy) do not have rests written out in full. Thus, the final grace note of the motif appears at the beginning of a bar empty even of rests, perhaps indirectly or even unintentionally suggesting that the full duration of the measure need not be observed.

Feldman's performance of *Intermission 5*, recorded in 1978,[33] has at least as great a dynamic range as Tudor's (the *fff* chords are extremely loud and *ppp* some times actually inaudible), but proceeds at a much slower pace. In general, the timing is more relaxed throughout, with a certain sense of unhurried flexibility that contrasts markedly with the rather rushed-along Tudor performance. Once again, I note two distinct deviations from the score as published:

- Feldman makes a cut from measure 16 to measure 22.
- Like Tudor, he plays the closing section in 5/8 instead of 3/8 + 3/8 (Figure 2.2).

The cut is rather alarming in terms of its implications for analysis of the work. Not only does it significantly alter the formal time-structure of this relatively short work, but it also interferes with the pitch content of the work at a crucial point, as we shall see. There are several possible explanations:

- It may have been a mistake, possibly caused by skipping from one system to the next inadvertently (in the published scores, measure 16 is directly above measure 22).
- It may have been an overly drastic tape edit (although none is definitively audible), perhaps to remove extraneous noise (there is minor traffic noise elsewhere in the recording).
- It may be a deliberate change made to the work subsequent to publication.

---

[33]   For Deutschlandfunk. See sleeve notes, *Morton Feldman*. CD.

Of these, the first and second would be the most convenient explanations, while serious consideration of the third certainly gives rise to the most difficulties. Unless further evidence comes to light (another manuscript with this cut indicated, for example), it is reasonable to assume that this strange deviation was either accidental or related to some problem with the recording itself. As we shall see, analysis of the work demonstrates that this cut destroys several important compositional structures, suggesting that it was most likely an unfortunate accident.

In contrast, the evidence of both Tudor and Feldman performing *Intermission 5* (in 1956 and 1978, respectively) with the timing of the last section purposefully and consistently altered in exactly the same way may not be so conveniently dismissed. While it is difficult to explain with any certainty why they both played in this way, or why the timing is not reflected in the published score, it seems that we must view this as a valid 'reading' of the closing section of the work. This is one instance, I would argue, where the primary-source recordings do actually add a new element to our understanding of the work, and any future edition of *Intermission 5* should offer this variant if it is to claim to represent the work accurately. As is so often the case with the examination of multiple sources for musical works, such a study tends to elucidate by increasing the richness and complexity of our understanding, rather than simplifying.

The un-notated rhythmic variant raises questions about performance practice, especially concerning Feldman's understanding of rhythm, and the manner in which he expected a performer to interpret his notations. In terms of the proportional partitioning of the time-duration of the work discussed in this chapter below, this rhythmic variant seems to cause problems: after all, the omission of one quaver from every second measure over 18 measures amounts to a substantial alteration of the overall time-canvas. Without pre-empting the analytical discussion to follow, let me here observe that it seems likely that Feldman's principal unit of time-measurement was the measure itself as notated (comparable in this sense to the square of Feldman's grid-based graphic scores), and that precise placement within the bar was a secondary consideration in the early stages of composition. (In Feldman's late works, a very flexible approach to the length and content of measures is a vital characteristic of style.) In this way we may appreciate that the variation of rhythm in the closing section is a kind of performed *rubato*, operating at a different level of organisation to the macro-structure of an 18-measure partition of the overall 72 measure 'on paper' duration of the work. Similarly, the *fermata* in measure 2 appears in the published scores, but is not present in any of the earlier manuscripts. Clearly, it was not a factor in the composition process, but added later as a performance-related embellishment of the local time-structure.

In terms of text material, as has been noted in Chapter 1, relatively little survives in Feldman's own words from the 1950s. Sebastian Claren lists only six small texts that may be dated to the 1950s period,[34] and none of these concerns

---

[34]   Sebastian Claren, 'Verzeichnis der Schriften, Vorträge und Gespräche Feldmans', in *Neither*, 577–8.

Intermission 5 specifically. While passing references to the work are to be found in the secondary literature, there is little detailed published analysis of *Intermission 5* – the writings of Borio and Undreiner being the exceptions.[35] A very significant (albeit brief) discussion of the work is contained in Gianmario Borio's 1996 essay on Feldman and abstract expressionism.[36] Here, Borio made an important breakthrough for the study of Feldman's music by demonstrating that there is an underlying mathematical structure to *Intermission 5*, and illustrating this with a complex analytical model. My interpretation of the structures – and the relationships between them – differs somewhat from Borio's analysis. His work does, however, set a precedent for my aims in this chapter: to demonstrate that in *Intermission 5* Feldman was intelligently manipulating the deployment of his musical material (rather than applying a purely chance-driven or intuitive procedure), and to show some of the ways in which this is most clearly evident.

Analysis i

Rausch, Borio and Claren have identified several features of *Intermission 5* that have immediate significance, namely, the use of cluster-like chords, the extreme dynamic range (*fff–ppp*), the instruction to hold both pedals down throughout, and the repeated motif that brings the work to a close.[37]

Among Feldman's works of the early 1950s are some that are entirely quiet, others that demand highly contrasted dynamics, and some in which dynamic decisions are left entirely to the performer. In this context, we may observe that *Intermission 5*'s published dynamic range from *fff* to *ppp* is at the extreme of Feldman's dynamic contrasts (in the sketch and the Tudor manuscript this was originally only *f* to *p*, but was expanded later on the sketch itself and in the published version). Other instances of notated dynamic contrasts (not uncommon in Feldman's work of this period) are to be found, for example, in *Intermission 4*, *Extensions 1*, dating from November 1951 and *Extensions 3*, composed shortly after *Intermission 5* in 1952.[38] In these cases, as with *Intermission 5*, the loud events tend to be isolated chords rather than extended passages – as is also the

---

[35] Gianmario Borio, 'Morton Feldman e l'Espressionismo astratto: La costruzione di tempo e suono nelle miniature pianistiche degli anni Cinquanta e Sessanta', in *Itinerari della musica americana* (Lucca: Una Cosa Rara, 1996), 119–34; Paul Stephen Undreiner, *Pitch Structure in Morton Feldman's Compositions of 1952* (PhD Dissertation, State University of New Jersey, 2009).

[36] Gianmario Borio, 'Morton Feldman e l'Espressionismo astratto'.

[37] Sebastian Claren, *Neither*, 61, 187; Ulrike Rausch, *Grenzgänge: Musik und Bildende Kunst im New York der 50er Jahre* (Saarbrücken: Pfau-Verlag, 1999), 31–9; Gianmario Borio, 'Morton Feldman e l'Espressionismo astratto'.

[38] The exact date of *Extensions 3* is uncertain, but the work was performed on 2 May 1952. Sebastian Claren, *Neither*, 553.

case with later works such as *Piano* (1977). The *Intersection* pieces, on the other hand, leave dynamics to the discretion of the performer, which, needless to say, most performers have understood to mean not entirely quiet. The violence of these highly contrasted sound-events suggests that there may be more even to Feldman's genuinely quiet music than is often assumed, or even that we may be misunderstanding it altogether.

In *Intermission 5*, Feldman asks for the damper-release and *una corda* pedals to be held down throughout (in the sketch he quaintly refers to them as 'soft and loud' pedals). One further aspect of the pedal indication is worth noting: that the combination of *una corda* pedal and *fff* chords makes for a subtly particular quality of sound, rather different to the effect of an *fff* chord played without *una corda*. Pedal indications are quite rare in Feldman's published piano music of the 1950s and 1960s. Such markings were generally omitted even in works that do have pedal indications in the sketches or early manuscripts. (Compare, for example, the published score of *Three Pieces for Piano* (1954) with the manuscript copies. This work certainly deserves a new, properly revised edition. The presently available published scores contain a number of serious note errors – some of which, for example, cause the sympathetic harmonic resonance of silently held notes to be ineffective.)[39]

Holding the right pedal down throughout *Intermission 5* serves two functions: firstly, it ensures that there is no silence in the piece (or virtually none – this depends to some extent on the instrument and the performance) and that rests in the notated score cannot be understood to represent silence. Even in sections where there are several consecutive measures without notes, the sounds of those played previously continue their entropic journeys. Secondly, the pedal helps to create the shape of the piece, amplifying and extending the resonance of the opening *fff* chord so that the first page of the work emerges from the gradually decaying chromatic field. The work is, in this sense, largely structured around the concept of drawing a select set of notes gradually out of the chromatic field (ultimately resolving themselves into the chromatic tetrachord that makes up the closing repeated motif). It is clear from annotations in Feldman's sketchbooks of the early 1950s that he was at this time including the decay of sounds in his conceptual model of musical composition:

> Structure then makes us ask what the basic materials are and what is unnecessary. Most important structure teaches us that these basic materials are in a state of complete equality. And we also deal with degradations of sound … immediately as we conceive a work.[40]

Intermission 5 begins, in the published version, with a very loud 14-note chord made up of 12 pitch-classes – an entire 12-tone aggregate unto itself (Figure 2.3).

---

[39]   Paul Sacher Foundation, Basel, Morton Feldman Collection.

[40]   Ibid.

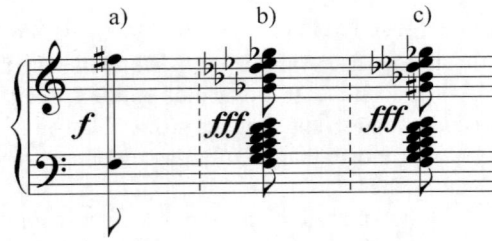

Figure 2.3   Feldman, *Intermission 5*. The opening chord as given in
              (a) the original sketch; (b) the sketch revision; and
              (c) the published score of 1962

Curiously, the manuscripts show that Feldman reworked the pitch-content of this
chord twice. In the original sketch of the opening, he notated the chord in cluster-
notation, specifying only the outer notes. In Tudor's copy, only the outer notes are
indicated, not the cluster, although in the 1956 recording he does in fact play the
cluster. Subsequently, the sketch shows that Feldman re-notated the two opening
measures on another system, with the chord spelt out fully. This sketched chord
would be a full 12-tone aggregate, except that it is missing the pitch-class G♯/A♭.
In copying the work for publication, Feldman corrected this error by changing
the right hand G♭4 to G♯4, demonstrating that he was conscious of the aggregate
content of the chord and its importance. Most importantly, Feldman's tinkering
with the pitch-content of the chord indicates that the details of pitch material
did matter to him, and that he was aware of the content and concerned about its
implications.[41] Clearly dissatisfied with the cluster-notation (which is interesting
in itself, given that he was occupied with writing graphic scores in the early 1950s
that seemingly do not specify pitch to even this degree of detail), Feldman felt
it necessary to notate the pitches making up the chord exactly, and had several
attempts at refining them.[42]

---

[41]   Note that in this analysis I treat enharmonics as equivalent. Feldman's use of
enharmonic spelling is interesting, and the worthwhile subject of another study. Certainly,
in most works of this period he makes many revisions of enharmonic spelling between
sketches, drafts and neat-copies.

[42]   The computer-engraved edition of the work published in 2000 introduces several
novel variants that have no basis in the manuscript sources. One of these is in the opening
chord, where the top note is given as G5 instead of Feldman's G♭5. Musical works, of
course, are not static objects, but constantly changing over time, much like paintings. The
surfaces of many abstract expressionist paintings today are not what the original audiences
saw in the 1950s, owing to the combined effects of degradation and restoration. For one
discussion of such conservation problems, see Harry F. Gaugh, *Franz Kline* (New York:

Each of the four very loud chords (Figure 2.4) has different pitch-content and pitch-class density; I suggest that what we are seeing here is not so much a flirtation with the notion of the cluster as a sound-effect, but the working out, in this very sketch, of Feldman's later concept of a controlled use of highly chromatic, cluster-like chords. This controlled approach to the composition of chords is evident in all of Feldman's pitch-notated scores, to the end of his life.

More than a decade after composing *Intermission 5*, Feldman spoke of some of his compositional concerns regarding chords vs clusters in the unpublished *Four Lectures: New York Style*. Here, discussing *Two Pieces for Three Pianos* (1965/66), it seems he felt that he had crossed a boundary between chords and clusters, and needed to rationalise what had been happening in his work up to this point:

> I found myself using chords of a thickness in density which I only hinted at earlier in my music. Before, I got my density in the conventional way – by altering the chord. What was unconventional – was that the chords did not follow, here I found myself using clusters – that is piling up sounds with the closest interval we have on the piano – minor seconds. But if I did this consistently – then it would be like this ex.[ample] I just gave about using all the 88 notes at one time instead of only 80 of them. In other words – I could then compose in such a way that I wouldn't even have to hear it – it would be just an idea – something that we legitimize and call conceptual.
>
> But I did hear something. Something that were neither chords nor were they clusters. Something in between. I invented a new term for this. A term that is already making the rounds. I called it altered clusters.[43]

There is a trajectory of thought leading to this conception of the 'altered cluster' – from the works of the early 1950s through the *Vertical Thoughts* series, the elegant (yet vertically massive) complexity of *Piano Piece (to Philip Guston)*, and on into the 1970s, with the great hovering and colliding sound-masses and planes of *Piano* (1977).[44] The opening 12-tone chord of *Intermission 5*, otherwise unique in Feldman's 1950s music, is not a true cluster, but a controlled chord of particular weight and density – and a precursor of the 1960s developments discussed in the

---

Abbeville Press, 1985), 155–62. Present and future pianists using the 2000 edition of *Intermission 5* perform a work containing notes that Feldman did not write – an interesting problem for future analysts. Morton Feldman, *Intermission 5*, in Volker Straebel (ed.), *Solo Piano Works 1950–64*, 3–4.

[43] Morton Feldman, *Four Lectures: New York Style* [unpublished manuscript ca 1967/68], Paul Sacher Foundation, Basel, Morton Feldman Collection.

[44] For a thoughtful analysis, incorporating material from interviews with Feldman, see Paula Ames, '*Piano* (1977)', in Thomas DeLio (ed.), *The Music of Morton Feldman* (Westport, CT: Greenwood Press, 1996), 99–143.

lecture quoted above. As early as 1936, Varèse was speaking of these things in terms strikingly similar to Feldman's sketchbook annotations:

> When new instruments will allow me to write music as I conceive it, the movement of sound-masses, of shifting planes, will be clearly perceived in my work, taking the place of the linear counterpoint.[45]

Unlike Varèse, Feldman was not very interested in new instruments (with the exception of the electric guitar),[46] but chords such as those in *Intermission 5* – carefully chosen from an almost infinite variety of possibilities of pitch-content, voicing and register – might be piled against one other, spaced to regulate the partitioning of the time-canvas or contrasted with single notes or simple intervals. They may be thus perceived to have almost painterly properties. As Feldman explained many years later, in significantly visual terms,

> I work very much like a painter, insofar as I'm watching the phenomena and I'm thickening and I'm thinning and I'm working in that way and just watching what it needs.[47]

It is useful to consider the connections between the four loud chords as a distinct plane (counterpoint) in the musical texture, not only because of their highly contrasted dynamic, but also with regard to pitch content (Figure 2.4). These chords seem to speak to each other in a common tongue, in which they carry out their own structured discourse (in part determined by an exchange of black and white notes between the pianist-composer's hands).

These four chords themselves may justifiably be understood as made up of two sub-domains, each of two chords. The first and third chords operate as 'altered' clusters (to use Feldman's term) and have a special relationship in terms of black and white notes on the keyboard), whereas the second and fourth are made of semitone dyads. The fourth chord is in fact a simple dyad, a single semitone made up of the pitches D♯ and E. In addition to being the last of the loud sound-events, this is the last appearance of the pitch-class E in the piece – and we hear this same

---

[45]   Edgard Varèse, 'The Liberation of Sound', in Elliott Schwartz and Barney Childs (eds), *Contemporary Composers on Contemporary Music* (New York: Holt, Rinehart and Winston, 1967), 197.

[46]   The only work that explicitly suggests a contemplated move in the direction of Varèse's sonic interests is *Marginal Intersection* (1951), for an orchestra that includes electrical oscillators and magnetic tape recordings. The later *Intersection for Magnetic Tape* (1953) is a distinctly more abstract score, less concerned with defined sonority than architectural design.

[47]   Morton Feldman, 'XXX Anecdotes and Drawings', in Walter Zimmermann (ed.), *Morton Feldman Essays* (Kerpen: Beginner Press, 1985), 168 [transcribed by Gerhard Westerrath from a seminar given in Frankfurt, 1984; translated by Hanfried Blume].

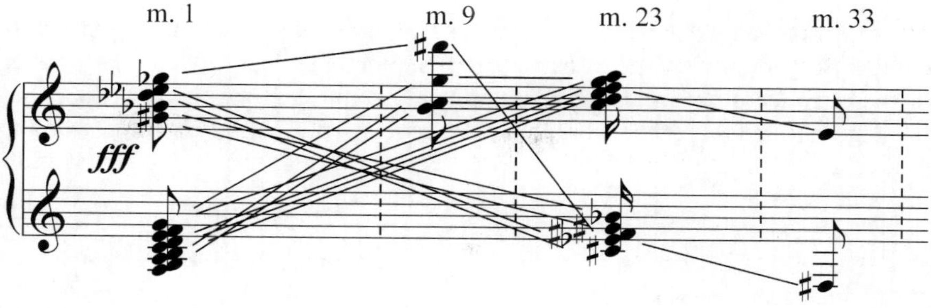

Figure 2.4   Feldman, *Intermission 5*. Registral exchanges between the four loud chords

dyad in measure 4, where the pitch-class E makes its first appearance subsequent to the opening chord. Spread over the first half of the work, these four chords of alternately higher and lower density convey an impression of succumbing to pitch-content-related entropy, mirroring the overall declining wedge-shape of the work. The final *fff* dyad reinforces this point of closure as the intersection of two planes, one of dynamic definition and the other of pitch-deployment.

One cannot help noticing that G♭/F♯, the upper boundary of the vertical pitch-space defined by the opening chord, is also the prominent highest pitch-class of the second. The bulk of the chords swing through a registral exchange spanning an octave, with a 1:1 still-point, or fulcrum, of B♭4–B4, which is itself curiously close to the 1:1 partition of the vertical pitch-space of the entire piece, at G♯4. One senses that the four chords are simultaneously standing out from the background texture in high relief, and also knitted into it firmly in terms of pitch-organisation and the structuring of vertical space.

The first loud chord, a gigantic cluster-like aggregation of pitch-classes, would be shocking in any context, coming at our ears out of silence with marked violence. The majority of sound-events in *Intermission 5* are extremely quiet – and it is the extreme contrast, as we have already noted, that is crucial to any understanding of Feldman's work in this period (*mezzo* dynamics were not part of Feldman's palette of sounds). Furthermore, it is immediately apparent that the listener will perceive these loud chords as somehow defining time-spaces within the overall 72-measure duration of the work, effectively partitioning the 'horizontal' time-canvas.

Similarly, the closing repetition-field defines a clearly audible partition of the work's duration, in the proportion 3:1. Such clearly defined repetition sections (prefiguring the vast repetition cycles of the late works) are not altogether uncommon in Feldman's work of the early 1950s (see, for example, works like *Structures* and *Extensions 3*), and the repetition-field as a closing section (or cadential figure) also appears in some works of the later 1950s, notably *Two Pianos* (1957). Here, and in *Intermission 5*, the listener has a clear sense not only of the section being defined by a repeated motif, but of the very limited pitch-class content of that motif, which is by this means effectively highlighted. The listener or score-reader is invited to speculate, not only about the time–space defined and its relation to the rest of the work, but also the relation of this pitch-class set to the pitch material of the rest of the work. As Feldman's teacher, Stefan Wolpe, said in 1959,

> Every pitch constellation smaller than the all-chromatic circuit is either a delay in completing the whole, or is an autonomous fragment which can exist outside the total circuit. It may be first unhinged as a part of the total circuit, later hinged back.[48]

As we shall see, Feldman's motif in the closing section of *Intermission 5* is indeed 'unhinged' from the total chromatic, rather than completely autonomous (in contrast, the repetition-field in *Structures* (1951) for string quartet is both unhinged and 'hinged back'). It functions as what more conventional composers might have called a *coda*; the first statement of the final motif completes the preceding chromatic field, but the time-structure, the large-scale rhythm of the work, requires that the unhinged fragment be repeated a further eight times to fill out the space.

It can be problematic to divide a relatively abstract work like *Intermission 5* into manageable segments for pitch-analysis.[49] For much of the work, segmentation by motif, phrase and even gesture seems dangerously arbitrary, given that we have little idea of how Feldman put the material together. The last 18 measures of the work, however, represent not only a distinctly visible and audible unit of time, but also a distinct pitch collection (Figure 2.5), and are thus a vital clue to Feldman's own partitioning of both pitch material and architectural time, through which we may begin to glimpse his compositional processes in action. Although one might choose to spell this as an ordered set (A, G♯, G, B♭), it is crucial to observe that the collection is a chromatic tetrachord. This particular kind of set held a special interest for Feldman throughout his career.[50]

There is also a sense in which the notes aurally group themselves (according to Feldman's disposition of them) as a pair of semitones: A and B♭, separated in time and space by the pair G♯ and G. Such well-defined groups of semitones are very much in evidence throughout the piece (as noted previously, for example, in two of the three loud chords). This reminds us of Wolpe's words of 1952: 'And thus the second ... has still (and I'm sure for a good while) the importance of a

---

[48]   Stefan Wolpe, 'Thinking Twice' [1959], in Elliott Schwartz and Barney Childs, *Contemporary Composer*, 287.

[49]   For discussion of the practical issues, see Christopher Hasty 'Segmentation and Process in Post-tonal Music', *Music Theory Spectrum*, 3 (Spring 1981), 54–73.

[50]   Morton Feldman, 'XXX Anecdotes and Drawings', p. 169. Seminar given in Frankfurt, February 1984.

Figure 2.5   Feldman, *Intermission 5*, mm. 55–72. Pitch content of closing motif

principal axis-interval'.[51] I might add at this point that there may well be a link between Feldman's set-construction, so often revealing an interest in chromatic segments, and a line of thought stemming from Webern's interest in the chromatic hexachord, via Wolpe.[52] As Milton Babbitt said in 1983,[53] discussing Webern's *Symphony*,

> Notice that he's using the same hexachord that he used in the *Piano Variations* – the chromatic hexachord; here, however, he uses it very differently … There are aspects of this passage which were extremely suggestive to later composers, many of whom are still alive.[54]

Feldman seems to have very rarely used such chromatic sets as partitions of ordered 12-tone rows[55] (of course it is possible that ordered material may be so

---

[51]   Stefan Wolpe, 'Thoughts on Pitch and some Considerations Connected with It' [Lecture given at Black Mountain College, August 1952], Austin Clarkson (ed.), *Perspectives of New Music*, 17/2 (Spring/Summer 1979), 53.

[52]   Additionally, it seems likely that Feldman was at least peripherally aware (via Cage and Tudor) of the discussions concerning Webern that took place at Darmstadt in the 1950s. Whether he also knew the theoretical writings published in *Die Reihe* is uncertain, and in any case these did not appear in English until the late 1950s.

[53]   There are numerous evidences for the frequently overlooked contact between Feldman and Babbitt, and their lifelong relationship certainly deserves close examination. See, for example, Morton Feldman, 'I met Heine on the Rue Fürstenberg', in B.H. Friedman (ed.), *Give My Regards to Eighth Street*, 114. Also, Cole Gagne and Tracy Caras, 'Soundpieces Interview', in Chris Villars, *Morton Feldman Says*, 87.

[54]   Milton Babbitt, *Words about Music*, Stephen Dembski and Joseph N Strauss (eds) (Madison, WI: University of Wisconsin Press, 1987), 42–3.

[55]   For discussion of ordered row material in *Why Patterns?* (1978), see Steven Johnson, 'Jasper Johns and Morton Feldman: Why Patterns?', in Steven Johnson (ed.), *The New York Schools of Music and the Visual Arts* (New York: Routledge, 2002), 235–40. A rare instance of Feldman speaking of such matters is recorded in the Gagne-Caras interview,

buried under other, unordered layers as to be unidentifiable), but he did use them to build 12-tone aggregates, or chromatic fields, spread over variable spaces of time. Consequently, we may observe that Feldman was conscious not only of the properties of the smaller sets he was using, chromatic or otherwise, but also of their complementary sets; their relation to the 'all-chromatic circuit' (in Wolpe's words). It is through the controlled manipulation of these basic pitch materials that Feldman formed his larger chromatic fields, which are in turn intimately related to the formal architecture of a given piece, as we shall see. Similarly, Feldman seems not to have been particularly interested in exploring the contrapuntal or combinatorial possibilities of such sets (as Babbitt was, for example), but he was nonetheless aware of them as distinct sets, for structural purposes, and even allowed them at times to form figural motifs, unhinged from the total chromatic. It is from this understanding of a sub-set of the aggregate deployed as a motif that Feldman might logically allow such a figure to fill an entire section of his designed structure, as in the closing section of *Intermission 5*.

Although motivic repetitions are common in Feldman's dance pieces of the 1950s,[56] the published concert works of the same period have much less a sense of having been actually built from such repetitions. Many of these 1950s pieces, in fact, have no obvious repetitions at all; when there are repetitions, they are often used in quite subtle ways, and for varied purposes in different contexts. One may suspect that, in the dance, theatre and film works,[57] Feldman was rather more closely following Cage's models – and this may well have been part of his reason for not publishing them when the opportunity arose. In *Intermission 5*, we have one of the most striking motivic repetition sections in Feldman's 1950s concert music.[58] *Intermissions 1–4*, for example, have no repetitions of this kind, and

---

where he speaks of two ordered rows in *Violin and Orchestra* (1979), one of which is a symbolic quotation from Webern. Cole Gagne and Tracy Caras, 'Soundpieces Interview', in Chris Villars, *Morton Feldman Says*, 92–3. The manuscript sketches of several works of the late 1970s and 1980s contain matrices for the serial ordering of not only 12-tone rows, but also rhythmic motifs, dynamics and even instrumentation. Our understanding of how Feldman actually uses this material in practice is as yet largely unformed. Describing such formations of pitch material in Feldman's music is problematic, however; they are perhaps better understood as linear aggregates rather than 'rows' in the conventional sense.

[56]   See, for example, the *Nature Pieces* (1951), or *Three Dances* (1950), or the later *Figure of Memory* (1958). The untitled piece for two pianos dating from 1958 is a rare example of this style in what may have been intended (though never published as such) to be a concert work. Manuscripts in Paul Sacher Foundation, Basel, Morton Feldman Collection.

[57]   See, for example, the music composed in 1951 for Hans Namuth and Paul Falkenberg's film *Jackson Pollock*.

[58]   Although it was pre-dated by the repetition-section in *Structures* for string quartet (March 1951), which sounds to twenty-first century ears as a strong premonition of Feldman's late style. Such repetition-fields are only one of many points of connection between the early and late Feldman works.

this is one of several factors that give them their characteristic flavour. Of other works composed *ca* 1952, we may observe that *Piano Piece 1952* does not have a repetition-field (although it does have recurring pitch-sets), while *Extensions 3* does. Given the importance of such repetitions in Feldman's late works, however, I would suggest that in *Intermission 5* we hear one of the earliest applications of a clearly structural motivic repetition in Feldman's concert works. This marks the beginning of the composer's interest in such repetitions that eventually gave rise to the late works, where the fields are woven into vast, carpet-inspired patterns of motifs.

The repetition-field in *Intermission 5* thus operates on several levels of significance. It has a structural significance, defining (on paper at least) exactly one-quarter of the duration of the work, and the section's internal structure of nine repetitions of a two-measure motif implies some deeper aspect of numerical significance. It has a narrative significance as the ending of the work, functioning as a sort of cadential figure, and is somehow audibly recognisable as such. Furthermore, the motif is one of the clearest instances in the early 1950s Feldman pieces of the composer's emphasis of a pitch collection by repetition; there can be no doubt for either listener or reader that Feldman wished to draw our attention to this small group of notes.

Analysis ii

Already, in consideration of some of these superficial aspects of the piece, we have noted points of structural interest that will bear further investigation. That the four very loud chords, more-or-less equally spaced, clearly fall only within the first half of the work certainly implies some sort of over-arching structure within which these chords operate. We have also observed that the work begins with a chord that may be understood to function as a 12-tone aggregate (the closed circuit, in Wolpe's terms, of the total chromatic), while also noting that other discrete parts of the piece are built from smaller pitch collections. In particular, the closing section, with its motivic repetition, highlights one such collection and also suggests a way of investigating the formal structures of the piece according to mathematical proportions.

On this basis, I identify at the outset two significant structural divisions. Firstly, the mid-point of the work at the end of measure 36 is clearly important in so far as it closes off that part of the work in which loud chords appear. It is also marked by three audibly notable repetitions of F♯7; these are the first explicit, uninterrupted repetitions in the work, introducing the element of repetition that (as we have seen) becomes increasingly significant in the second half of the piece. Secondly, the closing repetition-section appears to reinforce this binary structural division,

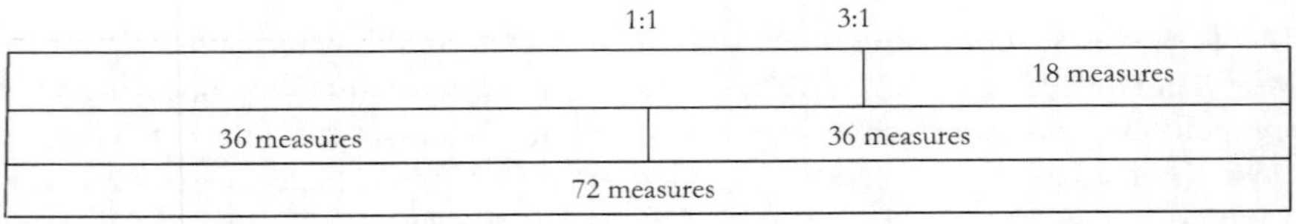

		1:1		3:1	

				18 measures
	36 measures		36 measures	
		72 measures		

Figure 2.6   Major time-partitions of *Intermission 5*

built out of a two-measure motif repeated nine times to fill 18 measures, exactly one-quarter of the piece.[59] We may begin to model the structures as in Figure 2.6.

Within the frame of this structure, Feldman has placed his four loud chords roughly every 10 measures through the first half of the piece (in measures 1, 9, 23, 33), decorated the 1:1 division with three high notes (F♯7), and filled the closing quarter of the work's duration with the repetition-field. Given that this field of motivic repetition also draws attention to a chromatic tetrachord (G, G♯, A, B♭), this may be a clue to the pitch-organisation of the work. Noticing that the notes of this set are markedly scarce in the systems preceding the closing section, we might wonder if this is some deliberate function of complementarity. If we search, working backwards from the closing section, for the completion of the 12-tone aggregate, we find that this occurs with the F4 grace-note at the end of measure 24 that is in fact the last F sounded in the piece.

The pitch-class F is also curiously scarce throughout the early part of the work, but rather common between measures 17 and 24. If one were to think of the opening chord as a chromatic field unto itself (I shall henceforth consider this entity to be the first chromatic field, a verticalised sounding of the total chromatic – see Figures 2.7 and 2.8), we find that the first subsequent F in the piece is actually that in measure 17, and that this event completes a 12-tone aggregate sounded between the second quaver of measure 1 and measure 17. Close examination of the section between measures 17 and 24 reveals that this also contains a complete chromatic aggregate.[60] Further, we may observe that the important dyad F–G♭ that marks the boundary of the third and fourth chromatic fields (measure 24) is also a prominent part of the chord marking the boundary between the first and second (measure 17).

Is there anything structurally or proportionally significant about these points at measures 17 and 24, where we hear the first and last distinct appearances of the

---

[59]   The corresponding one-quarter division of the first half of the work does not appear to mark anything so obviously significant, although it falls only one measure away from the commencement of the third chromatic field in m. 17 (Figure 2.8).

[60]   In the manuscript sketch, the section from m. 16 to m. 24 defined by the first and last appearances of pitch-class F occupies a full system. As an aside, we may note that the pitch-class B is likely to be significant here, as it is the only pitch-class missing from the *fff* chord in m. 23, and appears prominently in m. 21 – the mid-point of the third chromatic field. Paul Sacher Foundation, Basel, Morton Feldman Collection.

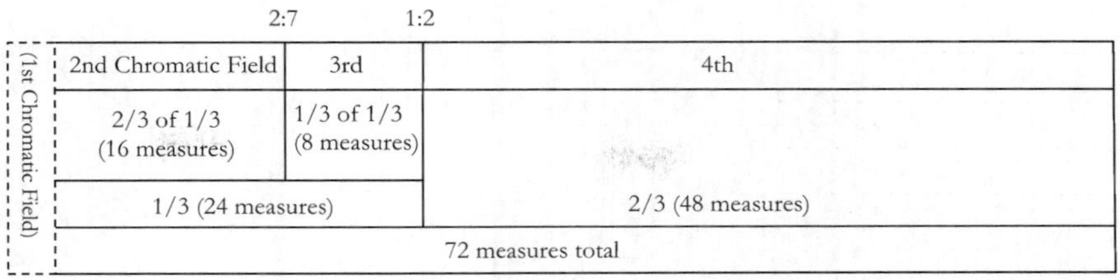

	2:7		1:2	

	2nd Chromatic Field	3rd	4th	
(1st Chromatic Field)	2/3 of 1/3 (16 measures)	1/3 of 1/3 (8 measures)		
	1/3 (24 measures)		2/3 (48 measures)	
	72 measures total			

Figure 2.7   Chromatic-field partitions of *Intermission 5*

pitch-class F? Indeed there is: the first third of the work (in terms of 'on paper' duration as a subdivision of the full 72 measures) ends at measure 24, while 24 divided itself by three is 8 – the number of measures spanned by the appearances of F. This enables us to map the underlying chromatic fields as framed by successive proportional subdivisions of the total duration, as in Figure 2.7.

This structure of underlying pitch organisation operates at a deeper level than the four loud chords, and the division of the piece by 2 and 4 as discussed above (Figure 2.6). Such well-defined structures are not likely to occur by accident or chance – this is a planned deployment of pitch materials within carefully structured subdivisions of the overall time-canvas.

To add weight to this argument, it is instructive to examine the internal structure of the fourth chromatic field. (I choose this because of the very explicit partitioning of the 12-tone aggregate evident in the last part of the work, which makes the deployment of materials on a smaller scale particularly clear.) If we examine this fourth and final chromatic field as a discrete entity of 48 measures, including the grace-note at the end of measure 24, we find that it may be subdivided into three parts of 16 measures each. The juncture of each of the two 16-measure divisions (at measures 40 and 56, respectively) is marked by significant pitch-related events. In measures 40 and 41, we hear three of the pitch-classes belonging to the closing repetition motif (A, G♯, A♯) introduced for the first time in this chromatic field (the other three pitch-classes of this gesture are an adjacent chromatic set, the whole thus forming a chromatic hexachord); these are not heard again until the closing section itself begins. Measure 56 marks the end of the initial statement of the repetition motif and, perhaps more importantly, at a deeper level it is also the point at which the chromatic field (when read forwards from the F in measure 24 to the end, rather than backwards) is completed by G5 in measure 55.

There are two significant things to note about this completion: firstly, it highlights the already-known fact that the closing repetition-field functions as a coda in terms of the pitch material, in so far as the entire chromatic field has been deployed and concluded at the initial statement in measures 55–56. Secondly, the crucial completion note (G5) almost exactly defines a 1:2 partition of the total vertical (pitch) space (see Figure 2.9) and in this sense has a strong relationship with the upper notes of the loud chords in measures 1 and 23. That we tend to

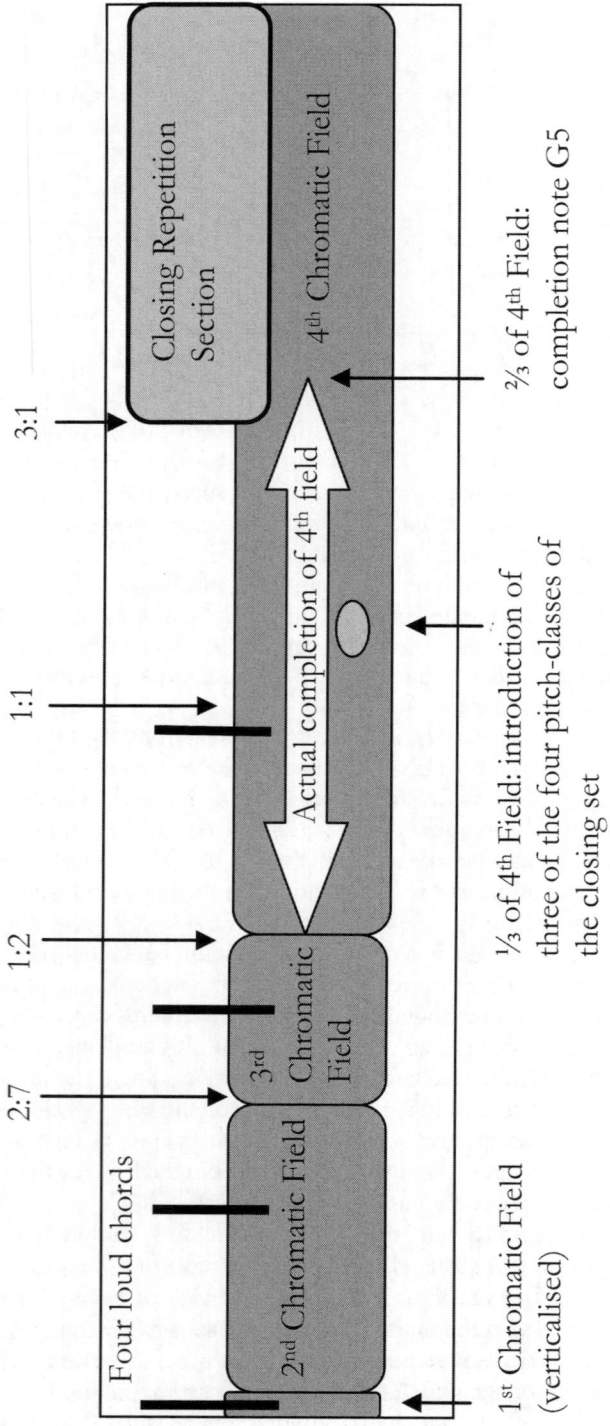

Four loud chords

3:1

Closing Repetition Section

1:1

1:2

2:7

Actual completion of 4th field

4th Chromatic Field

3rd Chromatic Field

2nd Chromatic Field

1st Chromatic Field (verticalised)

⅔ of 4th Field: completion note G5

⅓ of 4th Field: introduction of three of the four pitch-classes of the closing set

Figure 2.8   General model of *Intermission 5*, showing significant time-partitions

hear the closing section as cadential is not merely the effect of the repetitions – it is also the result of our apprehension of Feldman's deep organisation of pitch materials. From this we may also make one further important observation: in terms of its compositional structure, *Intermission 5* is founded upon the deployment of chromatic fields over structured spaces of time, and part of the aural experience depends upon a sensitivity (conscious or not) to the completion of such aggregates. Feldman is heard to be utilising both of Wolpe's methods of manipulating the total chromatic: delay in completion of the whole, and the strategic deployment of 'unhinged' sets.

We may sum up this survey of the larger structures of *Intermission 5* in diagrammatic form as in Figure 2.8. In this diagram, the crucial underlying structure is that of the four chromatic fields. The several planes of overlaid surface activity (the loud chords, the repetition section, and so forth) are all built out of the materials of the chromatic fields and thus inseparably knitted into these deep structures. All the obvious surface structures, however, are placed upon or around points of structural significance in terms of simple durational subdivisions of one-half or one-third, either of the whole work or a clearly defined part of the work.

Several of these nodal points may be understood in terms of more than one form of subdivision, and in some cases it is debatable which may have been the one used by Feldman to determine the placement. It is likely that Feldman was well aware of the fact that certain events are of significance to several planes of structural activity. An example of this may be found at measures 55–56, immediately after the first hearing of the repetition motif that completes the aggregate of the fourth chromatic field. This point may be understood as determined by two-thirds of the duration of the fourth chromatic field, or as a one-third division of the final third of the work as a whole (thus mirroring the point at which the third chromatic field begins). We might therefore argue that this moment of the work has significance for several layers of the composition's structure. Similarly, there is an interesting moment at measures 48–49, which is both two-thirds of the entire work and also half-way through the fourth chromatic field. Here, Feldman has draped across this region of the piece (measures 44–51) a threefold repetition of a two-note motif (the last repetition purposefully incomplete, creating a four-measure suspenseful silence before the repetition-field begins).

It was a common practice of Feldman's to organise a segment of activity around a point of structural significance. We shall see this again in the other analysed works, and we have already seen it in *Intermission 5* with the thrice-repeated F♯7 marking the mid-point of the work. (Threefold repetition itself seems to be rather an important motif in *Intermission 5* – in the sketch, as another example, the closing section is clearly constructed as three repetitions of three repetitions (3×3) of the motif.) Feldman's deployment of materials between, over and around the structural nodes certainly suggests that he is not simply using the partitioned sections of the time-frame as containers for material; his use of the mapped structure is flexible and non-systematic, although with a certain consistency of manner.

Intermission 5 is undoubtedly built around a complex network of quite simple proportional subdivisions of time duration (one-half, one-third, etc.). One might almost wonder if this formal architecture is merely one part of a comprehensive structuring method for all sound events in the piece; it is at least conceivable that Feldman used this proportional division and subdivision method to create both macro-structures (large-scale form) and micro (what we might conventionally understand as rhythm). Arguably, Feldman's large-scale form is a kind of rhythm, and we might put forward the possibility of understanding form as rhythm in a work like *Intermission 5*. Analytically, however, the point becomes harder to press the deeper one delves into the small-scale activity (a problem we will revisit later in this chapter); it is sufficient for the purpose of the present argument to establish the properties of the large-scale formal architecture.

This combination of pitch-deployment and proportional structure also has a bearing upon the rate at which an aggregate statement is played out; to put it another way, it is related to the variable density of the chromatic field. That Feldman knew this and used it as a natural part of his process, rather than subverting it, may be observed in the differences of density between the three or four main sections of the work. The longest section of the work, from measure 25 to measure 55, has clearly the lowest density of pitch content (diluted by empty measures and repetitions) and this is reflected in a low density of activity on other levels. The shortest section (between measures 17 and 24), on the other hand, is filled with the most compressed chromatic field and a correspondingly high level of general activity (while the opening chord reserves its exclusive status as the moment of maximum density). The pitch-density of the field is thus linked to perceived tempo.

In effect, from the analytical point of view, it is the field boundaries that mark out the broader structures, and we may observe how elegantly Feldman handles these boundaries: each aggregate statement is completed by placing one note across the bar-line of a structural division-point, and the result is seamless. This has many ramifications for our understanding of Feldman's compositional aesthetic and process, but most importantly it confirms that he had a conscious sensitivity to the completion of the aggregate, and that he applied this (at least in *Intermission 5*) in conjunction with proportional structures. The closing section, with only four pitch-classes rather than the full chromatic field, logically assumes characteristics of rhythmic and motivic stasis.

In summary, I suggest two ways of understanding the horizontal time-structures of *Intermission 5*; neither is exclusive and they complement each other as different perspectives of the same object. Firstly, we may say that the larger structures of *Intermission 5* are built around the broad division of the first third of the work into thirds, and the latter half by a half (this defines the closing section of 18 measures). The mid-point of the work remains significant as the pivot around which the divisional unit swings. Within these broad spatial divisions, we have also seen that there are complexes of other proportional subdivisions operating, all of which may be linked to the strategic deployment of pitch material. Alternatively, we may understand the works as comprising two layers of structure: a surface layer (defined by the most obvious features of the loud chords and the closing repetitions) constructed by division of the time-canvas in half, and in half again; and a deeper layer of design at the level of the chromatic fields, structured by a division of the time-canvas into thirds, and again into thirds.

Analysis iii *This in the golden Section for heavens sake. It also links to his relationship with the New york Painters and organisation of Colorfields.*

Curiously, there is very little evidence from Feldman's own utterances and writings of the implementation of numerical/proportional structures in his compositional practice. Indeed, it is worth reflecting upon the fact that Feldman seems to have very rarely spoken publicly of issues to do with formal structures at all – but then it is also true to say that he rarely spoke of any specific technical matters of composition. In this regard, the annotations in the 1950s period sketchbooks preserve some crucially important clues to the more practical aspects of the thinking behind the work. Here, we may catch glimpses of his concerns with (and I use Feldman's terminology here) methods of structuring time, space, tone, pitch, timbre and balance. While the precise origin or implementation of these musings is not always at all clear,[61] the sketchbook annotations remain crucial evidence for the nature of Feldman's compositional concerns at this period.

David Nicholls, discussing Feldman's conventionally notated works of the early 1950s in his 2002 essay 'Getting Rid of the Glue: The Music of the New York School', notes that, 'several also appear to be based in numerology (for want of a better word), at least in part'.[62] His examples, while they do not delve into the internal structure of works, illustrate that there are often remarkable correspondences between Feldman's metronome speeds and the measure-length of a piece, and also between measure-length and the date of composition. These kinds of numerological games present a considerable difficulty in analysis, as without the key to the code – such as a date–duration correspondence – it might often be almost impossible to determine what the structuring factor was. In the case of *Intermission 5*, for example, the exact date of composition is not known.[63]

Gianmario Borio has argued that *Intermission 5* is based upon the number six as the basic unit of control, and that the work's time-structures are based upon multiples of six (6×4, 6×7, 6×5, 6×2 and 6×9). Borio's analysis is based upon the eighth-note as the unit of measure, comparable to the measured *ictus* of

---

[61]   Many annotations seem to so closely echo the thinking and even the words and phrases of both Varèse and Wolpe, that one suspects they may be notes made of conversations rather than necessarily original thoughts.

[62]   David Nicholls, 'Getting Rid of the Glue: The Music of the New York School', in Steven Johnson (ed.), *The New York Schools*, 30.

[63]   One might speculate that the date could be deduced from analysis of the work.

the graphic scores. Importantly, he is able to show that this is a way of defining an underlying pattern of calculated time-structures that accounts for the placement of the loud chords, and also the proportion of the closing section beginning in measure 55.[64]

This is a neat solution to the problem of explaining the structural design of the work, but it does raise some other questions: where do the multiplier numbers come from (4, 7, 5, 2, 9), and what is the relationship between them? How do we explain other significant events in the work that do not so easily fit this model? The importance of Borio's analysis for Feldman's work of the 1950s is that, for the first time, it has been shown that there is some manner of numerical or mathematical control. As with my simpler half, third and quarter divisions discussed above, the model confirms an underlying pattern, but does not necessarily offer a complete solution. I suggest that in Borio's model we are still not seeing the control factor, but the superstructure of the formal design; effects of the system, rather than the system itself (which perhaps will never be entirely decipherable). The structures identified are real and observable phenomena, but there may be other ways of understanding the relationships between them. To explain, for example, the parameters of the closing section as a a quarter division of the whole is more straightforward than to say that it is defined by 6×9 *icti*, but both are valid explanations of the same identifiable structure.

The fact that we can arrive at several different explanations for a structural event in *Intermission 5*, some numerically more accurate than others, does not necessarily imply that we may begin to assemble a hierarchy of possibilities based upon relative accuracy. Stefan Wolpe's mathematical inexactitude is almost a feature of his compositional technique,[65] and we do not have any reason to suppose that his student Feldman was any more precise (in his later work, in fact, this planned inexactitude, or 'crippled symmetry',[66] is highly significant). Partly for this reason, I think there is an argument for taking the relatively simple, straightforward explanations in preference to the more complex.[67]

---

[64]   Gianmario Borio, 'Morton Feldman e l'Espressionismo astratto'.

[65]   As Andrew Kohn has observed, 'Wolpe's concept of symmetry was approximate at best. He was very fond of treating as functionally equivalent two quantities which differed by a factor of one. ... in the case of very large intervals, larger discrepancies are tolerated. This characteristic of Wolpe's can make it very difficult to analyze his music on his own terms, since the distinction between equal and unequal (or symmetric and asymmetric), which he held to be very important, can be unclear in practice.' Andrew Kohn, *The Development of Stefan Wolpe's Compositional Style 1948–1963 and the Role of Other Arts, with 'Never Any Jam Today' (Original Composition)* (PhD Dissertation, Univeristy of Pittsburgh, 1995), 14.

[66]   The title of a late Feldman work, *Crippled Symmetry* (1983) for flute, bass flute, glockenspiel, vibraphone, piano and celeste (three players).

[67]   It is important to recognise that this inexactitude or asymmetry was not the result of a lack of attention to detail, on either Wolpe or Feldman's part. As Paula Ames has noted, 'We recall Feldman's emphasis upon "aspects that make a piece which are not usually

Thus far, my analysis has been primarily concerned with the 'horizontal' axis of time-structures, and the deployment of pitch-classes in a manner that is integral to the time-structures. Is it possible to identify similar structuring of the vertical axis of timbre, or sounding pitch? If, as suggested by the diagrams in his sketchbooks, Feldman was thinking in terms of the placement of events in a two-dimensional space as a 'crystalline' formation, we might justifiably expect to find comparable partitioning of the vertical space – perhaps in similar proportions of half, third, quarter and so forth. We might also at this point recall Wolpe's theory of proportions, by which he described interactions between sounding pitch-classes (i.e. at sounding register) as either proportional subdivisions or expansions of intervals.[68]

One notable feature of the deployment of pitch material in *Intermission 5* is that it is not spread over the entire range of the piano; instead, we have a tessitura of E1–C8 (the highest note of the piano range). Irregular partitioning of the instrument range is common in Feldman's piano music (see also *Intermission 6*, for example), and there is very clear precedent for the contrived partitioning of the keyboard range in Wolpe's *Seven Pieces for Three Pianos* (1951), which Feldman must have known.[69] On one occasion, Feldman wrote in a sketchbook, 'Each instrument has its own illusory space-structure which I will think of as one space experience'.[70] Proportional subdivision of the full range of the piano to identify significant pitch-areas does suggest that there may be some sensitivity to the 'illusory space-structure' evident in *Intermission 5*: G5, for example, which is such an important pitch in terms of the four loud chords and also of the closing section, may be described as a one-third division of the available pitch-space. At the same time, however, we must recognise that the range of sounded pitches (E1–C8) as chosen by Feldman ought to give rise to a complex of further subdivisions; indeed, it is here that we find the most compelling evidence for Feldman's organisation of pitch by register.

---

considered significant." Among those features of *Piano* which may be listed in this category are his concept of the "notational image," and the minute variations to which he subjected even the simplest musical patterns. Feldman himself would have also included register and voicing.' Paula Ames, 'Piano (1977)', in Thomas DeLio (ed.), *The Music of Morton Feldman*, 141.

[68]   Stefan Wolpe, 'On Proportions' [1960], trans. Matthew Greenbaum, *Perspectives of New Music*, 34/2 (Summer 1996), 132–84 (Lecture given at Darmstadt, July 1960).

[69]   These pieces were originally composed as illustrations for the lecture (text now lost) 'Spatial Relations, Harmonic Structures and Shapes' given at Yale University in 1951. According to Austin Clarkson, Feldman was part of a group of Wolpe's students who sat on the stage during the lecture. See Austin Clarkson, 'Stefan Wolpe and Abstract Expressionism', in Steven Johnson (ed.), *The New York Schools*, 95. For Milton Babbitt's reminiscence of this lecture, see *Milton Babbitt, Recollections of Stefan Wolpe*, http://www.wolpe.org/page1/page10/page10.html#Milton%20Babbitt.

[70]   Paul Sacher Foundation, Basel, Morton Feldman Collection.

Dividing the interval of the overall vertical pitch-space of sounding notes used in *Intermission 5* by one-half, one-third and one-quarter highlights the following pitches (the one-third division not falling exactly upon a single note; Figure 2.9).[71]

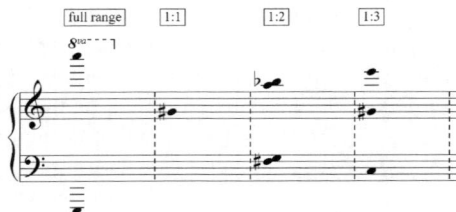

Figure 2.9   Feldman, *Intermission 5*. Major partition-boundaries of vertical (pitch) space

Is it possible that Feldman was using these pitches as proportional nodes in the vertical space comparable to those of the time-canvas? Are they activated in some way at significant structural points in the piece? The scope of the discussion that follows is for the most part limited to appearances of these proportions that are either exact or within a semitone or so of the exact pitch.[72] As already noted, one cannot be sure of the extent to which Feldman was concerned with such accuracy; perhaps he applied these proportions 'by eye' as estimated measurements. From an analytical point of view, however, my concern is to show that in at least some cases, it is clear that the exact (or near-exact) proportions appear at significant moments or in significant contexts in the work, suggesting that Feldman was quite aware of them even if he also at times allowed them to be a little smudged or blurred in terms of literal accuracy.

At the outset, it is surely no accident that the lowest pitch of the work (E1) appears only once – and this appearance is in measure 24 at the close of the third chromatic field, which is also the 1:3 division of the time-frame (see Figure 2.13). The highest pitch occurs three times early in the piece, between measures 1 and 11, although the B♭7 heard in measure 24 (immediately adjacent to the solitary E1) may be heard as a 'smudged' C8. B♭7 is of course also one of the four notes of the closing repetition-field, and in this section may also substitute for the C8 in approximating the extremity of the vertical pitch-space.

G♯4, which is the exact mid-point of the vertical pitch-space, appears 12 times in the piece, of which nine occur as part of the repetition section in measures 55–72. Each of the three earlier appearances is significantly placed, and we may observe that the note is extremely scarce outside of the final section and never heard alone.

<hr>

[71]   The one-sixth divisions (one-third of one-third) are conspicuously absent, except in one instance as the bass-note of the 'altered cluster' in m. 22.

[72]   As is consistent with Wolpe's practice. See footnote 66 of this chapter.

The note is first heard in the opening chord, which is not entirely surprising given this chord's cluster-like character; closer examination suggests, however, that the cluster-formation may well be built around the G♯4 as its central point – certainly, this is the kinetic centre of the chord in terms of the disposition of the hands upon the keyboard (see Figure 2.5). G♯4 is heard a second time in the third loud chord, in measure 23. One may also note that, in terms of the horizontal time-structure, this chord falls very close to the 1:2 division of the total duration, towards the close of the third chromatic field. This seems to take on a greater significance as we observe that the final appearance of the G♯4 (prior to the repetition-field) is as part of another cluster-like aggregation in measure 41 – indeed, G♯4 serves as the very foundation of this event. This sound-event has, as has already been noted, two other important aspects: it marks the boundary of the 1:2 partition of the fourth chromatic field (which falls between measures 40 and 41) and is also part of what seems to be a calculated premonition of the pitch-content of the repetition-motif, where the G♯4 ultimately appears a further nine times.

Of the quarter division pitches, E6 is heard only twice, both times within the opening four measures of the work. C3 is heard literally only once, in measure 40, at the crucial 1:2 time division of the fourth field. There is also an argument for considering the appearances of B2 (measures 15 and 30) as slightly less accurate substitutes. The relative scarcity of such pitches associated with proportional subdivisions of the vertical space is indeed part of their interest: in many cases one has the sense that Feldman is saving them for strategic moments, much in the same way as he rationed carefully the pitch-classes of the closing repetition-set through the earlier parts of the piece. In general, Feldman makes careful use of two methods of emphasis: repetition and contrived scarcity.

The two one-third division pitches appear first in measures 1 and 3, where they clearly frame the opening chord. A5 is the lowest pitch of the second chord, forming a distinct aural association with the F♯/G♭5 at the top of the opening chord. Similarly, when F♯3 is heard as the bass-note of the event at the beginning of measure 3, we also hear it as the first lower expansion of the register defined by the still-reverberating opening chord. We hear the two one-third divisions in close association again in measures 19–21 (the lower smudged by a semitone), where they form part of a discrete three-note formation in the middle of the third chromatic field. The third note of this formation (B4) may be heard as an approximation of a symmetrical subdivision of the interval defined by the other two (the exact 1:1 division is G♯4, which Feldman seems reluctant to use overtly until the later part of the work).

Most striking is the appearance of a more precise F♯/G♭3 at the end of measure 24; the 1:2 division of the pitch-space falling exactly upon the 1:2 division of the time-frame. This alone would be enough to suggest that Feldman is entirely conscious of the proportional divisions of his canvas in two dimensions (of pitch over time). Unsurprisingly, the 2:1 pitch-division (B♭/A5 expressed as C6) also features at the 1:2 time division of the fourth field in measure 41; here, the C has been drawn out of a close, cluster-like formation by octave transposition, as though to highlight it. Again, it is not surprising that the other one-third-division pitch (F♯/ G♭3) is featured in the section following this point up to the commencement of the repetition motif; in this region, G♭3 is part of a discrete two-note repeated motif. In a rare instance of explicit symmetry, at the approach to the 1:3 division of the time-frame (measures 18–19) the lower one-third pitch is followed by the higher, while in the later part of the work we hear the two pitches in reverse order as we move away from the 1:2 time-division of the fourth chromatic field.

Out of what seems at first a rather confusing picture, we here begin to discern a highly organised structure built in two dimensions through the partitioning of both time and pitch/register in similar, inter-connected ways. This method of structuring the disposition of musical materials enables Feldman to work in a distinctly abstract manner: 'a crystalized structural situation a purely sound experience divorced from harmony as well as counterpoint', as he noted in his sketchbook (echoing Varèse).[73] We might also note that this conceptual method enabled Feldman to compose without concern for either tonal or serial structures.

As we have seen, many individual sound-events and groups of events are clustered around important structural nodes (the 1:2 partition of the fourth chromatic field at measures 40–41, for example). In the analysis of rhythm/time, as noted earlier, it is difficult to progress from the relatively obvious large-scale formations to an understanding of the more detailed, micro-structures of rhythm and duration. In examination of the pitch material, however, and the associated vertical axis of structure, it is much easier to identify more detailed structures along the lines of Wolpe's symmetrical and asymmetrical proportions.[74] We have seen some of these already, operating across the larger scale of the total pitch-space, but Feldman was also working with networks of such proportional relations between intervals in the deployment of the pitch material down to the smallest scale of adjacent events and even the internal structure of individual chords. The opening chord, for example, may be understood to be built around a centre of G♯4, which is also the centre-pitch of the entire vertical space. Similarly, the three notes at measures 19–21 may be understood as a slightly looser Wolpean symmetrical proportion, while another very clear individual event of the symmetrical type is the chord at measure 40 (the 1:2 of the fourth chromatic field).

More than this, however, it may be demonstrated that various more intricate groupings of events have complex proportional interrelations, to the extent that almost every note of the piece may be understood as relating to its neighbours in simple half, third or quarter proportions. Figure 2.10, for example, shows the (vertical) proportional structure of the closing repetition motif, while Figure 2.11 shows the rather more intricate, interlocking formations of the opening system.

---

[73]   Paul Sacher Foundation, Basel, Morton Feldman Collection.

[74]   The classic text is Stefan Wolpe, 'On Proportions'. See also Matthew Greenbaum, 'The Proportions of Density 21.5: Wolpean Symmetries in the Music of Edgard Varese', in Austin Clarkson (ed.), *On the Music of Stefan Wolpe: Essays and Recollections* (Hillsdale, NY: Pendragon Press, 2003), 207–19.

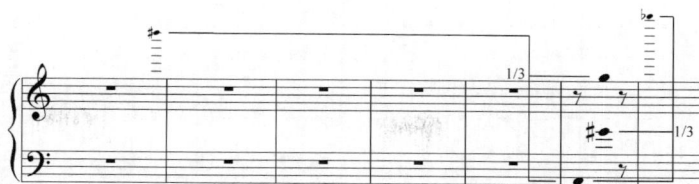

Figure 2.10   Feldman, *Intermission 5*, mm. 50–56, showing intervallic
proportions

Figure 2.11   Feldman, *Intermission 5*, first system, showing intervallic
proportions

In this way, it becomes possible to identify discrete domains, or 'phrases' of the piece, each of which represents a network, or crystalline structure, of such proportions. Furthermore, we can clearly see, in relation to the earlier discussion of chromatic fields, that Feldman was working with pitch materials on two levels simultaneously as defined by pitch-class and registral placement, respectively. Figure 2.12 shows another contiguous example of the second system.

One further example of a particularly significant moment in the piece, the 1:2 division-point at measure 24, illustrates a sophisticated apportioning of the vertical space (Figure 2.13). Here, the first two notes of the measure represent the high and low extremities of the pitch-space of the entire work, while the G♭3 is a one-third division of this all-encompassing interval and the F4 is the last appearance of the pitch-class F in the work. This F4 thus marks the commencement of the fourth and final chromatic field and also the one-half division of the total range (with only a two-semitone error margin, consistent with Wolpe's implementation of such structures over very wide intervals).

As noted previously, the extension of the proportional analysis of time from the large scale to the fine detail is problematic. In terms of pitch, there is an advantage in knowing the fundamental unit of measure (semitone), whereas the smallest unit of time-measure is not quite so self-evident (although the quaver seems the likely possibility, smudged slightly here and there by grace-notes and semiquavers). Similarly, we are faced with a problem of segmentation; the

Figure 2.12   Feldman, *Intermission 5*, second system, showing intervallic
               proportions

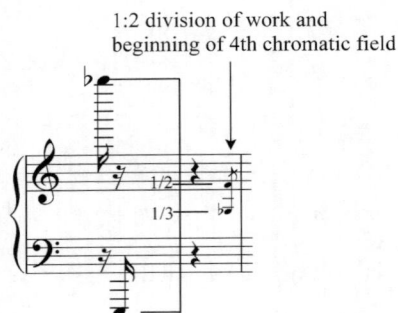

Figure 2.13   Feldman, *Intermission 5*, m. 24

relationships between differently scaled regions of time or layers of activity may be difficult to substantiate in analysis.

It may be observed, however, that the region between measures 17 and 24 (what I have called the third chromatic field – Figure 2.14) is clearly subdivided in a 1:1 proportion by the striking dyad at measure 21, which so distinctively stands apart from its surroundings. Additionally, as interval class 1 it is related to the sonorities at the beginning and end of the field in a manner that may be not coincidental. (The reader will recall that this field occupies, significantly, an entire system to itself in Feldman's original sketch.) Further, the crucial outburst of activity between the end of measure 22 and measure 25 (built, as discussed earlier, as though to emphasise the 1:2 partition of the entire work and the beginning of the final chromatic field) begins immediately after the 2:1 partition of the field's time-span. Very similar medium-scale time-structures may be observed in the segments given in figures 2.11 and 2.12. Beyond this level of detail, however, the analytical instrument is not sufficiently precise to offer explanation of the finer points of

Figure 2.14   Feldman, *Intermission 5*, mm. 17–25 (third chromatic field), showing possible proportional subdivisions

Feldman's placement of all individual sounds. (It would be possible, for example, to interpret this section of the piece as made up of four two-measure segments.) On this evidence, however, it does seem very likely that each note was placed carefully by Feldman with a sensitivity to its place in one or more layers of time-structure, and that the properties of each sound are thus designed in terms of such relationships.

Structure, Space, Design

This chapter does not, and cannot, present a comprehensive analysis of *Intermission 5*. At any point, the analysis of either the work itself, the sources or the historical context might be opened up to further investigation. In the light of Feldman's two-dimensional model of timbre/pitch over time, we have seen that the time-canvas of *Intermission 5* is explicitly partitioned, on several intersecting planes, by a network of relatively simple proportional subdivisions (half, quarter, third). It is also evident that the placement of significant structures (from the deep level of the chromatic fields, through to individual sound events and clusters of events) is highly integrated with the proportional time structures. Furthermore, examination of the registral deployment of pitches shows that Feldman was also sensitive to the proportional partitions of the vertical (pitch) space, and that the articulation of proportional relations between simultaneous or successive intervals (like Wolpean 'proportions') is an intricate aspect of the internal logic of the work. While there is more that might be said about the structures of this work, this much is clear: *Intermission 5* is indeed carefully and intelligently controlled with regard to structures of both pitch and time, and in the deployment of materials in the space defined by these axes, forms arise that may be described as 'crystalline'.

It is of particular note that many of the structures of this work are unusually explicit. For example, the clear partition of the final quarter of the time-span, together with the deployment in this space of a closely defined chromatic set emphasised by repetition, offers a point of leverage with which the analyst may begin to excavate the less obvious structures. In some other Feldman works (*Piano Piece 1952*, for example), the task is not so straightforward.

Additionally, we may appreciate that Feldman's language in this work is explicitly 12-tone (if not in the strict serial sense, at least in terms of his aesthetic and structural involvement with the total chromatic), and that he is working with a high degree of sensitivity to the completion of chromatic fields spread over varied spaces of time, and to their relative densities. One may easily imagine Feldman nodding agreement at Wolpe's words, 'Since the twelve-tone chromatic set has become the master set and the principal source of generating musical material, one acquiesces to the state of balance for which its closed circuit provides'.[75]

---

[75]   Stefan Wolpe, 'Thinking Twice' [1959], in Elliott Schwartz and Barney Childs (eds), *Contemporary Composers*, 276.

Like Wolpe, Feldman also had a deep sensitivity to the relics of tonal language; of intervals and triadic formations manipulated within the chromatic field.[76] He was not primarily concerned with strict ordering of pitch material in a serial sense but, again like Wolpe, interested in exploiting the fluid possibilities offered by the chromatic ground, from which varied and flexible subsets, motifs, pitch-classes and intervals may be in different contexts either highlighted (by repetition, for example) or suppressed – and all of these at all times are necessarily knitted to the background field, related to each other in terms of this common plane and the rate of unfolding of the chromatic field. Feldman's manner of manipulating subsets of the aggregate as motifs, some times audibly explicit and other times hidden, is a way not only of generating and organising localised pitch material but also of structuring the work.

Intermission 5 serves to illustrate Feldman's complex synthesis of compositional techniques and procedures drawn from a range of early influences – it is no coincidence that his composition teachers (Riegger and Wolpe) were both sophisticated 12-tone composers of an original and unconventional kind. A recognition of Feldman's purposeful control of pitch-content is fundamental to an understanding of this work. The sound-events that make up this piece are most certainly not selected by chance procedures, nor are they random in any sense.

In *Intermission 5*, form is rhythm, not merely a container for sound but the result of a process that is highly integrated with the deployment of pitch-materials, a process that may be understood and mapped through Feldman's model of a flat yet complex double-articulation, the two-dimensional canvas. Feldman's sketchbook annotations and notes are a record of his struggle with the structuring of musical materials within this two-dimensional frame. On at least one occasion, he positively declared his opposition to admitting a third dimension: 'the happening in time is the reality. Space in music is illusion.'[77] This is a curiously formalist point of view, which echoes formalist understandings of painting in the 1950s period,[78] and it is clear that this two-dimensional frame was comparable, in Feldman's mind, to the painter's canvas. In his sketchbook annotations Feldman wrote of this explicitly:

> If we think of music in terms of filling out a continuity, with pauses and places
> of rests, structure can not be constructed in the linear fashion but must be seen in
> its entirety. One must then work on the exact proportion. The time structure then
> makes it possible to create music as on a canvas [. . .].[79]

---

[76] For example, m. 8, or the structure deployed from the grace-note at the end of m. 24 to B2 in m. 30.

[77] Paul Sacher Foundation, Basel, Morton Feldman Collection.

[78] For a brief summary of the formalist agenda in twentieth-century art-criticism, see Pam Meecham and Julie Sheldon, Modern Art, 25–7.

[79] Paul Sacher Foundation, Basel, Morton Feldman Collection.

Clearly, Feldman aimed to conceptualise musical work as being founded upon a horizontal line, itself a visual metaphor for the linear time of a work's literal performance. Once on the page, this horizontal line, and the structures of sound (timbre and pitch in Feldman's terms) built upon it, may be viewed in their entirety, in a single view, 'as on a canvas'. The composer's experience of the time-canvas is thus not linear, but objectified (while the listener's complex perceptions of musical time are another matter again). Certainly, Feldman's two-dimensional model offers a way to 'read' his scores conceptually, as vertical structures of sound over horizontal structures of time (the terms vertical and horizontal are in this context metaphorical; they have no literal meaning in sound). In so far as this model seems almost built for the purpose of making analogical connections between musical and painterly structures, it serves as evidence that Feldman's interest in the visual arts was practical and concrete as much as aesthetic. As a purely musical model it is oddly limited (Varèse, in comparison, proposed a model with no fewer than four dimensions),[80] but as an engine for translating the visual canvas into sound, or indeed vice versa, it is ideal.

As a radical constriction of conventional models of musical structure, Feldman's model seems to resonate with the notion of the flattened picture-plane that Greenberg and others observed as characteristic of abstract expressionist painting in the late 1940s and 1950s. This concept of a unified picture plane is, however, rather more complex and sophisticated than it sounds. Greenberg's 1955 discussion of Jackson Pollock's work illustrates this well:

> Pollock has an instinct for bold oppositions of dark and light, and the capacity to bind the canvas rectangle and assert its ambiguous flatness and quite unambiguous shape as a single and whole image concentrating into one the several images distributed over it.[81]

Similarly, the two-dimensional model made it possible for Feldman to bind the rather diverse elements of *Intermission 5* to a unified conceptual plane. For Feldman as a composer, the analogical model of the picture- plane served as a way of conceptualising the organisation and structure of the musical work in quite specific ways. While demonstrated here in relation to *Intermission 5*, and in the context of Feldman's music of the early 1950s, the aesthetic and methodological implications of the two-dimensional model were of lifelong importance to Feldman. In 1984, at a seminar in Frankfurt, he explained:

---

[80]   Edgard Varèse, 'New Instruments and New Music', in Elliott Schwartz and Barney Childs (eds), *Contemporary Composers*, 197.

[81]   Clement Greenberg, '"American-Type" Painting', in Ellen Landau (ed.), *Reading Abstract Expressionism: Context and Critique* (New Haven, CT: Yale University Press, 2005), 205.

What I picked up from painting is what every art student knows. And it's called the picture plane. I substituted for my ears the aural plane and it's a kind of balance but it has nothing to do with foreground and background. It has to do with how do I keep it on the plane from falling off, from having the sound falling on the floor.[82]

Feldman's personal connections and aesthetic affinities with the New York abstract expressionist painters of the 1950s are well known, if not fully understood.[83] Crucially, the discovery of the two-dimensional model and its application in *Intermission 5* offer a unique mechanism for making direct, structural comparisons between musical and visual works. More specifically, the dramatic, asymmetrical broad gesture of *Intermission 5* is so clearly akin to the structures of very many of Guston's early 1950s paintings and drawings that a formal homology must be identified.[84]

Philip Guston was one of Feldman's closest friends, and in his pictures of the early 1950s we sense not only a building-up of colour and surface structure out of the ground of pale under-painting (the white-noise of the total chromatic), but also a tendency to form the larger structures around asymmetrical one-third or one-quarter divisions of the canvas. The result, while often subtle on the surface, is strong in structure. A typical example is found in *Attar* (1953), a painting that Feldman owned.[85] Here, the lower right of the canvas is dominated by a great pinkish-red form, cantilevered from a plinth built upon a 2:1 division of the base-line of the canvas. The eye is drawn diagonally across the canvas to the point where the cantilevered form strikes the middle of the left edge of the frame. Such structures are common in Guston's work of the early 1950s, both paintings and drawings.[86]

In a sense the structural analogy with Feldman's music is even clearer in Guston's drawings (many of which were sketches for paintings), where the viewer is less distracted by colour; here we may see the organisation of form and space in an explicit black-on-white medium. Among these works are many images of similar asymmetrical, cantilevered forms – and in the high-contrast of ink marks against white paper we can clearly see the almost architectural manner with which Guston engineers the structures from horizontal platforms, beams and vertical pillars. The division of the picture-plane into thirds, both horizontally and vertically, is frequently of explicit importance. Within these strongly built structures based upon

---

[82]   Morton Feldman, 'XXX Anecdotes and Drawings', p. 168.

[83]   See, for example, Jonathan Bernard, 'Feldman's Painters', in Steven Johnson (ed.), *The New York Schools*, 173–216.

[84]   Refer, for example, to Guston's *Attar* [1953], reproduced in Sebastian Claren, *Neither*, 290.

[85]   Ibid.

[86]   See Magdalena Dabrovski, *The Drawings of Philip Guston* (New York: The Museum of Modern Art, New York, 1988).

third-divisions, we may also note Guston's lighter sensitivity to the 1:1 divisions, as secondary structures hover around, or sometimes seem to veer towards or away from, the implicit centre-lines, as observed also in *Intermission 5*.

Very similar cantilevered forms are to be found in the early 1950s paintings of Franz Kline, another artist who was well known personally to Feldman. Some pieces are, in their structural elements, almost identical to the works of Guston discussed above. Kline's stark black and white style is of course utterly unlike Guston's painted pallette, and his very different way of approaching the canvas results in an equally different surface texture. Beneath this surface, however, the structures are more than just similar – although the 1:1 canvas-division is often more strongly defined in Kline than in Guston. Kline's *Painting No. 11* (1951)[87] is a particularly significant work in the context of the present discussion, in which the canvas is divided roughly in the proportion 1:2 by a horizontal line (slightly askew), and then each of these parts divided vertically, the lower into thirds and the upper in half. We might depict this structure schematically as in Figure 2.15.

This painting is a particularly explicit representation of the structural principles that inform the works of Feldman, Guston and Kline in the early 1950s: the canvas partitioned, and partitioned again, horizontally and vertically.[88] Note that one effect in this painting is to create two horizontal planes of organisation, one forming a spatial diptych, the other a triptych. This is directly comparable to the time-structures evident in *Intermission 5*, which are on the surface binary, but ternary on the deeper level of the chromatic field. In addition, there is a strong sense of controlled balance between horizontal and vertical forces, and an ambiguity in so far as neither quite dominates the space. That Feldman felt some particularly close affinity with the work of Guston and Kline in terms of structure, and that the three of them had this in common, was made explicit in a reminiscence contained in the 1972 essay 'A Compositional Problem'. Here, Feldman discusses by analogy the dichotomy in music between instrumental colour and structure:

---

[87]   Reproduced in Harry F. Gaugh, *Franz Kline* (New York: Abbeville Press, 1985), 100.

[88]   Another layer of significance in these forms is that both Feldman and Kline were, in the 1950s, engaged in a dialogue with the work of Mondrian. See Harry F. Gaugh, ibid., 97. The critic Thomas Hess described Kline's works of the early 1950s as 'melted Mondrians'. See Thomas Hess, 'Mondrian and New York Painting', in *Six Painters* (Houston, TX: University of St. Thomas, 1967), 12. Mondrian was the subject of an early disagreement between Feldman and Boulez (who preferred Klee). See Pierre Boulez and John Cage, Jean-Jacques Nattiez and Robert Samuels (eds), *The Boulez–Cage Correspondence* (Cambridge: Cambridge University Press, 1993).

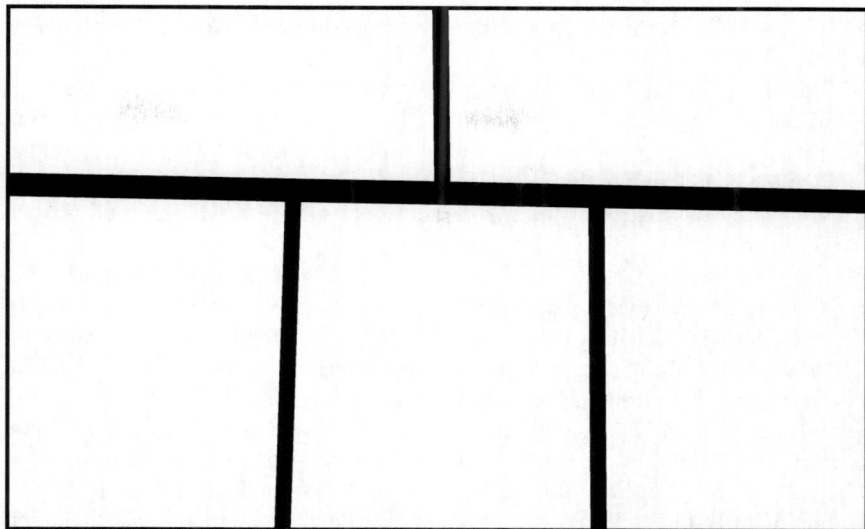

Figure 2.15   Diagrammatic representation of Franz Kline's *Painting No. 11*
              (1951)

> Franz Kline once told me that it was only rarely that color did not act as an
> intrusion into his painting. Guston, too, felt this. Most crucial to him was the
> immediacy of where the forms were placed.[89]

He added, 'I began to feel that the sounds were not concerned with my ideas of
symmetry and design, that they wanted to sing of other things'.[90] It would seem
that, for Feldman, as for Kline and Guston, there was a perception that colour
(whether of paint or of sound) might be in conflict with structure and form
('symmetry and design'). As Catherine Hirata has pointed out, the idea of the
emphasis of sound over structure has often been understood too simplistically in
relation to Feldman's work – and in any case might be more properly a Cagean
notion than one of prime importance to Feldman, who seems in so many ways to
have been resistant to the allure of the extravagant new sound-palettes explored
by his contemporaries.[91] I suggest that many of the difficulties in understanding
Feldman's 1950s music might be resolved through close examination of his
notions of 'symmetry and design'. The very phrase itself echoes Wolpe's teaching,

---

[89]   Morton Feldman, 'A Compositional Problem', in B.H. Friedman (ed.), *Give My
Regards to Eighth Street*, 110.

[90]   Ibid., 110–11.

[91]   Catherine Hirata, *Analyzing the Music of Morton Feldman* (PhD Dissertation,
Columbia University, 2003), 32, fn. 5.

and places Feldman firmly in a tradition that stems from Wolpe's involvement with the Bauhaus in the 1920s.[92]

While this present discussion is in many ways merely a beginning, on the basis of this analysis it is nevertheless possible to make some observations concerning Feldman's position in the field of cultural production at this time. For example, while much of Feldman's thinking clearly derived from Varèse (both directly and via Wolpe), in the matter of the two-dimensional model the thinking of the two composers diverged markedly. Perhaps most striking of all, however, the analysis reveals very clearly that this work and Cage's work of the period had much less in common than has been commonly supposed. *Intermission 5* exhibits none of the characteristics that Cage admired in Feldman's graphic scores. It shows no sign whatsoever of the application of chance procedures and does not allow for indeterminacy of performance in any unconventional way.

Even at this early stage of his career, Feldman was staking out his own territory in the field. In the establishment and maintenance of such a position in relation to colleagues/competitors, oppositions are as crucial as affinities. Just as the publicly personal link between Cage and Feldman was crucial to both, so too was the fundamental conflict evident in the work. In contrast, we may observe that *Intermission 5* has strong relationships with the contemporary work of both Feldman's teachers, Riegger and Wolpe. These affinities are many: the 12-tone materials; the counterpointed layers and planes; the visual analogy; and the abstraction of music in terms of crystalline forms suspended in a space between the vertical and horizontal axes of pitch over time.[93]

---

[92]   See Austin Clarkson, 'Stefan Wolpe and Abstract Expressionism', in Steven Johnson (ed.), *The New York Schools*, 76–7; Matthew Greenbaum, 'The Proportions of Density 21.5', 207–8; and also Clement Jewitt, 'Music at the Bauhaus, 1919–1933', *Tempo*, New Series, 213 (July 2000), 5–11.

[93]   A valuable insight into Riegger's compositional interests is offered by *New and Old: Twelve Pieces for Piano*, an album of piano pieces for students published with analytical notes by the composer. Crucially, this pedagogical work dates from the period of the early 1940s when Feldman was Riegger's composition student. In piece four, *The Twelve Tones*, Riegger illustrates a simple use of a row by dividing the row into two sets of eight and four notes each, and emphasising the four-note set by repetition. In piece six, *Twelve Upside Down*, which uses the row inverted, Riegger uses this same technique of repetition within a statement of the row/aggregate to bring subsets to the listener's attention. In both cases, he discusses this explicitly in his analytical notes. Another piece in the set relevant to Feldman's work is *Polytonality*. Here, Riegger is not simply writing layered voices in different keys; in fact the motives are not tonal at all, but constructed using sets of notes drawn from diatonic collections with different centres. It is rather more subtle than the title suggests, and in his notes, Riegger stresses the listener's experience. Does the listener hear one key as right and the other as wrong, or in conflict with it? Can a listener hear two keys/collections at once? Riegger suggests that all this is dependent upon the composer's handling of the 'situation', and that in this piece he anticipates that the listener will 'unconsciously' alternate between the two keys and in only one passage hear a 'genuine

Perhaps most important of all, however, is Feldman's unwillingness to give up the composer's prerogative of control (an individual exercise of will, in the nineteenth-century sense). Even as late as 1977, Feldman would tell an interviewer 'My biggest complaint – and I have to quote Nietzsche on this one – (quote) "The world of distinction is lost"'.[94] Feldman's sounds are, in this work at least, always carefully placed, with deliberation. In this, as also in his choice of instrument, one might argue that Feldman's work was both conservative (with all that the term implies) and nostalgic. Feldman was a middle-class New Yorker, with a finely tuned affinity for a lost European heritage of the imagination. In part, his music is concerned with the recovery (or better, reinvention) of that imagined heritage. Feldman's apparent political neutrality in fact reveals his true position, which is not so much neutral as (awkwardly) bourgeois. The space that Feldman occupied in the field, defined by allegiances and antagonisms of many kinds, is indeed complex and ambiguous. However, this is much more than just a space in which a career is acted out – it is above all the space of tensioned ambiguity within which the work itself resonates.

---

polytonality'. Note that Riegger uses these collections not only as two diatonic collections in opposition, but with a sense of their mutual function as subsets of the aggregate. Also of interest in terms of Feldman's later work is the piece demonstrating Seegerian 'dissonant counterpoint', while the piece concerned with clusters is chiefly notable for the fact that there are few genuine clusters in it at all – rather, Riegger is using carefully designed 'thick' chords. Wallingford Riegger, *New and Old: Twelve Pieces for Piano* (London: Boosey and Hawkes, 1944).

[94]   Stuart Morgan, 'Pie-slicing and Small Moves: Morton Feldman in Conversation with Stuart Morgan' [1977], in Chris Villars (ed.), *Morton Feldman Says*, 84. Nietzschean philosophy has been identified as one of the important influences on the abstract expressionist painters from the late 1940s. See Ellen Landau, 'Abstract Expressionism: Changing Methodologies for Interpreting Meaning', in Ellen Landau (ed.), *Reading Abstract Expressionism: Context and Critique* (New Haven, CT: Yale University Press, 2005), 9–10.

Chapter 3
Piano Piece 1952:
'a discipline of vagueness'[1]

A Broken Dialectic

Piano Piece 1952 is rather unusual among Feldman's works of the 1950s, and certainly among the piano pieces. Despite a richness of pitch-content, it presents a surface of implacably straight-jacketed rhythm and kinetic motion. In a sense, the piece may be said to be founded upon the simple alternation of right and left hands, note by note. Far from being relaxed and meditatively beautiful, the work's contrived and rigid system results in a surface structure that is almost unbearable, appalling even, for both performer and audience alike.

In the peculiar conceit of notating a piece entirely in dotted quarter-notes, this work is not quite alone in Feldman's 1950s music; *Intermission 6* was sketched in a somewhat similar manner (although the published version was re-notated), and as late as 1960 we find a similar notational device (albeit not so strict) in the unpublished *Piece for Seven Instruments*.[2] The effect with *Piano Piece 1952* is somewhat disorienting, in so far as it would not matter what note-value the sound-events were, as they are all of equal length. Feldman certainly did have a mysterious fascination with triple time (usually as 3/8 or 3/16) in the early and middle 1950s, but *Piano Piece 1952* seems a bizarre manifestation of this, as its smallest unit of measure is the dotted quarter-note; the triple-eighth note subdivision is purely abstract and conceptual. On the other hand, if there was ever a Feldman work that could be described as 'flat' (in a broader sense than simply quiet),[3] this is it: *Piano Piece 1952* is certainly flat in terms of the small-scale rhythmic articulation of the time-canvas, and perhaps of all Feldman's works the most comparable to Jackson Pollock's all-over painting.

---

[1]   Harold Rosenberg, 'The American Action Painters' [1952], in Ellen Landau (ed.), *Reading Abstract Expressionism: Context and Critique* (New Haven, CT: Yale University Press, 2005), 194.

[2]   Both manuscripts are in the Paul Sacher Foundation, Basel, Morton Feldman Collection. For discussion of *Intermission 6*, see Chapter 4 of this book.

[3]   Feldman explained to Paula Ames that he wanted the performer's interaction with the piano (any specific piano, not the generic one) to give rise to subtle variation of dynamic and tone-colour, even in passages marked as all quiet. Paula Ames, 'Piano (1977)', in Thomas DeLio (ed.), *The Music of Morton Feldman* (Westport, CT: Greenwood Press, 1996), 137–8.

My analytical interest in *Piano Piece 1952* began with puzzlement about what might be going on beneath the rhythmically blank surface; surely, I thought, the notes have come from somewhere, whether by a chance-driven procedure or something else. I am not the first to wonder about this piece, of course. It was specifically of *Piano Piece 1952* that Christian Wolff was writing when he voiced his often-quoted opinion that 'The music appears to be unanalyzable.'[4] More interesting, as noted in Chapter 1, is the fact that Wolff went on to write a page or so of quite perceptive analysis, noting a number of distinctly audible internal structures. In terms of pitch-content, it seems, the work is not featureless after all – there are indeed notable formations, and even recurring patterns. Experientially, Wolff took the view that the rhythmic stasis 'erases, as Feldman might have said, the memory of what precedes, or, one could say, stills the impulse to connect and the habit of conceptualising'.[5] Is it not also possible, however, that the effect might be quite the opposite for an active listener, as indeed Wolff was himself – that the rhythmic stasis might have the effect of throwing any such pitch-related patterns, structures or continuities into high relief, perhaps even some continuities of such subtlety that in a more rhythmically varied work they might pass unnoticed?

However, there is something even more peculiar about *Piano Piece 1952*: examination of the sketchbook manuscripts reveals that the work was originally composed – to a completed state – as a pair of contrasting pieces, of which the published work is the second. Luciano Berio, interestingly, remarked on the piece's 'dialectic' after an early performance,[6] which makes one wonder whether this performance included the unpublished companion piece. The event is otherwise undocumented, so there is no way to be sure, but it is certainly possible that Feldman deleted the first of the two pieces after hearing a performance.[7]

In this chapter, I examine *Piano Piece 1952* in the light of the structuring of time and pitch in *Intermission 5* as discussed in the previous chapter. This analysis demonstrates that a similar manner of proportional structuring of time and pitch is evident, but the unique qualities of *Piano Piece 1952* make it possible to examine closely the pitch organisation divorced, in a sense, from rhythm and also without the potential complication of vertically sounded aggregations (chords). We shall see that, while *Piano Piece 1952* is, like *Intermission 5*, built with a finely honed deployment of chromatic fields spread over spaces of time, there is also a clear

---

[4]   Christian Wolff, 'The Sound Doesn't Look Back (1995): On Morton Feldman's Piano Piece 1952', http://www.cnvill.net/mfwolff2.htm#wolff5. Originally published in Christian Wolff, *Cues: Writings and Conversations* (Köln: MusikTexte, 1998), 370–78.

[5]   Ibid.

[6]   Ibid.

[7]   Berio was at Tanglewood during the summer of 1952, and afterwards in New York before returning to Italy. The performance with Berio and Wolff present must have taken place during this time, in the late summer or autumn of 1952. See David Osmond-Smith, *Berio* (Oxford: Oxford University Press, 1991), 11.

layer of pitch-organisation that depends upon the recognition of smaller repeated sets (commonly dyads, trichords and tetrachords).

The discovery of the hitherto unknown (or at least lost) companion piece offers an unusual opportunity to investigate Feldman's decision-making as a composer in relation to the initial design of the work and the subsequent decision to delete the first of the two pieces. In the later 1950s, Feldman made more frequent essays in multi-movement form. (See, for example, *Three Pieces for Piano*, *Two Pieces for Two Pianos* and *Two Pieces for Six Instruments*). It is likely that Feldman's understanding of the two-part work was in some ways derived from Wolpe. In 1980, Feldman expressed a special interest in this aspect of Wolpe's work:

> I'm very interested in the two-movement form that he developed. I think that he developed a very interesting two-movement form that works fantastically for him. I don't think anyone else could work it as well as he did it. And I'm interested in *Music In Two Parts* [*sic*], and I'm interested in ... the *String Quartet* is a masterpiece.[8]

It seems possible, then, that the original two-movement form of *Piano Piece 1952* was an attempt on Feldman's part to construct a characteristically Wolpean form. For some reason, he subsequently deemed it necessary to dismember the work. This decision, rather than resulting from a perceived success or failure of the piece in its original form, may well have had something to do with Feldman's relationship with Wolpe at this time and indeed, more properly, the relation between Feldman's work and Wolpe's as positioned within the dynamic of the field of cultural production.

Sources and Dating

The undated sketch manuscript of *Piano Piece 1952* is in a fragmented state.[9] Several loose pages of autograph are contained in a sketchbook that contains material mostly from 1951. A further couple of pages are contained in a later sketchbook, from which, it appears, the loose pages were torn; this later sketchbook contains material from 1953–55. In addition to the complete sketch of the published *Piano Piece 1952*, I have identified two pages of material belonging to the unpublished work, one of which is the ending shown in Figure 3.1.[10] The other fragment (Figure 3.2) may or may not be contiguous with the final page.

---

[8]   Austin Clarkson, 'Conversation about Stefan Wolpe: 13 November 1980', in Chris Villars (ed.), *Morton Feldman Says: Selected Interviews and Lectures 1964–1987* (London: Hyphen Press, 2006), 105.

[9]   Paul Sacher Foundation, Basel, Morton Feldman Collection.

[10]   For legibility, I have given the examples in transcription, rather than as photographic reproduction. Feldman's layout and annotations have been retained.

Figure 3.1   Transcript of autograph page showing the closing section of
                the unpublished part of Feldman, *Piano Piece 1952*, together
                with the opening of the published work. System layout and
                annotations are Feldman's

Figure 3.2   Transcript of autograph page showing a fragment of the
                unpublished part of Feldman, *Piano Piece 1952*. System
                layout and annotations are Feldman's

There is an early copy of the piece in David Tudor's papers, which follows closely the sketch of *Piano Piece 1952* (the second piece only).[11] The Tudor copy retains the bar-lines, but has no tempo or dynamic markings.

Piano Piece 1952 was first published by Edition Peters (New York) in 1962.[12] As with other works discussed in this book, the piece has been published twice; the original edition was a holograph of a neat copy made by Feldman himself,[13] while a computer-engraved version published in 2000 is based directly and solely upon the previous edition.[14] Apart from the deletion of the first part, the major differences between the published scores and the sketch are the removal of bar-lines and metronome speed, and the omission of an *8ᵇᵃ* sign on the second note (most likely a copying error).[15] The published piece has no bar-lines and consists of an unbroken stream of 171 dotted quarter-notes, alternating strictly between right hand and left hand. In this sense it is perhaps the most rigidly systematic of all Feldman's compositions, obeying this conceptual (and kinetic) rule throughout.

Perhaps because of the lack of dynamic, rhythmic, textural or gestural variety, the work has been less often performed than other Feldman works of the 1950s, and there are few recordings of it. The first documented performance of the work (or, to be exact, a work with this title) took place in 1959, with David Tudor as pianist.[16] It is quite likely that the work had been heard before this, if only in a semi-private studio performance (Wolff and Berio may have heard such a performance)[17] – and

---

[11]   The Getty Research Institute, Los Angeles, David Tudor Papers, 980039, Series 1b, Box 186, 6.

[12]   Morton Feldman, *Piano Piece 1952* (New York: Edition Peters, 1962).

[13]   Music Library, University at Buffalo, The State University of New York, Buffalo, C.F. Peters Collection of Morton Feldman Manuscripts, 1961–69, Mus. Arc. 2.4, Box 2, 27.

[14]   Morton Feldman, *Piano Piece 1952*, in Volker Straebel (ed.), *Solo Piano Works 1950–64* (New York: Edition Peters, 2000), 6–7.

[15]   The Tudor copy conforms to the sketch in this instance. A strong case could be made for reinstating A1 as the second note of the work, rather than the published A2. Other minor discrepancies are as follows (while interesting and potentially relevant to performance, these do not have a great bearing on the analysis presented here): event 89 (F3 in published score) reads clearly G3 in sketch; event 18 (G♯2 in published score) reads G♯1 in sketchbook; event 32 (E♭1 in published score) reads C♯1 in sketch; the lowest note (B0 in published score) is B1 in sketch; event 59 (C♯7 in published score) reads clearly as E♯7 in sketch; event 62 (A3 published score) reads an octave lower in sketch as A2; also in the sketch, Feldman numbered the event at the end of each system. There is a descending diagonal line drawn from event 67 to 74 (G6–C♯4). This descending line occurs (oddly) over the ascending hand-crossing figure.

[16]   See Volker Straebel's notes to the new edition of the work published in *Morton Feldman: Solo Piano Works 1950–64* (New York: Edition Peters, 2000). Note, however, that he gives 1951 incorrectly instead of 1959. Claren gives the correct date of 2 March 1959. See Sebastian Claren, *Neither: Die Musik Morton Feldmans* (Hofheim: Wolke, 2000), 553.

[17]   Christian Wolff, 'The Sound Doesn't Look Back'.

we cannot be sure of its title before 1959. It is not possible to be certain when Feldman made the decision to delete the first piece, but it was most likely before the 1959 performance (for which the Tudor copy was presumably made), by which time the work had acquired its present title.

In my transcription of the manuscript (Figure 3.1) we can see the end of the unpublished work and the beginning of *Piano Piece 1952*. Note that, in the original manuscript (but not in my copy), the two systems showing the end of the unpublished work are heavily crossed out. We may observe that the first piece was completed; Feldman even indicates a timing of two minutes. Most important, however, is the annotation between the two pieces, where Feldman wrote 'The music is in II parts. The first explosive and fleeting in character the II quiet'. In the light of this, the peculiarly mechanistic flatness of the published *Piano Piece 1952* takes on a new significance: it is a work in which Feldman has as much as possible eliminated all contrast of dynamic and rhythmic gesture (and in so doing emphasised the elements of pitch, interval and register) for the express purpose of making a clear contrast with the unpublished piece. The published piece is quiet in more than just the dynamic sense; it is also gesturally, texturally and rhythmically 'quiet' in comparison with the other, unpublished part. This quietness, as Berio perceptively pointed out, is the direct result of a dialectic process – in Feldman's creative imagination (as far as the original diptych was concerned) the sounds were patently not all quiet, or slow. Part of the unease we feel listening to *Piano Piece 1952* as published may derive from an unconscious sense that something is missing, as though we are (as is indeed the case) hearing only one side of an argument.

Regarding the dating of the work, we are faced with a similar situation to that of *Intermission 5*. The manuscript described above, held by the Paul Sacher Stiftung, is undated and fragmentary. Further, it is scattered between two sketchbooks that range in material from 1951 through to 1955. Given that our first dated documentation of the work is as late as 1959, we should perhaps exercise caution in assuming that the work was actually composed in 1952, even though Feldman presumably thought that it had been; it is at least possible that the date was conjectural. Given the numerological tendency identified by David Nicholls,[18] the metronome marking of 52 may be a clue as to the date, or it may simply be what Feldman based his conjecture upon when preparing the work for publication in 1962 (the metronome marking was not retained in the published version of the piece). While many gestures of the unpublished work seem to hark back to *Intermission 1* and *Intermission 2* of 1950, the published piece, with its progress of unchanging dotted quarter-notes, most closely resembles the original sketch for *Intermission 6*, which is conventionally dated (on admittedly slim evidence) to 6

---

[18]   David Nicholls, 'Getting Rid of the Glue: The Music of the New York School', in Steven Johnson (ed.), *The New York Schools of Music and the Visual Arts* (New York: Routledge, 2002), 30.

November 1953.[19] *Piano Piece 1952* may have been composed in 1952, or indeed almost any time between 1951 and 1955. Feldman's later attribution of the work to 1952 seems to be supported by Christian Wolff's reminiscence of attending a performance with Berio in that year, but such anecdotal evidence cannot be relied upon without further corroboration.

Like *Intermission 5*, it was never released on LP record. In contrast, however, the piece has only appeared twice on CD to the time of writing,[20] compared with *Intermission 5*'s seven times – *Piano Piece 1952*, it would seem, is not popular Feldman. The two recordings differ gigantically in duration, one performance taking 8:47 (minutes:seconds), the other 3:35. There is no known primary-source recording of Feldman performing the work. For the sake of clarity in the analytical discussion which follows, I will refer to the two parts of the work as *Piano Piece 1952a* (the unpublished part), and *Piano Piece 1952b* (the published work).

Analysis i

Many of the crucial differences between the two pieces are immediately apparent. *Piano Piece 1952a* is not only designed to contrast with its fraternal twin, but is also explicitly concerned with contrasts; there is a relatively great range of note-durations, dynamics and gestures. I say relatively, because the variety is extreme only in comparison with *Piano Piece 1952b*, which has one note-duration, a flat dynamic level, and consists, one might argue, of a single uninterrupted gesture.[21] Compared with other piano music produced by Feldman's immediate circle at this time – John Cage's *Seven Haiku* (1951–52) and *4'33"* (1952), Earle Brown's *Perspectives* (1952), Wolpe's *Seven Pieces for Three Pianos*, Boulez's *Second Sonata* (composed 1948, first heard in New York 1950)[22] or Christian Wolff's *For Piano* (1952) – the palette of sounds and performance demands are strikingly conservative even as he aimed to create music that is 'explosive and fleeting' and to maximise contrast between the pair of pieces. Dynamics and articulations are hardly extravagant, rhythmic gestures are quite simple and straightforward, and there are no piano preparations or special playing techniques. Perhaps this may have been one factor in Feldman's decision to repress the unpublished work:

---

[19]   See Chapter 4 for discussion of the dating problems related to *Intermission 6*.

[20]   Steffen Schleiermacher, *Morton Feldman: Early Piano Works*, CD (hat[now]ART 138, 2003); John Tilbury, *Morton Feldman All Piano (1950–1986)*, 4 CD set (LondonHALL do13, 1999).

[21]   Comparison between the published score and the manuscript is illuminating: in the original sketch Feldman drew a bar-line after every note (implying a time signature of 3/8) whereas in the published version the entire work is presented literally as a single measure. Perhaps this change indicates some adjustment of vertical vs horizontal perception.

[22]   The Getty Research Institute, Los Angeles, David Tudor Papers, 980039, Series 1b, Box 70, f. 4.

it might not have been heard as sufficiently 'explosive' in comparison to the contemporary work of his colleagues. This perspective serves to highlight essential differences between Feldman's aesthetic outlook (and his approach to musical material) and that of his contemporary colleagues. It is also possible, however, to view the contrast between the two parts of *Piano Piece 1952* as echoing to some extent the developing aesthetic rift between Cage and Boulez. Feldman is perhaps striving to create and occupy a middle ground between the two extremes of Cage's *4'33"* on the one hand and Boulez' *Structures I* on the other (both composed in the period of 1951–52).

Despite the relatively subdued nature of Feldman's music, its conservatism even, the *forte/piano* contrasts in the unpublished work clearly associate it with a group of other early 1950s pieces exhibiting similarly extreme dynamic organisation: the *Extensions* series, *Intermission 4* and *Intermission 5*. The dynamic quietness of *Piano Piece 1952b* is similarly well precedented in previous works, and also the work of the later 1950s, which largely avoids dynamic contrast. In composing this pair of piano pieces Feldman was enacting a long-standing tension in his creative work; and in making the choice to delete the more gestural, contrasted piece, we witness a creative decision with deep and long-lasting consequences for Feldman's creative trajectory.

Given the fragmentary nature of the manuscript for the unpublished work, it is not possible to make comparisons in terms of the larger-scale architecture of the two works. It may be observed, however, that Feldman indicated a timing of two minutes for the unpublished work, and we may deduce from this that it was shorter than *Piano Piece 1952b*.

In range, *Piano Piece 1952b* as published spans 80 of the piano's 88 notes, of which only 65 are actually used. The usage of notes is heavily weighted to the central octaves of the keyboard, thinning out gradually in the higher range and more abruptly at the lower extreme. For three octaves across the mid-range every note is used at least once and some many times over. Few and used sparingly, the lowest notes in the piece are distinct outliers, if less dramatically so than the lowest notes of *Intermission 5*. (Analytically, it is tempting to hear these outlying, separated bass-notes as an independent line — either contrapuntally, or in the structural sense of a fundamental bass.)

The least conventional aspect of *Piano Piece 1952a* is the use of very long silences, and this is perhaps one aspect of the work that does show an influence of Cage and also has a connection to the contemporaneous work of Christian Wolff (who was Cage's student). I am thinking here of the Cagean notion that silence and sound are of equal importance as musical materials: 'But now there are silences and the words help make the silences ... We need not fear these silences – we may love them'.[23] Wolpe's observations regarding Wolff's *For Piano* are also applicable to Feldman's unpublished piece under discussion: 'Music of this kind

---

[23]   John Cage, 'Lecture on Nothing' [1949/50], in *Silence: Lectures and Writings by John Cage* (Middletown, CT: Wesleyan University Press, 1961), 109–10.

consists of a series of standstills, or of the last phases of a motion brought to rest'.[24] In contrast, the published *Piano Piece 1952*, despite its quiet slowness, has no still-points and its implacable motion is never brought to rest until the very end. From a Cagean perspective, moreover, we might say that the work takes on a peculiarly suffocated (or suffocating) quality owing to the lack of silences.

In the unpublished work, conversely, enormous silences, five and nine bars in length, break up the scattered note-gestures. There are also many rests of shorter duration, but while the smaller rests go together with the notes to make up musical gestures, the long silences are something altogether 'other'. These great silences are treated compositionally as quite distinct entities. The notes are mostly marked *piano* but on three occasions individual sound-events are marked *forte*, exploding out of a ground of quietness. Where *Piano Piece 1952b* is entirely made of quiet notes of uniform duration, the unpublished work has three materials: silence (of two kinds — pauses and rests), quiet sounds (of varied duration and spacing) and occasional loud sounds. (It is not at all clear which of these materials are foreground and background: do the outbursts of sound interrupt a ground of silence, or is it the other way round?)

The idea of *Piano Piece 1952b* was, as Feldman tells us explicitly, to be 'quiet', but this is not the whole story. When we reflect upon the way in which Feldman has here reduced his compositional space to a flat plane in every aspect except that of pitch, we can appreciate that this is also part of the intended contrast between the two pieces. This is made more dramatic by the knowledge that Feldman then eliminated the explicit contrast by deleting the first piece altogether; *Piano Piece 1952b* is in itself so peculiar, however, that implicit oppositions are powerfully present. If *Piano Piece 1952b* has any sort of figurative content at all, it is contained in the organisation of pitch, and in making the decision to repress the companion piece, Feldman indicated that, whatever he ultimately wanted to be heard in this work, it is contained in *Piano Piece 1952*. He did not require complex variety of rhythm, varied dynamic levels or notes to be grouped into clearly audible directional gestures – which leaves the element of abstracted pitch-organisation as the primary medium through which the composer is communicating. His message is inextricable from the aesthetic stance that this selection of materials implies.

Analysis ii

Despite the fragmentary nature of one of the pieces and the relative featureless-ness of the other, I seek to unravel the internal structures of the works, in the light of the observations made concerning *Intermission 5*. The two fragments of the unpublished work are, in a way, the easiest to manage. Since we cannot be sure

---

[24]   See Stefan Wolpe's discussion of Wolff's *For Piano* (1952) in Stefan Wolpe, 'On New (And Not-so-New) Music in America' [Darmstadt, 1956], trans. Austin Clarkson, *Journal of Music Theory*, 1/28 (Spring 1984), 25.

that these two pages are even consecutive, they are best considered as separate entities. Each page also contains a long multi-measure silence, which might perhaps be thought to divide passages of note-activity. Beyond this level of detail, we must conjecture and experiment; it is not necessarily clear whether the many shorter rests, for example, are divisions between figures or part of the figures. The complexities of pitch organisation in *Intermission 5*, within each chromatic field and also across larger areas of the piece (both horizontally (time) and vertically (register)), warn us to exercise caution. On the other hand, this unpublished work does have small, identifiable figures within what may be larger structures: the rising four-note figure, for example, which is repeated three times with different pitch collections. Neither of the pieces under consideration here (the published or unpublished parts of *Piano Piece 1952*) has an obvious section of motivic repetition, after the manner of *Intermission 5* or *Structures* (for string quartet), that might give a clue to one level of the pitch material's segmentation.

Let us begin with the broad structures. We may note that the closing fragment (Figure 3.1) presents the full chromatic field. Significantly, the pitch-class B is heard only once, as the first note on the page. Viewed from the end backwards, then, the field is completed by this note. Feldman (as seen in Chapter 2) did not necessarily compose from beginning to end, but rather viewed the time-span as a canvas upon which he could work back and forth, viewing the total image as it developed in a 'crystalline', objectified form.[25] In the other fragment of *Piano Piece 1952a* (Figure 3.2), a comparable chromatic density is evident; in the surviving fragments of the piece, then, we may observe a rather more consistent deployment of the chromatic fields than that of *Intermission 5* which was designed as a gradual thinning of the chromatic density over time. *Piano Piece 1952a* seems to be rather more obviously concerned with surface gesture (for example, the recurrent rising four-note motif, the long silences) than with the deep-level, controlled structuring of the chromatic field.

This is not to say, however, that there is no evidence of detailed manipulation of the pitch materials. On the contrary, we may observe that the chromatic fields are, as in *Intermission 5*, weighted by repetitions of individual pitch-classes – and it is difficult not to interpret this weighting as hierarchical. In effect, Feldman has defined repetition-sets, even if they are not as explicit as that of the closing section of *Intermission 5*. A powerful example of this is found in the final page of *Piano Piece 1952a* (Figure 3.3), where the trichord C♯–F–G♯ is not only made quite prominent through repetition of the individual pitch-classes, but also allowed to sound quite distinctly as a set. Between measures 3 and 4 of the fragment (see Figure 3.3), Feldman allows the set to rise to the very surface of the aural experience, as we hear the three pitch-classes sounded in the same register in the left hand,

25   See David Patterson, 'Cage and Beyond: An Annotated Interview with Christian Wolff', *Perspectives of New Music*, 32/2 (Summer 1994), 72; also Morton Feldman, 'XXX Anecdotes & Drawings', in Walter Zimmermann (ed.), *Morton Feldman Essays* (Kerpen: Beginner Press, 1985), 168.

at which point one cannot help but hear the set enharmonically as a major triad (C♯–E♯–G♯). Whether sets like this formed identifiable motifs on a wider scale in the piece, or how they may form part of the larger design, cannot be determined – although similar implied triadic formations are present in *Piano Piece 1952b* (as noted by Christian Wolff).[26] Without the complete manuscript of the unpublished work, it is impossible to speculate about how these fragments might relate to the (lost) whole. Similarly, we cannot know if there are proportional divisions forming the durational architecture of the piece.

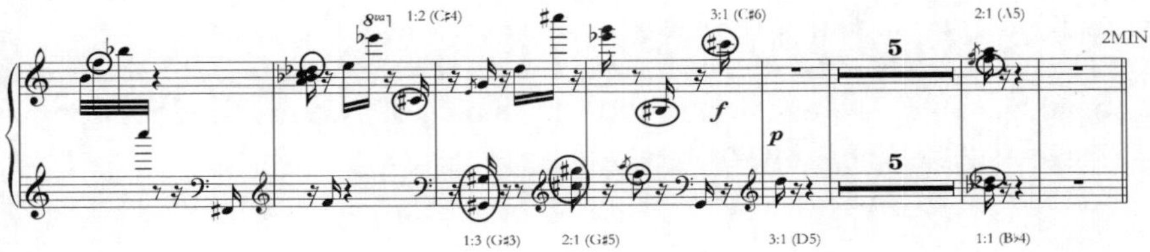

Figure 3.3   Closing section of Feldman, *Piano Piece 1952a*, with notes of the C♯–F–G♯ set circled and showing some proportional partitions of the vertical space

It is certainly possible to identify aspects of the activation of certain registers as partitions of the vertical space at significant moments. Even at the very broad level of partitions of the total vertical space as sounded in one of these fragments, we may find suggestive activations of 1:1, 1:2 and 1:3 proportions (Figure 3.3). Bear in mind that the closing fragment in Figure 3.3 represents a complete chromatic field as mapped from the end of the piece. In addition, there is evidence of localised deployment of Wolpean proportions, similar to those observed in *Intermission 5* (for example, Figure 3.3, measures 4–5).

In the published *Piano Piece 1952b*, however, there are no discrete gestures, rhythmic motifs, silences or other convenient segmentation points. Aurally, the piece seems an endless string of notes; yet this perception of a string, a line, already hints that we are not dealing with something purely abstract. Mysterious figures, melodic fragments and chords are glimpsed beneath the work's surface in such a way that the listener cannot always be certain whether they are truly present or illusory. Feldman, as Wolpe observed in 1956, may have been interested in 'the remnants of shapes that are barely heard at a distance'.[27] There are, however, a few significantly identifiable features that may be useful:

---

26   Christian Wolff, 'The Sound Doesn't Look Back'.
27   Stefan Wolpe, 'On New (And Not-so-New) Music in America', 25.

- the notes at the extremes of the piece's pitch-range are quite audibly prominent in their contexts, the lowest note in particular;
- there are two points where the relentless right/left-hand, treble/bass alternations cross over each other in register;
- at one point the hands meet at semitone-adjacent notes but do not cross.

To consider each of these in turn, it is interesting that the highest and lowest notes of the piece occur quite close to each other in the first three systems (this is similar to *Intermission 5*). The highest note is an F♯7 in the second system, while the lowest is B0 in the third system. Thinking of the A–E–A bass-line of *Intermission 5*, we may observe the similar IC5[28] relationship between these two notes.

The crossings between the two hands are also clearly visible in the score, and distinctly audible. The first occurs at the beginning of system 5, and results in a four-note rising gesture (Figure 3.4).

Figure 3.4   Feldman, *Piano Piece 1952b*. The ascending and descending gestures

Such a gesture is impossible in the right-hand/left-hand system Feldman has set up for the work unless, as here, the hands cross over each other. It is worth reflecting upon the observable fact that the piece's fundamental motion as determined by the strict alternation of hands is one of high–low–high–low, etc., so the extended single-direction movement made possible by the crossing of hands is highly significant and clearly audible. That Feldman was quite aware of this significance is demonstrated by the very sparing use of the hand-crossing gesture

---

[28]   Interval Class 5, to describe the relation of a fourth or fifth (its inversion) in traditional terminology.

(and, curiously, he drew a diagonally falling line above the first hand-crossing in the sketch). It should hardly come as a surprise, given the balanced deliberation which seems to be behind so much of Feldman's compositional processes that the second hand-crossing, in the very last system, results in a four-note downward gesture. It is also not insignificant that these two rare four-note gestures share two pitch-classes (G, B♭).

Between these rising and falling figures, the meeting of hands in system 7 is a point where chromatically adjacent notes are sounded by each hand in turn (Figure 3.5). This meeting is, moreover, emphasised by the two hands hovering around the meeting point for at least six notes (the line is arguably projected further); it may be heard as a distinct levelling of the jagged, irregular leaps that characterise the rest of the piece. Centred on D4/E♭4, this plateau also highlights the exact 1:1 (symmetrical) partition of the vertical pitch-space. Importantly, the listener has a momentary sense of linearity developing out of the relentless verticality of the high–low–high–low motion. There are several places in the piece where such linearities are allowed to become audible (the two instances of hand crossing, for example, certainly have such an implication), although this is by far the most explicit.

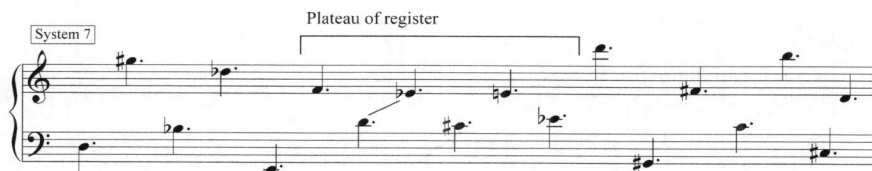

Figure 3.5   Feldman, *Piano Piece 1952b*, system 7

A few of the other points at which aspects of linearity seem to arise out of the abstraction (to my ears, at least) may be summarised:

- My attention is drawn to a triadic figure in the left hand of system 2 (G♯2–C3–E♭3) and this seems to create, for a few moments, a tenor-register voice that continues via the next note (B2) to the D3 a little further on (Figure 3.6). This has the effect of suddenly crystallising a sense of proliferating voices, as the left hand breaks into several distinct registers around this line.
- Overlaying this is the left hand's grandiose plunge through two minor ninths which, starting from a tenor register E♭4, descends to E♭1, the second-lowest note in the piece. There is, moreover, an elegant economy about the two chromatically adjacent notes (in terms of pitch-class) that form the bridge between the two E♭s, defining a chromatic trichord. These downward leaps

function as preparation for the more abrupt leap to the lowest note of all (B0) in the next system. Although abrupt in terms of register, it is surely no coincidence that this leap is also a minor ninth expanded by an octave (Figure 3.7).The entire structure intersects with the symmetrical rise and fall of the pitch-classes E and F♯ in the right hand.

- All this left-hand activity tends to draw some attention away from the piece's highest note (F♯7 in system 2), but the lowest note, in system 3, stands out dramatically. The descending fourth interval E–B (IC5) in the left hand of system 5 seems to echo and reinforce this memorable B sonority (Figure 3.8), rather like the fundamental A sonority in the bass of *Intermission 5*.[29]

Figure 3.6   Feldman, *Piano Piece 1952b*, system 2. Lines mark some aurally perceived 'voices'

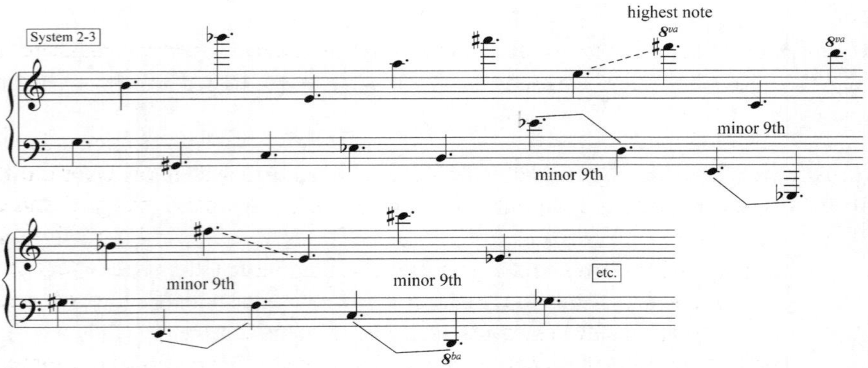

Figure 3.7   Feldman, *Piano Piece 1952b*, systems 2–3

---

[29]   IC5, as used here and in the bass-line of *Intermission 5*, clearly has powerful implications of tonality (in a harmonic, cadential sense), of which Feldman was no doubt conscious.

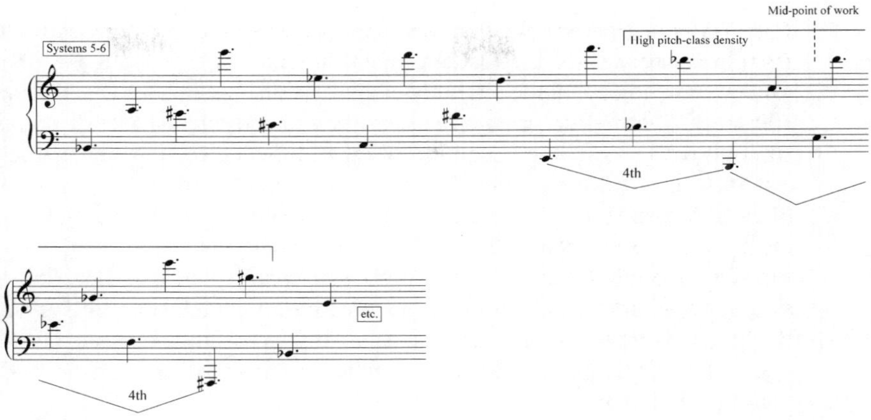

Figure 3.8   Feldman, *Piano Piece 1952b*, systems 5–6

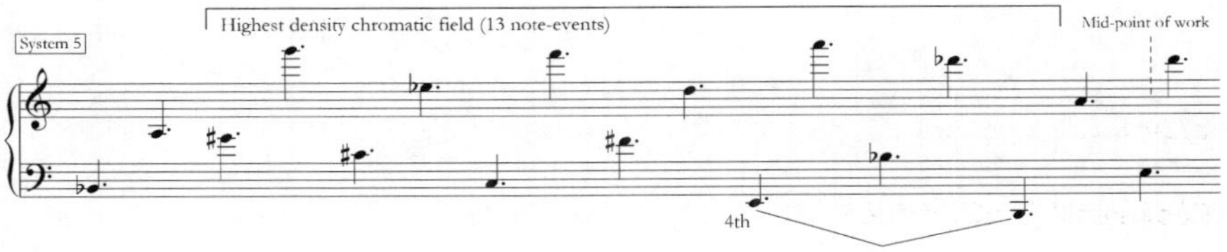

Figure 3.9   Feldman, *Piano Piece 1952b*, system 5

- Heralded by this E–B descending fourth, I hear a brief section of high chromatic density, beginning from note 82 (B♭3 in system 5). Over the 12 note-events from this point on, we hear every pitch-class except C and G (IC5) – while F♯/G♭ and E are repeated. This section of high pitch-class density falls directly over the mid-point of the piece (E3 at note-event 86). It is surely not a simple coincidence that the pitch-class F♯ is here repeated, just as it was over the mid-point of *Intermission 5*.
- Further investigation reveals that this 12-note, 10-pitch-class segment intersects with another section of very high pitch-class density to form a complete 12-tone aggregate over 13 notes between note-events 72 and 84 (Figure 3.9). Repeating only one pitch-class (C♯/D♭ in this case – forming, with the F♯/G♭ mentioned above, another IC5 relationship), this aggregate field shares three notes with the 10-pitch-class field that follows (B♭, D♭,

B).[30] We may also observe that the aggregate structure is otherwise built from chromatic dyads (G♯–G, C♯–C, E♭–D, etc.).

- We have already noted the pitch-plateau in system 7, which attracts the ear while highlighting the symmetrical partition of the pitch-space. In doing so, it projects a middle-range voice into the following section, and creates a three-voiced texture (Figure 3.10). We may aurally follow this through to the C♯4 in the middle of system 8, at which point an extraordinary thing happens: the outer voices fall away as the middle voice splits into two. These two newly revealed voices unfold in contrary motion, describing symmetrical arcs as they return to the middle of the pitch-space in system 9. Similar contrary-motion figures occur elsewhere in the piece (as in system 6, for example), but this instance is particularly dramatic – both on the page, and to the ear.

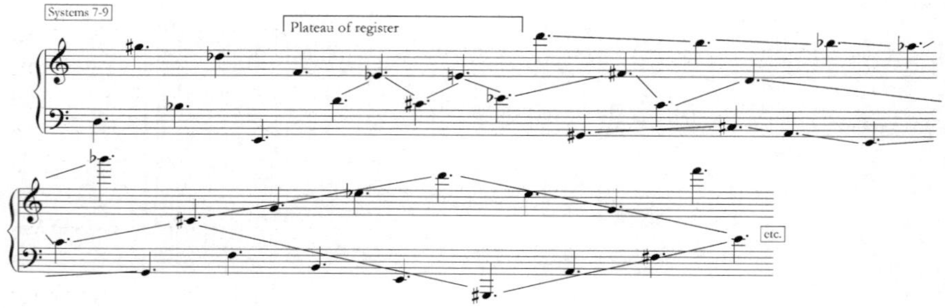

Figure 3.10   Feldman, *Piano Piece 1952b*, systems 7–9

Many of these features, figures and gestures fall upon points of obvious proportional significance in terms of the proportional subdivision of the work's duration. Most dramatically, the levelling out represented by the meeting of hands in system 7 falls directly over the point of 2:1 division (two-thirds of the duration of the work has elapsed at this point). Among other significantly placed audible structures, we may note that the highest note in the piece falls as close as can be possible to the 1:5 division of the piece (1/6), while the lowest is only about

---

[30]   These three pitch-classes are of the set-type 013, and we may note at this point that trichords of the pattern 013, 014, 015, etc., are common in Feldman's music – as both DeLio and Undreiner have shown. Thomas DeLio noted in his detailed examination of *Last Pieces #3* (1959) that interval classes 1 and 3 are of special significance in this work. Thomas Delio, '*Last Pieces* #3 (1959)', in Thomas DeLio (ed.), *The Music of Morton Feldman*; Paul Stephen Undreiner, *Pitch Structure in Morton Feldman's Compositions of 1952* (PhD Dissertation, State University of New Jersey, 2009).

one note removed from the 1:3 (one-quarter) division-point. In so far as they represent a mixture of proportions, this manner of structuring time is similar to that observed in *Intermission 5*. The significant features identified at this stage of our investigation are represented diagrammatically in Figure 3.11.

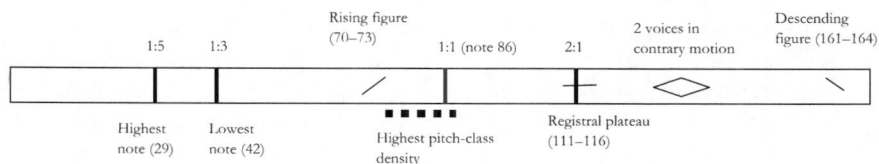

Figure 3.11   Feldman, *Piano Piece 1952b*. Significant surface structures

At first glance (or first hearing), *Piano Piece 1952* might perhaps give an impression of an almost random selection of notes. I think it is already clear, however, that closer listening and examination quickly reveal quite distinct and strategically positioned structures. As one delves further into the details of the work's fabric, this sensation of intelligent organisation deftly implemented is confirmed on every level.

Shape and interval were clearly important factors in Feldman's composition of this work, as indeed of other works of the 1950s. It is no coincidence that both aspects, of shape and interval, were crucial elements in the thinking and teaching of Wolpe. Even at the very end of his life, Feldman would write, 'I want to thank … Stefan Wolpe for teaching me the plastic possibilities of musical shape'[31] – and we might think of the remarkable geometric figures found in *Piano Piece 1952b*.

Wolpe spoke of intervals with great intensity and passion. In his 1952 lecture 'Thoughts on Pitch and Some Considerations Connected with It', Wolpe observed of Interval Class 1,

> … the second (and all that goes with it)
> has lost much of its original beauty.
> But beauty, as always, is a matter of coordinated equivalents,
> among which this interval has still (and I'm sure for a good while)
> the importance of a principal axis-interval.[32]

---

[31]   Morton Feldman, 'I Want to Thank' [1986], in B.H. Friedman (ed.), *Give My Regards to Eighth Street: Collected Writings of Morton Feldman* (Cambridge, MA: Exact Change, 2000), 202.

[32]   Stefan Wolpe, 'Thoughts on Pitch and some Considerations Connected with It' [1952], *Perspectives of New Music*, 17/2 (1979), 55 [pages un-numbered].

Meanwhile, 'a third is a third and sounds like it' (interval class 3 or 4).[33] Elliott Carter has written of witnessing Wolpe give a similar lecture at Dartington in 1959. His description is worth quoting at some length, because it gives a vivid insight into Wolpe's teaching on this very subject of interval:

> At once, sitting at the piano, he was caught up in a meditation on how wonderful these primary materials, intervals, were; playing each over and over again on the piano, singing, roaring, humming them, loudly, softly, quickly, slowly, short and detached or drawn out and expressive. All of us forgot time passing, when the class was to finish. As he led us from the smallest one, a minor second, to the largest, a major seventh – which took all afternoon – music was reborn, new light dawned, we all knew we would never again listen to music as we had. Stefan had made each of us experience very directly the living power of these primary elements.[34]

Perhaps this is how we should try to hear Feldman's music – not passively as a succession of random, isolated sounds, but with a great intensity of vivid experience expressed in all the complex relations between all the sounds within the frame of time and pitch.

Analysis iii

In the previous chapter, we saw that Feldman formed the broad structures of *Intermission 5* around proportional divisions, each space thus defined associated with the deployment of a chromatic field. *Piano Piece 1952b* is made up of seven or eight chromatic fields rather than the three broad fields of *Intermission 5*. The work as a whole may be understood to have the chromatic field (in abstract) as its ground, at the same time as we may define a fairly regular cycling through the field as more-or-less distinct parts of the work – what I have identified as smaller-scale deployment of the chromatic field. This indicates a greater consistency of pitch-class density, relative to the earlier work, and a significant regularity of maintaining the aggregate 'in play' as it were, which strongly implies deliberate control rather than accident. The fields would average approximately 21–24 notes each, were they of equal density (approximating a 1:1 dilution of the total chromatic in terms of repetitions); in fact, however, they are slightly irregular. As we have already seen, the middle of the piece has a relatively high pitch-class density (for example, the 12 pitch-classes over 13 notes between note-events 72 and 84).

In the absence of obvious structural features, such as the motives and gestures in *Intermission 5*, it is difficult to be certain where the exact boundaries of the

---

[33]   Ibid., 57 [pages un-numbered].
[34]   Elliott Carter, *Recollections of Stefan Wolpe*, http://www.wolpe.org/page1/page10/page10.html#Elliott%20Carter.

Rising figure
(70–73)

1:5   1:3   1:1 (note 86)   2:1

2 voices in
contrary motion

Descending
figure (161–164)

Highest
note (29)

Lowest
note (42)

Highest pitch-class
density

Registral plateau
(111–116)

18   46   79   104   131   157

Chromatic Fields mapped from beginning of work

No F, G#, B

16   44   72   85   119   138

No G, B   Chromatic Fields mapped from end of work

16   44   72   85   115   133   157

No G, B   Chromatic Fields mapped from the 2:1 partition of duration   No F, G#, B

16–17   44   73   100   131   157

No G, B   Chromatic Fields mapped from the 1:1 partition of duration   No F, G#, B

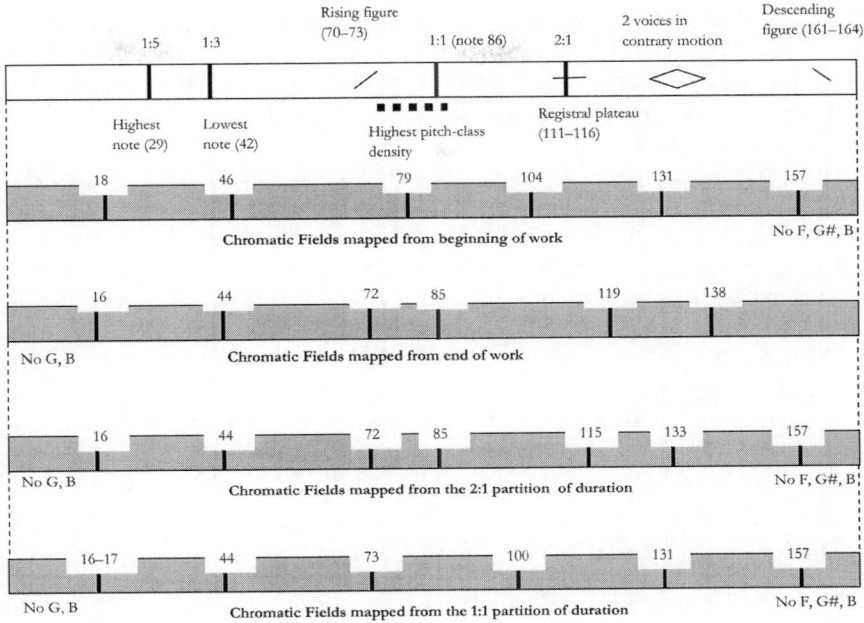

Figure 3.12   Feldman, *Piano Piece 1952b*. Several possible mappings of the chromatic fields

aggregate fields fall in *Piano Piece 1952b*. Mapping them out from the beginning of the piece, perhaps the most obvious experimental solution, gives the structure shown in the second line of Figure 3.12.[35]

Although this gives a rough impression of the broad layout of the fields, they seem not to intersect with the significant features outlined above (Analysis ii) in any particularly noteworthy manner. It is noteworthy, however, that the last field is not complete, but missing F, G♯ and B (a diminished triad). The only way to (analytically) complete the final field is to map the fields from the end backwards (see Figure 3.12 again).

The problem here, obviously, is that the first field in this case is incomplete. Crucially, however, the two notes needed to complete the opening field (G, B) are in fact note-events 16 and 17, immediately subsequent. The first two fields may thus be understood to share these notes and overlap. Notice also that the field boundaries in the first half of the piece are not dissimilar to those of the preceding figure, suggesting that in some parts of the piece the models may be approximating Feldman's compositional structures. The boundary at note-event 44 is particularly interesting in that it coincides with the 1:3 division of the

---

35   The numbers given in the figures indicate the note-event at which a new field begins.

piece, and is also placed very close to the lowest note of the piece (42) that we have already noted as aurally significant.

For the sake of comparison, Figure 3.12 also illustrates the division points as if deployed around the 2:1 point (marked by the registral plateau at 114–15). This confirms two things: first, our conjectured division points for the first half of the piece are accurate to a reasonable degree; and second, the 2:1 point is somehow part of the pitch structure. Given that our attempts at division have also consistently indicated some structural/pitch node around note-event 131–8, I would suggest that the passage of two voices in contrary motion (as discussed above) is also proving to be important. Similarly, there seems to be a point of consistency around 156–7, where the final incomplete field begins in most solutions.

After much experiment with these and other possibilities, I have developed a model of the aggregate field boundaries that is built around the mid-point of the piece (see Figure 3.12). This generates boundary points that are particularly useful and that fit well with many of the features and structures identified as significant. For example, sound-events 16–17 are exactly the point at which I have proposed that the first two fields intersect, event 73 is the high point of the rising figure, while 131 is the commencement of the contrary-motion figure.

This incorporates the boundaries at 16, 44, 73, 131 and 157 that other division methods have already revealed as important. It is also interesting that the fields thus mapped are remarkably consistent in length, with the exception of the first and last, which have already been shown to be elided or simply incomplete. (There is precedent for this – I would argue, for example, that the final section of the first of Wolpe's *Seven Pieces for Three Pianos* (1951) represents a similarly incomplete chromatic field, in a work where the 12-tone aggregate is deployed in a structural manner very similar to that observed in *Intermission 5* and *Piano Piece 1952*.) The mid-point field of *Piano Piece 1952b*, built symmetrically around note-event 86, also displays marked symmetries of pitch. Note, for example, that the pitch-class G which completes the field as worked out from the midpoint is represented by the thirteenth note-event on either side of the mid-point, thus forming both the field boundaries. This central field also incorporates the region of highest pitch-class density in the entire work (*ca* 72–93).

This method of division does produce clear correspondences with the simple kinds of proportions that Feldman used in *Intermission 5*. The 1:3 point (note-event 43), for example, is one note removed from the lowest note in the piece and marks a chromatic field boundary in my model (the reader will recall that the lowest pitch of *Intermission 5* forms part of a complex structure built upon the 1:2 division of time). It is also clear, however, that in *Piano Piece 1952b*, quite a few other points of significance are placed at the exact mid-points of a field, just as the mid-point of the fourth field is the mid-point of the piece (see Figure 3.12 again).

With this diagram of the chromatic fields deployed around the 1:1 time-partition, we have arrived at a working model providing an explanatory framework for all the significant features identified so far in terms of both chromatic fields and proportional time-structure. To this point, my analysis is replicating and confirming the argument presented in the previous chapter: namely, that Feldman was building his pieces at this time around proportional divisions of duration in synchronisation with the deployment of 12-tone chromatic fields. Seemingly an unstructured expanse of unrelated notes, *Piano Piece 1952b* is in fact decisively structured and markedly symmetrical at the chromatic field level. Although we cannot know exactly the compositional procedures that gave rise to this intricate structural organisation, the model does reflect a reality of observable phenomena in the work. On this basis I will adopt the model of field boundaries outlined above as the foundation for further investigation of Feldman's manipulation of pitch material at a more detailed level. I aim to demonstrate here that, even at the most detailed level of examination, we may discern the traces of the composer's hand controlling the pitch material (as Jackson Pollock said, 'I can control the flow of the paint. There is no accident').[36] Thus, we may show that the work is not only structured in the broad frame of time and pitch, but also that there are planned relationships between individual notes and sets of notes.

Analysis iv

As we excavate the details of *Piano Piece 1952*, an archaeology of Feldman's pitch management, I am not trying to create the impression that Feldman's compositional practice may be reduced to some kind of formula. Rather, what we are exploring here are simply the basic materials of his craft and art, analogous perhaps to a painter's materials, and some of the consistent, identifiable ways in which those materials are handled. Feldman, like the abstract expressionist painters he knew, was an accomplished and well-trained artist who had a highly developed understanding of the nature and possibilities of his materials.

Within each of Feldman's chromatic fields, we have noted that some pitch-classes are sounded more than once. This serves to emphasise select subsets of the chromatic aggregate. Precedent for the use of irregular serial rows, with pitch-classes either omitted or repeated, may be found also in Schoenberg (op. 23 and op. 24) and also commonly in the works of Feldman's teacher Riegger (not to mention later examples in the work of Stravinsky, Berio and others). There is a superficial similarity to Babbitt's much later concept of the 'weighted aggregate', although there is most likely little connection in a technical sense.[37] Babbitt's weighted aggregates are produced by certain manipulations of an array of 12-tone rows and result in formations which repeat pitch-classes and also omit pitch-classes. In reality, these are not 12-tone materials in the literal sense, although

---

[36]   Pollock is heard to say this in the soundtrack to Hans Namuth's film, *Jackson Pollock*. The soundtrack, including Pollock speaking, is available on CD: *Feldman Edition 2: First Recordings* (Mode 66, 1999).

[37]   For a brief discussion see Milton Babbitt, *Words About Music*, ed. Stephen Dembski and Joseph N. Straus (Madison, WI: The University of Wisconsin Press, 1987), 100–101.

derived therefrom, and in this lies their chief interest for Babbitt. Feldman's chromatic fields, on the other hand, are more usually complete aggregates – with only rare exceptions, such as the ending of *Piano Piece 1952b* – and there is no solid evidence that he was deriving his material from any kind of serial array in this period of his work. We may note here a likeness (at the aesthetic rather than systemic level) to Cage's system for composing *Music of Changes*, in which he allowed pitch-classes to be repeated, but stipulated that all 12 must be present.[38]

Table 3.1   Pitch-classes repeated in each chromatic field

Aggregate field	Pitch-classes repeated (in order of repetition, spelled as they appear)
I	F♯, A, B♭, E, C♯
II	B, A♯, E♭, E, C, D, G♯, B♭
III	B♭, E, G♯, G, A, D, E♭, B
IV	D♭, A, E, D, E♭, G♭, F, B♭, G
V	C, D, E, E♭, C♯, G♯, B
VI	E, G, F, E♭, B, C♯, A, C, F♯
VII	C♯, D, A, B♭, G

If we isolate the repeated pitch-classes from each field in *Piano Piece 1952b* (using the 1:1 partition model shown in Figure 3.12), the pitch-class sets Table 3.1 are revealed. This is a rather crude analytical instrument, but it does reveal some further evidence that the repetition-sets are controlled rather than randomly selected. We can observe here a broad symmetry over the whole work, with the smallest repetition-sets at beginning and end, while the largest is in the middle (this despite the middle area, as we have already observed, having also the highest pitch-class density). The first and sixth repetition-sets end with a trichord which forms a diminished triad (B♭, E, C♯ and A, C, F♯), and in the first case these notes appear consecutively in the work. The fourth repetition group begins by outlining a major triad, and again the notes appear in close succession in the work. Here, embedded in the pitch material at a deep level, we can see the origins of some of the triadic formations heard by Christian Wolff.[39] The fifth set begins with a five-note chromatic segment (C, D, E, E♭, C♯), which forms the registral plateau at the 2:1 division-point. In another curiously symmetrical arrangement, the fourth and

[38]   David W. Bernstein, 'Cage and High Modernism', in David Nicholls (ed.), *The Cambridge Companion to John Cage* (Cambridge: Cambridge University Press, 2002), 204–5.

[39]   Christian Wolff, 'The Sound Doesn't Look Back'.

seventh sets outline a tritone C♯–G; the fourth field ends with the enharmonically equivalent notes D♭–G (note-events 98 and 99), while the seventh field ends G–C♯.

One could speculate further about various patterns in these sets, their types and complements; however, I wish to draw attention here to the evidence suggesting that Feldman was working with sets of specific pitch-classes. This is not to suggest that he was unconscious of the more abstract intervallic properties of such materials. My primary purpose, however, is to investigate whether these sets may provide clues to the structuring of motivic elements or identifiable figures in the work itself. Examination of the way in which the repetition-set is deployed in the first chromatic field serves to highlight a clear figure in repetition, made up of the trichord A, B♭, C♯ [014] (Figure 3.13).

Figure 3.13   Feldman, *Piano Piece 1952b*, system 1. The first complete
                    chromatic field

Notice that the last note of the repetition-set to be heard for the first time is E, which marks the exact mid-point of the field and heralds the immediate commencement of the repetitions. Although the A–B♭–C♯ group keeps its order, the other two notes (E, F♯ – also significant in Figure 3.7) are disordered although remaining closely associated with the main figure. Noting that the C♯ of the repeated figure is fixed in register while the A-B♭ is transposed upward (two octaves and one octave, respectively) draws attention to the next sounding of these two pitch-classes in the second system (refer to Figure 3.7). Here they are transposed up one more octave and the B♭ is disguised as an A♯. The C♯, however, is missing; I would argue that we hear the high F♯ (event 29 – the highest note in the piece and also the exact mid-point of the second aggregate field) as gestural completion of the motive (if not the set) in this third repetition. (Once again, we note the IC5 relationship.) It transpires that the fixed-pitch C♯7 is heard only one more time in the piece, at note-event 59. Most significantly, the full A–B♭–C♯ motif is heard here again, at the original register but sounding in reverse order (Figure 3.14). This occurs immediately after the completion of the first third of the work's duration at note-event 58 (A3, heard only once in the entire work), which is also the exact mid-point of the third aggregate field. Examination of this trichord thus reveals a carefully planned and deployed pitch-structure spanning the first four systems of the work.

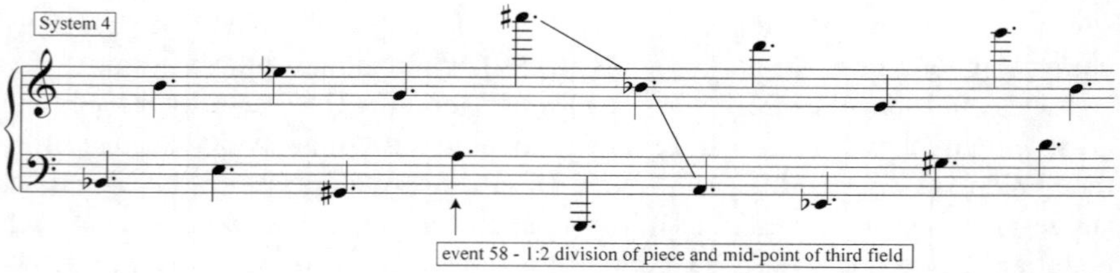

Figure 3.14   Feldman, *Piano Piece 1952b*, system 4

This trichord figure is not heard again in its original configuration, although it is present as a set of pitch-classes in close succession six more times. Of particular interest (refer to Figure 3.15):

- In the fourth field it is heard once only, immediately before the exact mid-point of the piece.
- It marks the boundary between the fifth and sixth chromatic fields, where C♯ begins the contrary-motion figure.
- It marks the boundary between the sixth and seventh fields.
- In the seventh and final field it is heard three times in close succession, echoing the opening.
- When heard for the last time (the final C♯ of the set is also the final note of the piece), the figure is accompanied by the F♯ and E, which were the other two notes of the repetition-set in the first field.

Having identified and examined even just this one motif from the work, it is already clear that the repetition-sets are related to motivic figures that Feldman deploys strategically within the frame of proportional time-structure. These pitch-class sets and figures operate integrally with the time-structures, in so far as they are very frequently associated with points of structural significance on the time-axis.

A related trichord (sharing two pitch-classes), E♭–A–B♭ [016], which occurs at the very beginning as the first three notes of the piece, also recurs towards the end – actually marking the beginning of the final field. Here, however, it is heard in reverse order. Together with the operation of the A–B♭–C♯ trichord, this creates the symmetrical pitch-structure that is largely responsible for the otherwise inexplicable sense of imminent closure that pervades the final field. This trichord is also heard once in each of the second and third fields.

The dyad E–E♭ is reasonably common throughout the piece, and E is the most commonly repeated pitch-class in the work. Furthermore, this dyad quite often occurs accompanied by C [034, inversion of 014]. The first occurrence is in the second chromatic field, where the trichord is heard three times; notice especially the elegant butterfly effect of the trichord intersecting with itself across the boundary of fields 2 and 3 (Figure 3.16)

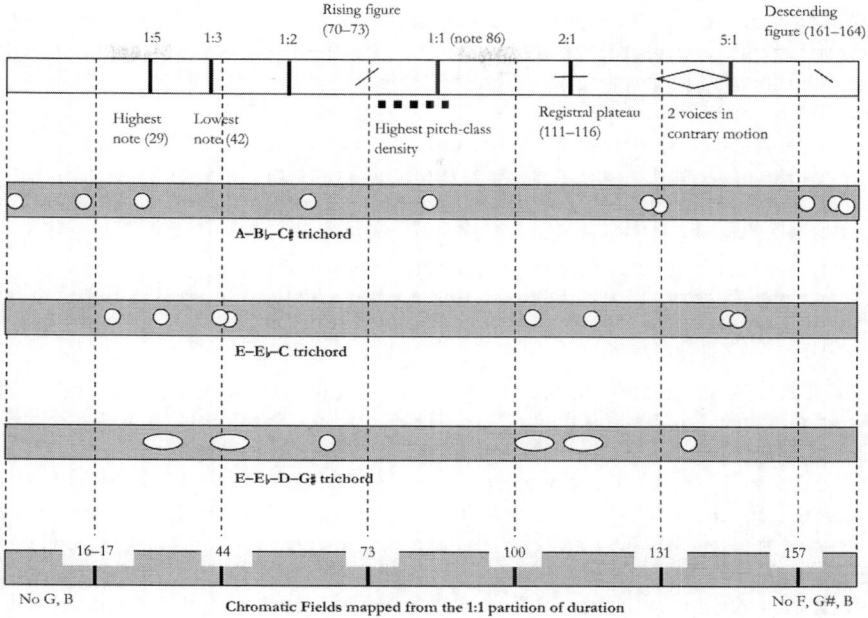

Figure 3.15   Feldman, *Piano Piece 1952b*. Occurrences of several notable trichord motifs

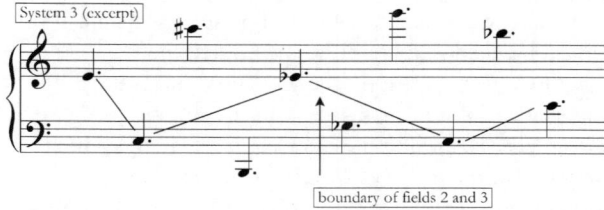

Figure 3.16   Feldman, *Piano Piece 1952b*. 'Butterfly' structure in system 3
Copyright © 1962 by C.F. Peters Corporation. All rights reserved. Used by permission.

This trichord disappears from view through the middle part of the piece, but reappears at the beginning of the fourth field, and again as part of the registral plateau structure at the 2:1 point. Finally, we may observe a second interlocked pair in the sixth field, beginning at the 5:1 point. This set is not heard as an explicit entity in the first or last fields (see Figure 3.15).

An expanded version of this trichord as the set E–E♭–C–D–G♯ [02348] may also be observed quite frequently in various forms; in some areas of the piece the

C is omitted from the set. If, for the sake of comparison, we identify the E–E♭–D–G♯ [0126] set as a discrete entity, we find that this four-note set is strongly present at the following places (see also Figure 3.15):

- the region surrounding the 1:5 point (where the highest note occurs);
- the early part of the third field, from the 1:3 point;
- strongly at both the first- and second-level 'golden section' points (around note-events 105 and 65 respectively);
- dominating the 2:1 point, including the registral plateau;
- clearly forming the climax of the contrary motion figure (the figure at its widest extent).

There can be no doubt that Feldman was using this pitch-class set as a motif at strategic, structurally significant points in the work. The formal purpose of this set overlaps to some extent with the E–E♭–C trichord, but works complementarily with the A–B♭–C♯ set to delineate structures along the time-axis (the two smaller sets also having a symmetrical relationship: 014 and 034). In their emphasis of selected subsets of the total chromatic at significant moments, these repeated figures throw the otherwise hidden structures of the work into relief, casting pitch-class shadows that reveal formal architecture which might otherwise remain obscure, and accentuating the symmetry of the work's design.

Each of these motifs, and there are others, is shown to operate on a structural level, reinforcing the strategically placed aggregate-field boundaries, or helping to distinguish one field from another by creating a difference of weighting in the repetitions within the aggregate. Similarly, many instances of motif repetition are designed to mark out other points of significance in the proportional time-durations of the work. It should be further noted that there are obvious symmetries in the deployment of each of these sets, as shown in Figure 3.15. Sadly, there is not enough material of *Piano Piece 1952a* surviving to make a direct comparison between the two pieces regarding the interplay of time- and pitch-structures.

In many ways, *Piano Piece 1952b* may be understood as being built from an immensely long chain of Wolpean proportions (Figure 3.17). Strikingly different to Wolpe's usage, however, is the way in which Feldman allows them to blur into each other seemingly without distinction, and to intersect and overlap with other pitch structures like the motifs discussed above. One is reminded of Dore Ashton's description of Guston's late 1940s paintings: 'Forms lay on a precisely defined picture plane with only flat overlays suggesting a modicum of depth'.[40] It is precisely the lack of defining gesture (of rhythm, most particularly) that makes this possible; any silences or other variances of the rigid system of *Piano Piece 1952* would immediately begin to unravel the complex structures into an audible

---

[40]   Dore Ashton, *Yes, but ...: A Critical Study of Philip Guston* (New York: Viking Press, 1976), 75.

hierarchy,[41] adding spatial depth to perception (to continue the visual analogy). As it stands, however, the work is experienced by the listener as a bewildering proliferation of possibilities, despite the flatness of dynamic and gesture. Christian Wolff suggested that in *Piano Piece 1952*, 'Each sound is simply itself'.[42] I would argue, in contrast, that each sound is many (indeed manifold), according to the ways in which the listener perceives it as relating to other sounds. None is ever 'simply itself'. Rather, the attentive listener will find that, despite the complexity of the surface, certain patterns, projections, motifs, sets and repetitions will stand out (even if only in a flattened low-relief).

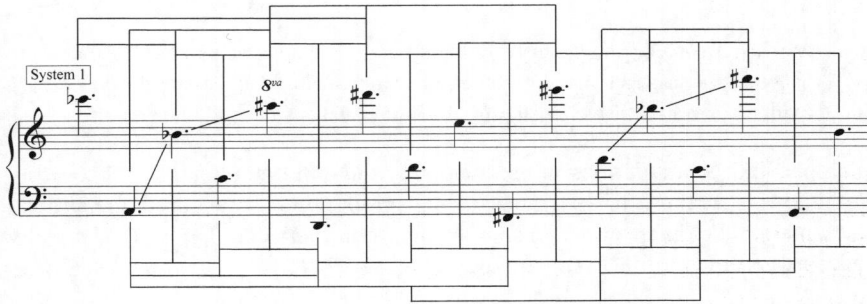

Figure 3.17   Some three-note Wolpean proportions audible in the opening
                     passage of Feldman's *Piano Piece 1952b* (not exhaustive)

For composers of the 1950s, the concept of a musical 'now' moment was an aspect of compositional practice, of performance, and of hearing (we might think not only of Cage's adaptations of Zen, but also of Stockhausen's 'moment form'). From the distance of the twenty-first century, we may appreciate that the concept pertains not only to the practice and experience of the internal structures of a work, but also to the politics of the musical field. In questioning whether the apprehension of an autonomous sound-event is even possible, Christopher Hasty has drawn this link between the works of this time, and the field within which they were produced:

> It may be that this pursuit of autonomy and novelty is in some way a reflection of
> the avant-garde's ambition for an absolutely new art completely dissociated from

---

[41]   This, as the architect Paul Rudolph has observed, is also characteristic of such 1950s New York architecture as the Seagram Building. Paul Rudolph, 'To Enrich Our Architecture', *Journal of Architectural Education*, 13/1 (Spring, 1958), 10.

[42]   Christian Wolff, 'The Sound Doesn't Look Back'.

tradition (and perhaps protected from a future of becoming old – certainly, the designation of postwar music as "the new music," like the earlier "music of the future," bespeaks a desire for perpetual novelty and originality). But from either perspective – history or "immediate," unmediated experience – we must ask if "now" can be cut off from becoming in an unconditional "present" moment.[43]

In Feldman's music, this very ambiguity is made manifest, and an attempt to hear his works as successions of unrelated autonomous moments is inherently problematic. This stimulating ambiguity is evident even in Feldman's sketchbook annotations of the period, and is often at the root of their seemingly confused nature:

> Art when divorced from the historical and lives in the now moment of decision, chance action can then breath freely on the world rather than having the world breath on ones neck. I feel great progress in my analysis.[44]

Such peculiar contradictions in Feldman's writing are homologous to the deeply ambiguous structures of his music. The ambiguity has coloured the critical assessment of Feldman's work in similar ways to the very comparable (and equally awkward) problem of 'action painting' in the visual arts.[45]

Ghostly Figures

Somewhat surprisingly, given the peculiarly featureless surface of *Piano Piece 1952b*, this investigation reveals that the work was composed with comparable materials and methods to *Intermission 5*, and by similar processes. In comparing these two works we may make correlation between the manner of partitioning the time-frame, and the sensitivities to the deployment of both pitch-class and register. In addition, however, we have also identified here a structurally significant deployment of pitch-class sets (as subsets of the total chromatic), which in some cases were used as recognisable, recurrent motifs – often loosely symmetrical. Compared with *Intermission 5*, *Piano Piece 1952* is markedly more symmetrical in construction on all levels.

---

[43]   Christopher Hasty, *Meter as Rhythm* (New York: Oxford University Press, 1997), 298.

[44]   Morton Feldman, sketchbook annotation dated 'Jan 28', most likely of 1952. Paul Sacher Foundation, Basel, Morton Feldman Collection.

[45]   The classic text on this subject is Harold Rosenberg, 'The American Action Painters', 189–98. Among the many problematic areas related to the concept of action painting is that of the explicitly gendered nature of the original discourse; see Lisa Saltzman, 'Reconsidering the Stain: on Gender, Identity, and New York School Painting', in Ellen Landau (ed.), *Reading Abstract Expressionism*, 564–5.

Analysis of Feldman's work quickly shows that his technical methods and procedures of composition owe a very great deal to Wolpe, and even interests in such things as the visual arts and Webern must have developed in Feldman through the mediation of Wolpe's teaching and aesthetic influence. Having said that, however, we should not discount the importance of Riegger, Feldman's earlier composition teacher, an interesting figure in his own right who must have laid the foundations of Feldman's sensitivity to the chromatic field and its manipulations, and to the understanding of music as built with many layers of conceptually unified material. While Riegger might have called this latter aspect 'counterpoint', of which he was an acknowledged master,[46] for Feldman it developed into a subtle appreciation of the planes of 'crystalline' structures. The 'thickening and thinning' activity of the composer upon his two-dimensional conceptual canvas may be understood as a nested construction, floating, held in place by the ambiguous and subtle tensions of the horizontal and vertical space.

Of crucial interest in the case of *Piano Piece 1952*, however, is what Berio perceptively noted as a 'dialectic'. Feldman was never very enthusiastic about the notion of Hegelian, Marxist or musical dialectic, and indeed some of his most caustic remarks were directed at those composers he considered to be pursuing a Hegelian logic in their work. 'Stockhausen', he wrote, 'believes in Hegel; I believe in God'.[47] Curiously, while Stockhausen seems to have always put Feldman in mind of 'systems' of thought, these in turn were frequently associated in his writings with war. In the 1965 essay 'The Anxiety of Art', Feldman likened his own work of the 1950s to the American Revolution which, he argued, 'was never appreciated ... There was no blood bath, no built-in terror'. In this story of Feldman's, Europeans were still the enemy: 'Our work did not have the authoritarianism, I might almost say, the terror, inherent in the teachings of Boulez, Schoenberg, and now Stockhausen'.[48]

Yet there is a dialectic in Feldman's work, which Feldman himself acknowledged had been learnt from Wolpe.[49] Feldman is not commonly thought of as a composer interested in oppositions, opposites, extremes, so it is a little surprising to find him saying to Austin Clarkson, 'He [Wolpe] also being a dialectical materialist, he also liked opposites. The world of opposites also in the sense that he brought to

---

[46]   In addition, Riegger was considered (in the late 1940s and early 1950s) to be one of America's most technically accomplished 12-tone composers. See Henry Cowell, 'Wallingford Riegger: *String Quartet No. 1*, Op. 30' [review], *Notes*, 2nd Series 3/4 (June 1947), 358–9; and Frederick Dorian, 'Wallingford Riegger: *Symphony No. 3* for orchestra' [review], *Notes*, 2nd Series, 4/6 (September 1949), 637–8.

[47]   Morton Feldman, 'A Life Without Bach and Beethoven' [1964], in B.H. Friedman (ed.), *Give My Regards to Eighth Street*, 18.

[48]   Morton Feldman, 'The Anxiety of Art' [1965], in ibid., 22. See also Morton Feldman, 'The Future of Local Music' [1984], in ibid., 174–5.

[49]   Austin Clarkson, 'Conversation about Stefan Wolpe: 13 November 1980', p. 101.

me – and I never think of my thinking about that – helped me tremendously'.[50] We have already caught glimpses of this in the extreme dynamics of Feldman's 1950s music, in the relations between subsets of the chromatic field and the field itself, between vast silences and abrupt complexes of sound activity, in the repetitive and non-repetitive sections of *Intermission 5*, in the right-hand/left-hand system of *Piano Piece 1952b*, in the clarity of Feldman's two-dimensional model which does not permit the confusion of depth or distance, only vertical and horizontal.

Most explicit of all, however, is the long-lost, abortive twin to *Piano Piece 1952b*, the discovery of which reveals that the essential subject of the work, at the point of composition, was a dialectical opposition – an internal, formal contradiction. This contradiction is no less present (if less explicit) in the published form of the work, where we literally hear only one side of the argument, and it is this that Berio may have sensed, and which puzzled Wolff. *Piano Piece 1952b* (the published work) is not, despite the 'quiet' surface (and I am not referring exclusively to dynamics here) simply intuitive or passive; it is an active, planned argument presented in the composer's chosen conceptual frame. It is, as analysis reveals, a complex, crystalline structure that is in many ways perhaps Feldman's most radical work of the 1950s. It is an argument against the ubiquity of rhythmically varied gestures; against tonal, chance-driven and serial systems; against new instruments and sound-materials; against the spectacle of virtuosity; against spatial depth, perhaps even against the audience. Of all Feldman's works, this is most like the all-over paintings that Pollock produced in the late 1940s and early 1950s, both in its expression of a flattened 'picture plane' and in the sense of intricate, seemingly infinite possibilities of proliferated significance. We are reminded of Greenberg, yet again:

> the capacity to bind the canvas rectangle and assert its ambiguous flatness and quite unambiguous shape as a single and whole image concentrating into one the several images distributed over it.[51]

Pollock, however, was not the only artist concerned with the flattening of the picture plane. Equally, parallel may be made with the work and thinking of Feldman's close friend Philip Guston. Dore Ashton, who was friendly with both Guston and Feldman, and having a similar Jewish migrant family background, quoted Guston speaking of his work of the late-1940s thus: 'Much of our talk was about the holocaust and how to allegorize it'. Guston told Ashton that he 'was searching for the plastic condition, where the compressed forms and spaces themselves expressed my feelings about the holocaust', and she later remarked

50 Ibid.
51 Clement Greenberg, '"American-Type" Painting', in Ellen Landau (ed.), *Reading Abstract Expressionism*, 205.

that this profoundly affected his work for the rest of his life.[52] Of Guston's late-1940s work, Ashton wrote,

> He adopted a new way of indicating space. Since the space he wished to depict was claustrophobic, confined as a narrow prison cell, the recession in depth had to be truncated. Forms lay on a precisely defined picture plane with only flat overlays suggesting a modicum of depth.[53]

To stress the idea that this was not a passive flattening of the picture plane, Ashton described the effect in rather violent terms: 'There is enormous pressure from the foreplane to the rear', and 'buildings (in which the windows are barred) are steamrollered flat'. She further likened the figures in the paintings, with their 'gestures of despair' to the 'unforgettable photographs of prisoners liberated from concentration camps'.[54]

In his own writings, Feldman did not discuss openly any specific influence of post-holocaust thinking upon his work of this 1940s–50s period, but at the very least he must surely have been aware of the importance to his friends and colleagues. References even to matters of Jewishness are generally rare in Feldman's writing, but we should not necessarily dismiss this, therefore, as irrelevant. On one rare occasion, in an interview with Heinz-Klaus Metzger in the early 1970s, Feldman did speak of this subject directly, if hesitantly:

> But what my music is [is] mourning, I just don't know what to say. I just said earlier, that perhaps just mourning ... I must say you did bring up something that I particularly don't want to talk about publicly, but I do talk privately.
>
> To some degree I do believe for example, like George Steiner,[55] that after Hitler perhaps there should no longer be art. Those thoughts are always in my mind. There was a hypocrisy, a delusion to continue, because those values proved to me nothing. They have no longer any moral basis. And what are our morals in music? Our moral in music is 19th century German music, isn't it?[56]

Feldman's anxiety in discussing this subject, and the parallel between his mourning and the atmosphere of despair that many critics besides Ashton have identified in the works of Guston and Rothko, suggests that this may be a fruitful area of investigation. What is uniquely important about Ashton's analysis of Guston's

---

[52] Dore Ashton, *Yes, but...: A Critical Study of Philip Guston*, 74.

[53] Ibid., 75.

[54] Ibid., 75, 76.

[55] See also Theodor Adorno, 'Cultural Criticism and Society' [1951], trans. Samuel and Sherry Weber, in *Prisms* (Cambridge, MA: MIT Press, 1983), 34.

[56] Heinz-Klaus Metzger, 'Prolog: über Jiddishkeit' (text in German and English), in Walter Zimmermann (ed.), *Morton Feldman Essays*, 7.

work is the fact that she was prepared to extend this beyond the atmospheric to the structural; the picture plane itself, as a 'disturbingly indeterminate but confined space', was for her directly symbolic.[57]

There is a curious sense of decisive indecision in *Piano Piece 1952*, as a substantial two-movement work mutilated subsequent to composition (crushed into a markedly flatter frame), which perhaps explains some of the uncomfortable ambiguity we sense. The work is on the one hand built from rather elegantly constructed complexes of pitch material, yet these are difficult to grasp and unravel in hearing; the structures remain mere shadows, seemingly without continuity of logic. The structures are actually present, but Feldman would have us hear them as illusory. Wolff's wonderfully (and appropriately) contradictory essay about the piece reveals his concern at the lack of apparent continuity and also his search for pattern; his identification of patterns and structures of organisation, together with his unwillingness to ascribe any intent to Feldman in their creation ('strictly speaking, I'd say he had nothing in mind').[58] This is not simple perversity on Wolff's part, it is an analysis of the structure of the field from Wolff's perspective (and Wolff's place in it in relation to Feldman) viewed through the window of the work itself.

The importance of the shadowy ambiguity of Feldman's musical structures was sensitively perceived by Wolpe, who explained to the Darmstadt audience of 1956 that 'He [Feldman] is interested in surfaces that are as spare as possible and in the remnants of shapes that are barely heard at a distance. Can I express this more precisely? No!'[59] Of course this combination of flat surface and ghostly figures might be read in a number of ways. While Wolpe chose to hear Feldman's music in terms of mysterious, shadowy figures, only half-recognisable, for Wolff 'the sound is simply present. It doesn't look back. That's what makes this music utopian'.[60] Certainly, we have already seen that Feldman understood his musical work as an opposition to the ordinary world, and in this sense we must appreciate that every note Feldman wrote was in a sense a dialectical critique of that ordinary, everyday world, its society and politics (albeit from a position tending toward the *bourgeois*). It suited Cage and Wolff, defending their own positions in the field of cultural production, to understand Feldman's work as utopian and forward-looking. Bourdieu reminds us that the fundamental activity in the field of cultural production is the struggle to attain and maintain a position;[61] while composers like Cage, Wolff and Feldman may have been friends at a personal level, their works are necessarily antagonistic to each other in some respects.

57   Dore Ashton, *Yes, but...: A Critical Study of Philip Guston*, 76.
58   Christian Wolff, 'The Sound Doesn't Look Back'.
59   Stefan Wolpe, 'On New (And Not-so-New) Music in America', 25.
60   Christian Wolff, 'The Sound Doesn't Look Back'.
61   Pierre Bourdieu, 'The Field of Cultural Production, or: The Economic World Reversed' [1983], in Randal Johnson (ed.), *The Field Of Cultural Production: Essays on Art and Literature* (New York: Columbia University Press, 1993), 30.

As noted in the introduction to this chapter, *Piano Piece 1952b* is, despite the seeming harmlessness of its rather conservative sounds, at the same time awful and forbidding. Feldman has denied the audience even the conceptual comfort that the explicit dialectic between the original pair of pieces might have offered. The piece is haunted not only by the ghosts of structures, shapes and figures, but also by that of its murdered twin, heavily crossed out in the sketch manuscript and literally dismembered page by page. This music is actively composed (rather than passively) and the work as we hear it today is heavily coloured by the violence of the composer's vandalism of his own creation. While it may well be a dialectal critique of the music, art, society and politics of its time, it is also nostalgic rather than utopian, possessed to a large degree by the bitter memory of a failed pre-war modernism, largely European.[62]

Feldman's ghostly figures are not necessarily friendly, angelic guides to some future utopia, but perhaps the reproachful, anxious ghosts of the holocaust. As in Guston's paintings, these are the ghostly, pale shadows of figures, inhabiting a terrible space that has been steamrollered flat. Such beauty as we find may be compared with the dark light cast by Rothko's sublime (and I use the word with appreciation of its full weight of import) burnt offerings of the later 1950s and 1960s.[63] In his 1950s notebooks Feldman wrote that 'for me art is insecurity' and 'space is an illusion'. By the 1980s, as noted above, he explained his music as 'mourning', yet was curiously uncomfortable about discussing this in any detail. Secrecy and ambiguity were also crucial aspects of Feldman's artistic expression, and indeed of the maintenance of his position in the field. In 1972, he wrote proudly of his friend Frank O'Hara, 'He admired my music because its methodology was hidden'.[64]

With *Piano Piece 1952* as published, Feldman took away the means for us to understand the pitch relationships in the usual ways, in relation to rhythm, explicit motif, development or obvious repetition. We might expect in this situation to find that the pitch relationships become meaningless, and structures (if there are any) disappear. On the contrary, however, the experience of listening to the piece is rather the opposite – the relationships proliferate in all directions. What is on one level the most simple and straightforward (even banal) of compositions becomes an experience of immense richness and complexity; rather than a single line of notes, we seem to hear many lines interwoven, many figures and gestures, shapes, intervals, chords, constantly changing in our perception of their relationships.

---

[62]   See Frederic Jameson, *Postmodernism, or, The Cultural Logic of Late Capitalism* (London: Verso, 1991), 1.

[63]   One is reminded of Karol Berger's discussion of 'dark modernity'. See Karol Berger, 'Time's Arrow and the Advent of Musical Modernity', in Karol Berger and Anthony Newcomb (eds), *Music and the Aesthetics of Modernity: Essays* (Cambridge, MA: Harvard University Press, 2005), 5.

[64]   Morton Feldman, 'Frank O'Hara: Lost Times and Future Hopes' [1972], in B.H. Friedman (ed.), *Give My Regards to Eighth Street*, 104.

There is a deep tension between the distinct sound of each event and the complex web of its relationships to other sounds.

Feldman's erstwhile teacher and mentor Wolpe seems to have understood very well the internal contradictions of the work: 'Brought to the brink of dissolution this music is a diabolic test of beauty'.[65] It is not simply a test of beauty in the sense of this particular work, or even of Feldman's work as a whole, but for the field of musical production itself; in this challenge, Feldman claimed a space of his own.[66]

---

[65]   Stefan Wolpe, 'On New (And Not-so-New) Music in America', 25.

[66]   In Bourdieu's understanding, such challenges, internal contradictions and ambiguities (planned or otherwise), are also a homological map of the field of cultural production.

Chapter 4

Intermission 6 (1953):
'the outlines of becoming'

Mobility and Determinacy

Intermission 6 is unique among Morton Feldman's piano works in that it has flexible instrumentation (for one or two pianos).[1] The other pieces in the *Intermission* series (numbers 1–5), for example, are for solo piano – and are more conventionally notated. Flexible instrumentation (always within strictly limited parameters) is in any case quite rare in Feldman's work, and otherwise confined to graphic scores (see, for example, *Intersection I* for orchestra, of 1951). More dramatically, the published piece is unique among all of Feldman's works in so far as it is notated as a mobile score (Figure 4.1). In this regard, it is the first of the four works discussed in this book that possesses an aspect of indeterminacy beyond the commonplace (by commonplace indeterminacy, I refer to pedalling, *fermatas*, and so forth).

It is often thought a truism to say that Feldman disapproved of music produced within the frame of what he termed a 'system'. So much so, that many who would argue for a more sophisticated view have adopted a rather apologetic (or defensive) tone. Herman Sabbe, as recently as 1996, felt it necessary to say 'Let me, therefore, right away and for the sake of clearness state explicitly that, to my mind Feldman does not leave anything to chance.'[2] That composers as diverse as Riegger, Wolpe, Babbitt and Cage were all on friendly terms with Feldman rather clouds any aesthetic demarcation (and indeed even Boulez and Stockhausen had close contact with Feldman at various times). However, what does it mean for our understanding of a mobile score such as *Intermission 6*, if even here 'nothing' is left to chance? Earle Brown believed very strongly that a performer playing from a graphic or mobile score was not 'taking a chance' but making decisions,

---

[1]   There is no indication on the autograph sketch or the David Tudor copies regarding the possibility of realisation with two pianos; it is likely that this idea was developed at the time of the performance in 1958 (for further discussion of this performance and dating of the work, see below in this chapter). Paul Sacher Foundation, Basel, Morton Feldman Collection; The Getty Research Institute, Los Angeles, Tudor Papers, 980039, Box 186, 4.

[2]   Herman Sabbe, 'The Feldman Paradoxes: a Deconstructionist View of Musical Aesthetics', in Thomas DeLio (ed.), *The Music of Morton Feldman* (Westport, CT: Greenwood Press, 1996), 10.

implementing decisive actions based on what they believed to be the next 'right' event (within the frame of the composer's directions).[3]

In fact, Feldman did not use the term 'system' pejoratively in his few surviving 1950s writings. In the 1958 essay 'Sound, Noise, Varèse, Boulez',[4] for example, he was primarily concerned with attacking Boulez for being an 'academician' (which may or may not have something to do with systems), and in pursuing this argument he hit even John Cage with some (presumably) friendly fire: 'What is calculated is for me academic. Chance is the most academic procedure yet arrived at, for it defines itself as a technique immediately'.[5] It is clear that a view based upon the binary opposition of system and non-system is not especially helpful. Feldman's lifelong involvement with the music of Webern (as documented in his writings, lectures and interviews) is illustrative of this complexity – and a shared interest in Webern was precisely what Feldman and Cage had in common when they first met in 1950.[6] The ambiguity of Feldman's attitude to systems of composition was further complicated by his explicit adaptation of serial matrices for his own procedural purposes in works of the late 1970s and 1980s, to organise pitch, dynamics, the ordering of repetition cells and even instrumentation.[7]

The unpublished notes, tables and diagrams in Feldman's sketchbooks of the 1950s are primarily concerned with structure in various guises.[8] In these writings, we may observe Feldman grappling with fundamental issues pertaining to the structuring of non-tonal music – problems concerning the organisation of tone, pitch, time, duration, timbre and texture. In my analyses of *Intermission 5* and *Piano Piece 1952*, I have shown that Feldman's music is evidently carefully designed with regard to both the architecture of time and pitch-organisation, and that these two elements are on some levels interconnected in his compositional practice *ca* 1951–53.

In the 1950s period with which this present study is concerned, the fragments of writing that survive in Feldman's notebooks discuss problems like 'decisive

---

[3]   See Richard Dufallo, *Trackings: Composers Speak with Richard Dufallo* (New York: Oxford University Press, 1989), 114–15. For a recent discussion of related matters, see Clemens Gresser, 'Earle Brown's "Creative Ambiguity" and Ideas of Co-creatorship in Selected Works', *Contemporary Music Review*, 26/3–4 (June 2007), 377–94.

[4]   Morton Feldman, 'Sound, Noise, Varèse, Boulez', in B.H. Friedman (ed.), *Give My Regards to Eighth Street: Collected Writings of Morton Feldman* (Cambridge, MA: Exact Change, 2000), 1–2.

[5]   Ibid., 1.

[6]   The story of Feldman's first meeting with Cage has been retold many times. The earliest version in Feldman's own words dates from 1962, see 'Liner Notes', in ibid., 4. For a review of the concert at which they met, see H.T., 'Hisses, Applause for Webern Opus', *New York Times* (27 January 1950).

[7]   Refer to sketches for works of this period. Paul Sacher Foundation, Basel, Morton Feldman Collection.

[8]   Paul Sacher Foundation, Basel, Morton Feldman Collection.

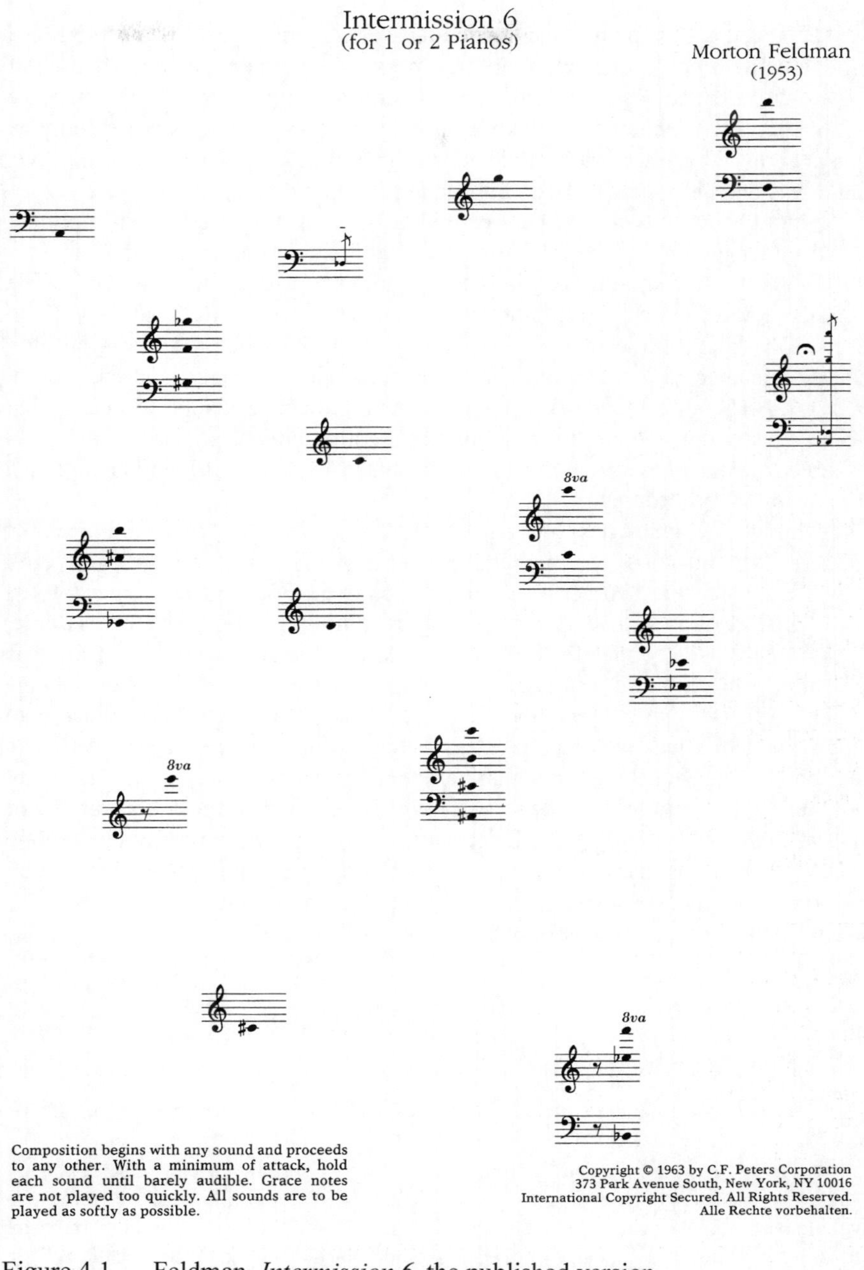
Intermission 6
(for 1 or 2 Pianos)
Morton Feldman
(1953)
8va
8va
8va
Composition begins with any sound and proceeds to any other. With a minimum of attack, hold each sound until barely audible. Grace notes are not played too quickly. All sounds are to be played as softly as possible.
Copyright © 1963 by C.F. Peters Corporation
373 Park Avenue South, New York, NY 10016
International Copyright Secured. All Rights Reserved.
Alle Rechte vorbehalten.

Figure 4.1 Feldman, *Intermission 6*, the published version

need', 'insecurity', structure and 'basic materials', the pursuit of a 'a crystallized structural situation',[9] not to mention the struggle (described in a June 1953 letter to David Tudor) to make 'music like violently boiling water'.[10] This evidence demonstrates that Feldman's thinking in relation to his work was more complex than is allowed by any easy generalisation – it was not simply passive or intuitive, and it was not simply concerned with sound for its own sake.

Certainly, *Intermission 6* is a tremendously interesting work, and important for an understanding of the development of Feldman's thinking in the early-to-mid-1950s, but we should keep its place in his output in clear perspective. The work is not technically or aesthetically representative of Feldman's work in terms of being a mobile score – it is the only such work he produced – but it is exactly this aberration which makes it a useful subject of analysis in the present study. Superficially, the work seems so unstructured, arguably formless, that we might wonder if there are any underlying structures at all, or whether it is possible to identify evidence for the implementation of any of Feldman's known compositional procedures.

Although Feldman has often been spoken of broadly as a composer of indeterminate music (at least with respect to his 1950s work), it was clear to both Cowell and Cage that he practised a very prescriptive kind of indeterminacy.[11] Even in his graphic scores, instruments, dynamics, timing and timbres (for example, *pizzicato*) are usually specified. Feldman's close association with John Cage has led some commentators to assume that Feldman was applying Cagean systems of chance in his own compositions, although there is little concrete evidence to suggest that this was ever the case. As Feldman himself reminded questioners after one of Cage's lectures, in which Feldman's music was discussed, 'That's not me; that's John'.[12] In this chapter, I will investigate whether our understanding of *Intermission 6* (seemingly quite indeterminate in its published form as a mobile score) may be revised in the context of the argument regarding pitch-organisation and formal architecture that has been developed here through the two previously discussed analyses, of *Intermission 5* and *Piano Piece 1952*.

---

    [9]   Ibid.

    [10]   The Getty Research Institute, Los Angeles, David Tudor Papers, Series 1b, 980039, Box 53, f.

    [11]   Henry Cowell, 'Current Chronicle', in *The Musical Quarterly*, 38/1 (January 1952), 131; John Cage, 'Indeterminacy', in *Silence: Lectures and Writings by John Cage* (Middletown, CT: Wesleyan University Press, 1961), 35–40. For discussion in more recent literature, see Steven Johnson, 'Jasper Johns and Morton Feldman: Why Patterns?', in Steven Johnson (ed.), *The New York Schools of Music and the Visual Arts* (New York: Routledge, 2002), 217–47; and the several analytical essays in Thomas DeLio (ed.), *The Music of Morton Feldman*.

    [12]   John Cage, *Silence*, 128.

Sources and Chronology

Intermission 6 is conventionally dated to 1953. Feldman himself, at the time of publishing the work in 1963, gave it this date,[13] although the extant sketch is dated simply 'Nov 6'.[14] Given that the earliest documented performance took place in 1958 (John Cage and David Tudor performing),[15] we must acknowledge that the dating is uncertain. Strictly on the basis of the documentary evidence, we may say that the work was most likely composed sometime between 6 November 1952 (following the first performances of *Intermission 3*, *Intermission 4* and *Intermission 5* earlier that year)[16] and 6 November 1957. In some ways, considering especially the scoring for 'one or two pianos', the piece does seem related to the series of multiple-pianist works begun in 1957.[17] On the other hand, to return to the *Intermission* series after a five-year interval would be quite inconsistent with Feldman's usual practice. More commonly, he had a tendency to produce a series of related works in quick succession, only to abandon them when his interests took a new turn, or the motivating concept of the series seemed to have exhausted itself. Examples of this are the *Intersection* series itself and the *Vertical Thoughts* series, both abandoned at a stage of having further pieces planned or even sketched.[18]

There are three published versions of the work, which do not differ greatly from one another. All published versions have the same pitch material in the same graphic arrangement – a single page, with 15 sound-events spaced irregularly around the page on broken staves (Figure 4.1).[19] The sketch is written quite roughly on a loose leaf pasted into one of the sketchbooks, on the lower part of

---

[13]   Morton Feldman, *Intermission 6* (New York: Edition Peters, 1963).

[14]   Paul Sacher Foundation, Basel, Morton Feldman Collection.

[15]   Sebastian Claren, *Neither: Die Musik Morton Feldmans* (Hofheim: Wolke, 2000), 554. Cage tells of this concert in *A Year from Monday* (Middletown, CT: Wesleyan University Press, 1967), 134.

[16]   David Tudor performed *Intermissions 3, 4* and *5* in a recital on 10 February 1952, Cherry Lane Theater, New York. See John Holzaepfel, 'Reminiscences of a Twentieth-century Pianist: An Interview with David Tudor', *Musical Quarterly*, 78/3 (Autumn 1994), 629.

[17]   *Piece for Four Pianos* (1957), *Piano (Three Hands)* (1957), *Two Pianos* (1957), *Piano Four Hands* (1958). There is also a stylistically inconsistent unpublished work for two pianos, dated April 1958. Paul Sacher Foundation, Basel, Morton Feldman Collection.

[18]   The extraordinary graphic score known as *Intersection +* was never performed or published. The *Vertical Thoughts* series, on the other hand, ends with preliminary sketches for *Vertical Thoughts VI* and *VII*, but these were abandoned with Feldman writing across the page 'REDUNDENT!!!!!!'. Paul Sacher Foundation, Basel, Morton Feldman Collection.

[19]   Morton Feldman, '*Marginal Intersection* (1951), *Intersection 2* (1951), *Intermission 6*', *Kulchur*, 3/11 (Autumn 1963), 33–6. Morton Feldman, *Intermission 6*. Republished in Volker Straebel (ed.), *Morton Feldman: Solo Piano Works 1950–64* (New York: Edition Peters, 2000), 5.

the final page of sketch material for *Intermission 5*.[20] We know that *Intermission 5* was first performed in February 1952, suggesting that *Intermission 6* was most likely composed after this date, rather than in November 1951. The ink on vellum manuscript used for the holograph reproduction of the 1963 Peters Edition is held by SUNY Buffalo.[21] As it is an identical source to the published edition, it will be disregarded for the purpose of the present discussion. There are two further extant manuscript copies of the work, in the David Tudor Papers held by The Getty Research Institute, Los Angeles.[22] It is likely that these copies are those used by Tudor and Cage for the 1958 performances of *Intermission 6*. Most importantly, all three of these manuscripts (the sketch and the two Tudor copies) differ substantially from the published versions of the work in so far as the sound-events are not graphically arranged on the page but notated on conventional systems, the events separated by double bar-lines.[23]

The published version is thus not merely an arrangement of the material, but a graphic re-arrangement. Furthermore, the published versions contain only 15 sound-events, whereas the earlier manuscripts and the sketch contain 19. There is a strong implication of conscious deliberation in this very act of rearrangement and selection of materials for the published version. There are several differences between the various scores in terms of annotations, which may be best summarised in a table (refer to Table 4.1).

Before embarking upon formal analysis of *Intermission 6*, we may outline a conjectural reconstruction of the composition process over a period of 10 years, based upon the evidence of primary-source materials. The piece was probably first sketched on 6 November 1952 (the date of 1953 seems rather less likely, as this would place it almost two years after *Intermission 5*). Unperformed at this time, as far as we know, the work was revived and copied without substantial alteration around 1957–58 for performances by Tudor and Cage. The piece is known to have been performed in the context of a concert of new 'indeterminate' music for two pianos, and this is the first indication that the work might be performed by two pianists, a decision very likely made at this time.[24] In 1963, Feldman made further copies for publication and at this time he made substantial changes: re-organising the pitch material, reducing the number of sound-events and, most importantly, re-presenting the individual sound-events in a graphic arrangement of broken staves. Lacking a formal record, Feldman perhaps estimated the original composition date to be 1953.

---

[20]   Paul Sacher Foundation, Basel, Morton Feldman Collection.

[21]   Music Library, University at Buffalo, The State University of New York, Buffalo, C.F. Peters Collection of Morton Feldman Manuscripts, 1961–69, Mus. Arc. 2.4, Box 2, 34.

[22]   The Getty Research Institute, Los Angeles, David Tudor Papers, Series 1b, 980039, Box 186, 4.

[23]   Feldman sketched the work using dotted quarter notes (which gives superficially a similar appearance to *Piano Piece 1952*), although in the published score they are reduced to un-dotted stemless note-heads.

[24]   Sebastian Claren, *Neither*, 554. Cage tells of this concert in *A Year from Monday*, 134.

Table 4.1   Comparison of sources for *Intermission 6*

Source	Sketch (Paul Sacher Stiftung, Basel, Sammlung Morton Feldman)	MS (The Getty Research Institute, Los Angeles, David Tudor Papers)	MS (The Getty Research Institute, Los Angeles, David Tudor Papers)	Published (*Kulchur* 3/11 (Autumn 1963) 36)	Published (New York, Edition Peters, EP6928, 1963)
Dated	6 Nov	No	No	1953	1953
Title	*Intermission #6*	*Intermission #6*	*Intermission #6*	*Intermission 6a* – Piano Solo, *Intermission 6b* – two pianos	*Intermission 6* (for one or two pianos)
Other annotations	'Hold each [measure?] until completely inaudible' 'This piece is about the out line of becoming. It can start anywhere go anywhere within the reference of sounds and may be any length.'	'This piece is about the outlines of becoming. It can start anywhere, go anywhere within these references of sounds and may be any length. Hold each meas. until barely audible.'	None	'Intermission VI (for one or two pianos) was written in 1953. The pianist, or pianists, begins with any sound on the page, will hold until barely audible, then proceed to whichever other sound he may choose. Sounds may be repeated. Dynamics throughout are soft as possible.'	'Composition begins with any sound and proceeds to any other. With a minimum of attack, hold each sound until barely audible. Grace notes are not played too quickly. All sounds are to be played as softly as possible.'
Number of sound-events	19	19	19	15	15
Style of score	Conventional, dotted quarter-notes, bar-lines	Conventional, dotted quarter-notes, bar-lines	Conventional, dotted quarter-notes, bar-lines	Graphic, stemless note-heads, no bar-lines	Graphic, stemless note-heads, no bar-lines

Aspects of Performance

Intermission 6 is not only about the 'outlines of becoming' as Feldman suggested in his annotations to the early manuscripts (see Table 4.1). It is also about points of tension between control and freedom. Of this, his only mobile-form work, we might say that it represents the furthest extent to which he was willing to relinquish control of the precise succession of sounds over time. The individual, isolated sound-events may be played in any order; in Feldman's words, 'The composition begins with any sound and proceeds to any other'. *Intermission 6* is (roughly) contemporaneous with other ground-breaking mobile scores of the 1950s, such as Boulez's *Third Piano Sonata* (begun around 1955) and Stockhausen's *Klavierstück XI* (1956). Earle Brown's works dating from 1952–53 are clearly even more closely related to *Intermission 6*; several Brown pieces of this period allow for performance on 'one or more instruments' and *25 Pages* (1953) is arguably the pioneering mobile score of the era. If *Intermission 6* was first sketched in 1952 or 1953, as seems likely, then it is almost exactly contemporary with Brown's first mobile scores.

The contextual situation is complicated by the fact that Brown and Feldman had fallen out during 1953 and were not reconciled until around 1963.[25] It is significant, in this context, that Feldman did not pursue the idea of mobile scoring in subsequent pieces. This decision may have been connected to the rift with Brown or, more likely, the result of a deeper tension of which the public argument was another manifestation. Feldman seems to have been satisfied with *Intermission 6*, however, as he was happy to publish the work 10 years later while suppressing certain other works from the early 1950s (*Intermission 3* and *Intermission 4* for example), but he never again relinquished direct control of the horizontal line (the placement of sound-events in time) to such an extent. Feldman's consciousness of these precise issues is explicit in his writings of the 1960s: 'The question continually on my mind all these years is: to what degree does one give up control, and still keep that last vestige where one can call the work one's own?'[26] It is interesting to observe that, even as he made the final change of layout in 1963, to give the work its published form as a semi-graphic score, he was refining the performance instructions to be ever more prescriptive.

The experiment of leaving the choice of the number of instruments up to performers is rare among Feldman's works, but it is clear that the choice is strictly limited: the instruments must be pianos, and there may be either one or two only. Furthermore, we are not talking about simple doubling of a part, but the permissible addition of a second pianist playing the score independently of the

---

[25]   Sebastian Claren, 'A Feldman Chronology', in Chris Villars (ed.), *Morton Feldman Says: Selected Interviews and Lectures 1964–1987* (London: Hyphen Press, 2006), 262, 265.

[26]   Morton Feldman, 'The Anxiety of Art' [1965], in B.H. Friedman (ed.), *Give My Regards to Eighth Street*, 30.

other. In *Intermission 6*, it might almost seem that Feldman took his compositional work to the very brink of post-modern performative multiplicity. He allowed the performer(s) to create, within strictly defined parameters, the linear structure of the piece and there is, of course, the real likelihood that the superposition of the two lines may give rise to un-notated (if not necessarily unforeseen) combinatorial simultaneities.

The sound-events of *Intermission 6* are variously single notes or groups of up to four simultaneously sounded notes. In the published version, one event includes a *fermata*, two include a quaver rest, and at the foot of the page, Feldman gives the instruction,

> Composition begins with any sound and proceeds to any other. With a minimum of attack, hold each sound until barely audible. Grace notes are not played too quickly. All sounds are to be played as softly as possible.[27]

The opening sentence here seems to overturn our deeply ingrained notion of the composer as being in control of form – and not just large-scale architecture, but the linear progression from one sound to another. Even today, when the work is half a century old, this open ordering of events gives rise to a range of anxieties among performers (who may feel uncomfortable about a score that seemingly has no linear structure), audiences (who, if they are aware of the nature of the score may feel that the composer is not entirely serious) and analysts (who may feel that there is not quite enough of the work on the page for a serious investigation to be made). No doubt the composer experienced anxieties of his own – but it is perhaps more significant that his instructions cause everyone else involved with the work to feel insecure as well. In a sense, *Intermission 6* is a frame for our insecurities and anxieties rather than simply Feldman's alone. Without invoking the intentionalist fallacy, we may suggest that this was part of Feldman's design: in the very sketchbook that contains the original draft of *Intermission 6*, Feldman wrote 'For me art is insecurity'.[28] I would suggest that this insecurity is not only a suggestive impression or affect but also structural; perhaps, in the work of Feldman, it is fruitful to think in terms of 'insecurity' rather than indeterminacy. In this context, it is worthwhile to examine closely the performance instructions for *Intermission 6*, which define the parameters of this insecurity:

- Feldman indicates a particular kind of approach to the keyboard action ('with a minimum of attack').
- Durations are determined ('hold each sound until barely audible'). Far from being a negation of rhythmic control, this instructs the performer to make specifically defined decisions about the duration of notes according to the length of the decaying sound.

27 Morton Feldman, *Intermission 6* (New York: Edition Peters, 1963).
28 Paul Sacher Foundation, Basel, Morton Feldman Collection.

- Feldman instructs that grace notes should not be played too quickly – by implication, this also makes it clear that grace notes should proceed directly to the next event, without waiting for the sound to decay. This overrules the previous instruction, unless one chooses to interpret it as also having pedal implications: one might proceed directly from a grace note to another event (not too quickly, though!), but sustain the grace note with the pedal until it has decayed.
- It is interesting to note that Feldman considered the last instruction ('All sounds are to be played as softly as possible') as distinct from the earlier 'With a minimum of attack'. He was making a distinction between dynamic level and quality of attack, which has far-reaching implications for performance practice of Feldman's piano music generally.[29]

The question of pedalling, also a rather important issue with respect to performance practice, is problematic. Feldman's published piano scores of the 1950s and 1960s almost never indicate pedalling (*Intermission 5* is a rare exception). To add to the difficulties of trying to establish a standard of practice for pedalling in Feldman's piano music, some of the sketches (*Three Pieces for Piano*, for example, from 1954) do carry pedal indications that were not included in the published version.[30] For the purpose of the present study, and this discussion of *Intermission 6* in particular, the precise nature of pedalling required (if any) remains open to speculation.

As we have seen, Feldman's annotations to the original sketch, and one of the Tudor copies, instruct the performer to hold each sound 'until completely inaudible'. Altering this in 1963 to read 'barely audible', Feldman effectively and appreciably increased the tempo. It is the kind of refining decision that one may easily imagine was made after a hearing of the piece (most likely after the 1958 performance).

Likewise, the sketch offers no advice concerning dynamic level. The published score's instruction to play 'as softly as possible' relates directly to overall tempo and duration, since Feldman has linked the duration of individual sounds to the perceived length of decay. It would seem that a specifically quiet dynamic was not crucially important to Feldman in 1952–53, but that it did seem important in 1963, which apart from practical considerations to do with durations (and indeed the duration of the piece), may also be indicative of certain developments in Feldman's personal aesthetic of pianoforte sound during the intervening years. In 1952–53 he commonly demanded extremes of dynamic from performers (as with *Intermission 4*, *Intermission 5* and *Extensions 3*) or, alternatively, left such decisions entirely to the performer (*Intersections 2* and *Intersections 3*). When

---

[29]   Feldman's interest in the subtlest distinctions of attack, voicing and dynamic is shown in his discussion with Paula Ames. See Paula Ames, '*Piano* (1977)', in Thomas DeLio (ed.), *The Music of Morton Feldman*, 137–8.

[30]   Paul Sacher Foundation, Basel, Morton Feldman Collection.

notating specific dynamics in the 1950s, Feldman was concerned with extremes of contrast; he had little interest in *mezzo* dynamic levels. Similarly, in those works that leave dynamic decisions to the performer, he surely had in mind the likely outcome of David Tudor making the decisions which, to judge from the recorded legacy of his performances, was extravagantly energetic, intense and complex. Feldman's attitude to sound by the 1960s was notably different – certainly with regard to the piano works, all extreme dynamic contrast was eliminated during the later 1950s, until by 1963 we find *Intermission 6* adorned with the instructions 'with a minimum of attack', 'as softly as possible'.[31]

In the published score, Feldman crucially failed to indicate whether each sound should be played only once, or whether they may be repeated. In practice, it might be difficult to remember which sounds have been played in order to not repeat them, unless a pre-performance plan has been decided upon. Judging from the evidence of Tudor's written-out realisations of Feldman's graphic scores, the composer would not have been opposed to this sort of preparation.[32] On the other hand, many performers have interpreted the instructions for *Intermission 6* as allowing repetitions – Steffen Schleiermacher's recorded performance, for example, stretches over more than nine minutes.[33] Again, if we may continue to draw a parallel between *Intermission 6* and the graphic scores, we should recall Feldman writing 'I had never thought of the graph as an art of improvisation, but more as a totally abstract sonic adventure'.[34] It seems that Feldman was less interested in a specific realisation of a work in the living moment of performance than in the fact that the performer was forced to make certain decisions in order for the performance to be possible.

The sketch material for the work provides evidential support for Schleiermacher's interpretation of the score. Feldman wrote across the bottom of the page, 'It can start anywhere go anywhere within the reference of sounds and may be any length'. More explicitly, in the notes accompanying the piece as published in the journal *Kulchur*, Feldman did specify that 'sounds may be repeated' (see Table 4.1).[35] It is curious that he chose not to include this clarification in the Peters score – one aspect of the work where Feldman's later instructions were less prescriptive than earlier.

---

[31]   Loud dynamics do reappear in Feldman's later work, however, although usually in isolated instances (see for example *Piano* of 1977).

[32]   See John Holzaepfel, 'Painting by Numbers: The *Intersections* of Morton Feldman and David Tudor', in Steven Johnson (ed.), *The New York Schools*, 159–72.

[33]   Steffen Schleiermacher, *Morton Feldman: Early Piano Works*, CD (hat[now]ART 138, 2003).

[34]   Morton Feldman, 'Liner Notes', in B.H. Friedman (ed.), *Give My Regards to Eighth Street*, 6.

[35]   Morton Feldman, '*Marginal Intersection* (1951), *Intersection 2* (1951), *Intermission 6*', 33–6.

The overall duration of the work is thus to a certain extent variable, although perhaps less so than the above discussion would lead us to believe. If each sound-event is heard only once, the duration will still be somewhat variable according to certain factors influencing the decay of the sound (relative dynamic, string length in relation to register and size of piano, room acoustic), but the relation of one event's duration to the others will be generally similar from one performance to another. Even a fully notated work like *Intermission 5* or *Piano Piece 1952* may vary considerably in duration from one performance to another, but the inner structural architecture of the work remains proportionally the same.

In a way, instructing the performer to determine the tempo of the work according to the physical decay of sound is more precise than to simply suggest 'slow', which is rather open to a wide range of interpretations (as may be heard, for example, in the recorded performances of *Intermission 5*). The only other difference between these other works and *Intermission 6* is that here the order of sounds is also variable. In the case of a performance that does allow repetition, the overall duration of the work is determined by the performer. Nevertheless, the relation of one sound-event's duration to all the others is still fixed by the rate of decay, and is revealed to the audience over time. As the sounds are heard repeatedly in changing contexts, it gradually becomes clearer that the duration of each individual sound is proportionally fixed and largely independent of immediate context.

Defining the Analysis

How does one set about analysing such a work as *Intermission 6*? More specifically, how are we to relate it to the understanding of *Intermission 5* and *Piano Piece 1952* developed in the previous chapters, where I argued a case for Feldman's concern with the integration of time- and pitch-organisation? In translating this argument to *Intermission 6*, which seems at first glance such a different material proposition, I will discuss first the element of form then examine pitch-organisation. Almost immediately, however, we will find that the two are necessarily related.

To discuss formal architecture at all in relation to *Intermission 6* seems almost nonsensical. Yet, one might argue that there can be no such thing as music without form, in which case there must be some way to identify something for analytical purposes. Discussing the distinction between form and content, Varèse argued a formalist position: 'There is no difference. Form and content are one. Take away form and there is no content, and if there is no content, there is only a rearrangement of musical patterns, but no form'.[36] Given Feldman's supposedly long-standing personal acquaintance with Varèse ('Since I was 18 years old I saw

---

[36]   Edgard Varèse, 'Rhythm, Form and Content' [1959], in Elliott Schwartz and Barney Childs (eds), *Contemporary Composers on Contemporary Music* (New York: Holt, Rinehart and Winston, 1967), 203–4.

Varèse at least once a week.'),[37] and his known admiration for Varèse's work,[38] what was he aiming to do in *Intermission 6*? Is this work merely 'a rearrangement of musical patterns, but no form'?

Such an interpretation might conform to notions of Feldman as 'passive, unsystematic',[39] and it also opens a convenient space for discussion of the work as being performative in its very essence. This might even allow us to dismiss concerns about how Feldman understood the work, or meant for it to be understood, and concentrate on the way the work exists in performance, as the result of a performative process. However, the piece remains Feldman's (rather than the performer's) precisely because of the structures and parameters he imposes – the very structures that give the work its broad formal characteristics.

Over and above the inherent formal structure imposed by instrumentation, and by the frame of Feldman's instructions for performance, we may identify a number of fundamental ways in which the work exhibits formal attributes:

- In terms of pitch materials (Feldman's 'reference of sounds'):

    a. the 12-tone aggregate or chromatic field as 'ground';
    b. partition by subset (chords, for example, are aggregated subsets of the total chromatic);
    c. partition by register (of vertical/pitch space);
    d. the hierarchy of pitch-classes implied by repetitions.

- In terms of relative durations (each sound-event has a more-or-less fixed duration as a result of its inherent acoustic properties).
- In terms of the ordering of sound-events (which is in no sense random):

    a. the performer makes active decisions;
    b. decisions are influenced (among other things) by the pitch material itself and also the layout of the score.

The work, as we have already seen, is of a reasonably predictable length if played without repetitions and of unlimited length with repetitions. Both possibilities are complicated by the fact that the performer may play the sound-events in any order. Has Feldman given any clues to possible favoured ordering? Does he manipulate the performer's decision-making in any way? To answer, we may begin by looking at the published score, where the sound-events are

---

[37] Morton Feldman, 'Darmstadt Lecture' [1984], in Chris Villars (ed.), *Morton Feldman Says*, 196.

[38] For some early published evidence, see Morton Feldman, 'Sound, Noise, Varèse, Boulez' [1958], in B.H. Friedman (ed.) *Give My Regards to Eighth Street*, 1–2.

[39] Amy Beal, '"Time Canvases": Morton Feldman and the Painters of the New York School', in James Leggio (ed.), *Music and Modern Art* (London: Routledge, 2001), 231.

irregularly placed around the page. For the performer, this is not a random arrangement. Rather, it is a visual ordering of the material, which does influence the way we might perform our way through, or around, the notation. The design leads the eye around the page following a clear spiral formation, from the outer edges of the page to the centre and vice versa. There is a point of rest, to which the eye is drawn by this formation, which is the sound-event of two Cs, slightly to right of horizontal centre in the vertical middle of the page. There is a distinct similarity of visual structure between this and Earle Brown's *December 1952*, a famous graphic score that Feldman must have known (one wonders if Brown's enthusiastic running away with Feldman's idea of the graphic score may have been part of the reason for Feldman's dislike of Brown in the 1950s). We may observe that where Feldman's graphic scores are always easily readable as musical scores – as the organised deployment of sound events over time[40] – Brown's are often not. In this respect, however, *Intermission 6* represents the closest point of comparability between Feldman's work and Brown's – composed in almost the exact moment at which their personal rift commenced.[41]

Of course each performer will respond differently to a score like *Intermission 6*, and one might at times be led by the seductively suggestive visual structure or resist it (knowingly or unknowingly). Either way, the performer makes decisions based upon a formal structure, however unconventional. The insecurity of art, in the case of *Intermission 6*, may be seen to reside explicitly in this decision-making – an anxiety about what to do next. The performer cannot just play anything, but must make an informed decision at every moment.

Given the variable ordering of the sound-events, it is clearly not possible to analyse the formal architecture of *Intermission 6* in the same way that we might a fully notated work, or even a graphic score – at this point some of our conventional analytical tools fail. In its published form, it is not possible to subdivide the larger durations of the work according to mathematical proportions, as was possible with *Intermission 5* and *Piano Piece 1952*. Hypothetically, if we could hear the work performed many times over by different pianists, it would be possible to formulate a statistically probable realisation of the work. In all likelihood, this would reveal the subtle promptings of the score as frequently recurring patterns of sound-events.

Pitch and Time

As we have seen, *Intermission 6* as published does possess an observable complex of formal properties, and cannot accurately be described as formless. The variable ordering of the material, however, makes it difficult to make more detailed analysis. The sketch and the early manuscript copies, in contrast, preserve the

---

40   With the possible exception of the unpublished *Intersection* + (1953).
41   According to Claren, this occurred in 1952. Sebastian Claren, *Neither*, 530.

original ordering of the material as it was composed (see figures 4.3 and 4.4). The significance of this cannot be overstated.

Figure 4.2   Morton Feldman, *Intermission 6.* Showing two measures deleted between Events 2 and 3

In addition to 19 sounding events, the sketch manuscript also shows two measures that were deleted, between Events 2 and 3 (in my numbering; see Figure 4.2). From what remains legible here, it is easy to identify the way in which these measures differ from the rest of the piece: they embark on a more linear idea, with all the implications of thematic motif that that implies. Feldman appears to have decided to resist these dual temptations. Of the remaining events, five were deleted in preparing the published score (Events 8 and 12–15), and a new one added at the same time (see Figure 4.4). Finally, Event 2 was changed from a D to an E in the published score.

Figure 4.3   Morton Feldman, *Intermission 6*, as it appears in the sketch, showing some proportional divisions

Figure 4.3 shows some of the proportional subdivisions of the conceptual time-frame of the piece as sketched. It is immediately clear that many of the proportions mark points of significance to the compositional structure in a manner not unlike that observed in both *Intermission 5* and *Piano Piece 1952*. Bear in mind that this proportional analysis is not based upon real-time duration in performance, but the succession of events as constructed on paper. The 1:1 division falls at Event 10, while the 1:3 divisions fall around Events 5 and 15, respectively. The proportions of 1:2 fall just after Event 6 and just before Event 14. These divisions draw attention to a structure that would in any case be rather obvious; namely, that the work falls into three sections with the middle part defined by a registral plateau very like that observed in *Piano Piece 1952*. The end of the plateau is exactly coincident with the 3:1 proportion, while the equivalent 1:3 proportion (in combination with the 1:2) draws our attention to the dramatic descending interval spanned by Events 5 and 6.

The pitch content of *Intermission 6* is deployed in ways that interact closely with the proportions outlined above. The chord at Event 1 is a chromatic set (B♭, B, C, C♯ – curiously, *Intermission 5* ends with a conjunct four-note chromatic set of G, G♯, A, B♭), and the subsequent Event 2 adds a further adjacent pitch-class (D) to form a five-note chromatic set. We should bear in mind at this point that the very middle of the work at 1:1 is marked by the pitch-class D. Event 3, while repeating the pitch-class C♯, adds to the chromatic set three further notes, forming a total chromatic set of eight notes, outlining a perfect fifth (G, G♯, A, B♭, B, C, C♯, D). This entire pitch structure, then, is clearly not accidental or randomly constructed.[42] Event 4 seems to break the pattern; it would add a further three pitch-classes to the set, but for the fact that it is missing an E. So at this point, approaching the significant 1:3 division, the work changes direction in terms of pitch content. Event 4 is also the first occurrence of octave doubling, a feature that becomes more frequent towards the end of the sketch. Events 4–6 are, rather obviously, a whole-tone set, contrasting with the preceding chromatic structure. Curiously, however, we may note that Events 4–7 would form a chromatic set, except that they are missing an E. The pitch-class E, in this reading of the work, is becoming significant through notable omissions.

After the introduction of the new whole-tone pitch-set at Event 4, our attention is drawn to the fact that Events 5 and 6 represent the first occurrence of two adjacent single notes in the piece so far. One is tempted to read the dramatically descending interval as part of a Wolpean proportion crucially requiring a third note to be defined.[43] It can surely be no coincidence that the exact 1:1 symmetrical

---

[42]   This method of building up the chromatic field with cumulative chromatic sets has also been observed in *Three Clarinets, Cello, and Piano* (1971). See Michael Hamman, '*Three Clarinets, Cello, and Piano* (1971)', in Thomas DeLio (ed.), *The Music of Morton Feldman*, 71–95. The opening section of *For Bunita Marcus* (1985) is another example.

[43]   Stefan Wolpe, 'On Proportions', trans. Matthew Greenbaum, *Perspectives of New Music*, 34/2 (Summer 1996), 132–84.

division of the interval (Wolpe's 'symmetrical proportion') is D4, as heard in Event 10, the 1:1 divisional time-proportion of the entire piece. Here we have exactly the kind of evidence we had hoped to find for the methodical intersection of pitch deployment and durational structures in the composition process. The fact that such compositional structures are not clearly evident in performance, or are seriously distorted in performance by the re-ordering of the material, and were revised anyway in the published version, does not alter the fact that they are visible in all the early manuscripts. One wonders whether part of Feldman's reason for graphically rearranging the sound-events in the published version was to conceal the highly organised nature of the work's essential material, rendering the form and content of the work ambiguous (an organised ambiguity).

Between Events 8 and 15, the organisational activity quiets down a little. This is the relative rest-period of the registral plateau of single notes, draped over the resolution of the symmetrical proportion (Event 10 as discussed above). Note also that this passage is built from a four-note chromatic set (C, C♯, D, E♭), like the opening chord, and indeed that it intersects with the opening set, with which it shares two pitch-classes. It is likely that this particular set's proximity to the suspiciously absent E pitch-class is also significant. At Event 15, we strike the 3:1 proportional division and the registral plateau is abruptly abandoned (it ends with the smallest possible symmetrical proportion, clearly stated: C, D, C♯). It is surely not coincidental that the 1:3 and 3:1 division-points are each marked by a symmetrical proportion, one over a large span and the other of the smallest possible. The two are further related in that the smaller proportion reiterates the mid-point of the larger.

The organisational thinking behind the pitch content of Events 16–19 is not as explicit as in the opening section. I may suggest two ways of hearing it, however, which each indicate that there is a comparable organisational practice employed. Firstly, Events 17–19 taken together form a diatonic set (B♭, C, D, E♭, F) which has a number of features in common with the opening material. Most notably, it is built upon the same B♭ as Event 1 (sounded even in the same register as B♭2) and, like the material of Events 1–3, it outlines a perfect fifth. Given Feldman's sensitivity to matters of 'symmetry and design', there is too much correspondence for this to be accidental. Secondly, the material of Events 15–19 taken together would form a nine-note chromatic set (from B♭ to G♭), but for the fact that it is missing an E (!).

Pitch Class and Aggregate Completion

At this point it is useful to observe that the pitch material of *Intermission 6* as sketched, taken in its entirety, is a complete 12-tone aggregate (or chromatic field), but for missing the E pitch-class altogether. Perhaps this E carries some special, literally occult significance; it represents, at the very least, an interesting problem. Given that my analyses of *Intermission 5* and *Piano Piece 1952* have shown that

Feldman was indeed working with a sensitivity to aggregate completion, how are we to understand this curious omission? Was it purposeful? The several segments of the piece where the omission is obvious may have been intended to highlight this fact. Or was it an accident, a mistake? In the latter case, we might ask how the error happened and even whether it is possible to conjecture about where the E should have been? One thing at least is certain: when Feldman revised the piece in 1963 for publication, he 'corrected' the problem by changing Event 2 from D to E. This action proves conclusively that Feldman was consciously involved with the deployment of pitch-classes in both the processes of composition and of revision (not only at the time of composition in the 1950s, but also in the 1960s). It also demonstrates (at the very least with regard to his manner of thinking in 1963) that chromatic field completion was important to him.

In composing *Intermission 6* Feldman may have been working from some manner of 12-tone plan (even if just a simple one like a list of the 12 notes, ticking them off as he went along, as was his habit in later years),[44] possibly a plan indicating certain weightings of the aggregate by repetition. After Event 2, the piece went briefly off course (in terms of gestural consistency), but was quickly brought back under control and continued. It is possible, however, that Feldman forgot that he had in fact just deleted two appearances of the E pitch-class, and failed to compensate for this as he continued. In the early 1960s, revisiting the work, he dismantled the pitch material and rebuilt the work, making several alterations, including correction of the missing pitch-class. While it is hardly the aim of this analysis to presume to correct the composer, it seems rather likely that the E should have appeared around Event 4, as it is in this area of the piece (Events 4–7) that it is first conspicuously absent – and indeed Event 4 is made up of the two neighbour pitch-classes to E (E♭, F). The D at Event 2, on the other hand, formed part of a unified chromatic set stretching over Events 1–3, which was in turn destroyed by the 1960s revision. Such collateral damage, it seems, was ultimately justifiable in pursuit of the chromatic field completion.

There is of course an alternate possibility: that, at the time of initial composition, Feldman intended *Intermission 6* to be missing one pitch-class. There is precedent for this problem of intent with regard to aggregates in Feldman's music of 1952 – we have already seen that the opening chord of *Intermission 5* in the second-stage sketch is an 11-note set also missing one pitch-class of the 12-tone aggregate. Each of these taken alone is perhaps easy to explain as a mistake; considered together, we may feel less certain. The idea that Feldman may have been quite deliberately interested in 'incomplete' aggregates at this time is rather appealing. It is not, after all, so very difficult to maintain control of 12 notes in a single chord, or over the duration of such a tiny piece as *Intermission 6*. Could Feldman really have been so careless?

---

[44]   This was Feldman's common practice in composing the late works of the later 1970s and 1980s. See, for example, the sketches for *Violin and Orchestra*, or *For Samuel Beckett*. Paul Sacher Foundation, Basel, Morton Feldman Collection.

In the case of the opening chord of *Intermission 5*, the sketch itself reveals that he revised the chord at least twice. *Intermission 6*, on the other hand, was copied for performance later in the 1950s but apparently not revised or redesigned until the time of publication. If the incomplete aggregate in *Intermission 6* was originally intentional, then we must assume that when revising the work in the 1960s Feldman had either forgotten that he had intended the E to be missing, or this approach to the aggregate no longer seemed appropriate. We may sum up with the observation that there can be no doubt that in 1963 Feldman decided that the aggregate completion was important. Furthermore, regardless of whether the original omission of E was deliberate or accidental, it is evident that in 1952 Feldman was sensitive to the 12-tone aggregate (with or without its full complement of pitch-classes). The worst we can say is that in the 1950s he may possibly have been a little careless – but there is even then something appropriate in terms of what this piece represents, a fleeting intermission in the busy life of a middle class working New Yorker.

Aggregate Weighting

To reiterate briefly: in the sketch, Feldman's material consists of 19 events (and two measures that have been deleted) of which three are exact repetitions – these repetitions were later removed from the work when the later version was prepared for publication (refer to Figure 4.4). At the same time, the E♭ at Event 12 was also deleted, while Event 2 was changed from D to E (completing the chromatic field). Finally, the grace-note D♭ (Event 20, for the sake of convenience) was added.

It is clear that at the time of revision Feldman was concerned to complete the aggregate, but what else was he doing? Why was he removing some notes and not others? Why add the D♭? At least in part, this seems to be a matter of eliminating particular pitch-class repetitions, and it also had the effect of altering the balance between single notes and chords (all the events deleted are single notes). Is this some adjustment of the weighting of pitch-classes within the aggregate (the hierarchy established by repetition)? Comparison of pitch-class weighting between the sketch and the published score reveals something startling: in making these various changes to the material, the range of contrast of weighting has been reduced but the overall pattern is retained. This is best appreciated in graphic form (Figure 4.5). Perhaps mirroring the reduction of dynamic contrast, Feldman has rather carefully reduced the extremes of contrast in the weighting of the aggregate without actually changing the pattern of the weighting. One might draw an analogy with the flattened picture-plane that was an interest for many of the abstract expressionist painters. Here once again is a feature of Feldman's musical composition that reminds us of Ashton's description of the flattened spaces and imprisoned, ghostly figures, in Guston's painting. Likewise, in Feldman the

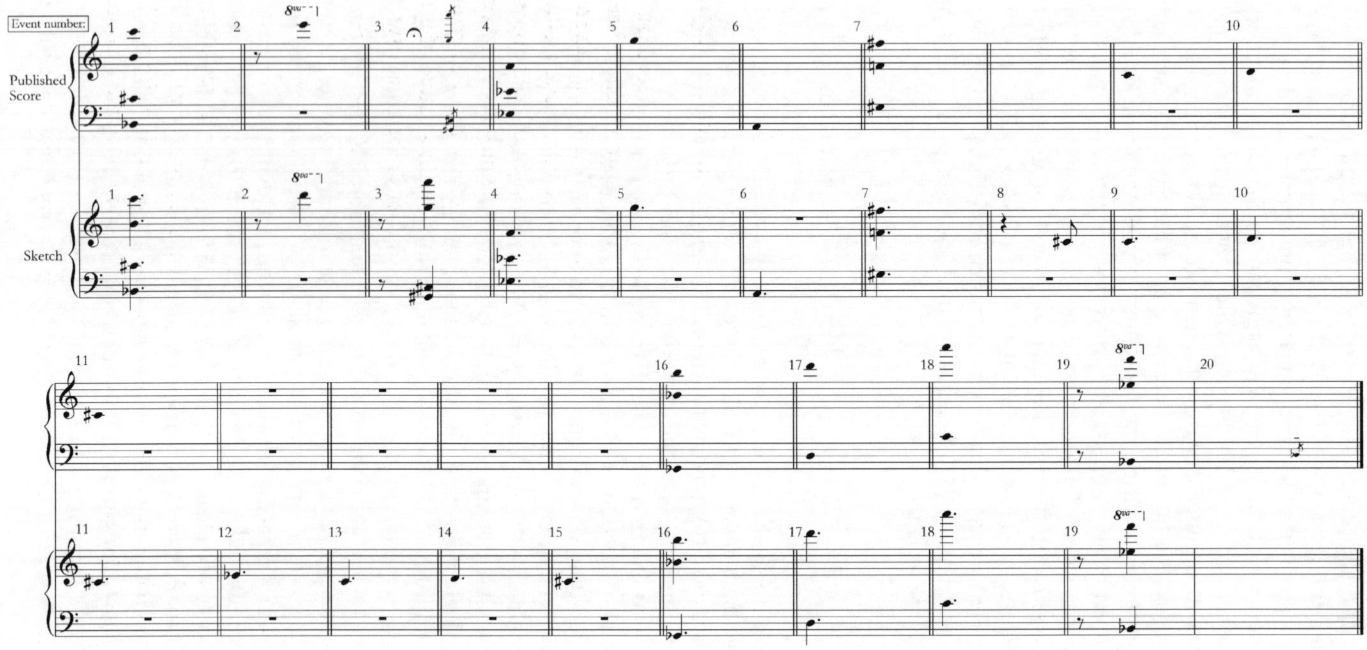

Figure 4.4   Morton Feldman, *Intermission 6*. Comparison of published score and sketch, with the material ordered as in the sketch

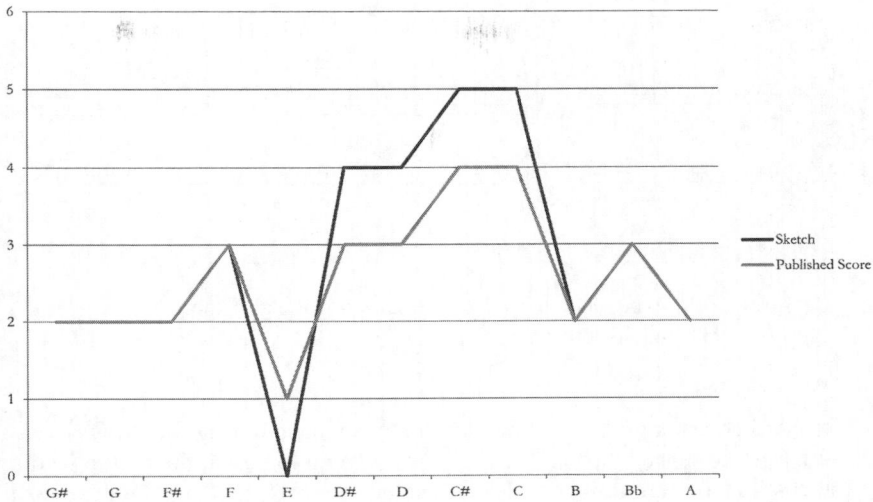

Figure 4.5   Morton Feldman, *Intermission 6*. Graphic representation of comparative aggregate weighting

flatness is not merely about quietness but equally in this case about the active 'steamrollering' of crystalline formations.[45]

Feldman's aggregates are always weighted (except, arguably, in rare localised instances of high chromatic density within a larger work), and the ordering of his pitch material remains fluid. Here, in preparing his revised score of *Intermission 6*, Feldman is effectively narrowing the range of his weighted aggregate, reducing the parameters of the frame of the 'reference of sounds' through which the performer chooses a path. While the effective ordering of the material remains in the hands of the performer, with the greatest degree of compositional fluidity that Feldman could tolerate, these revisions reveal his careful, almost anxious, fine-tuning of the frame within which the performer makes decisions. We can sense the composer's reluctance to allow the performer any more freedom than absolutely necessary.

Larger-scale (Implicit) Structures

The vertical pitch-space of *Intermission 6* spans just less than five octaves of the piano's range (see Figure 4.6). Conforming to the precedent set by *Intermission 5*, it is an essentially restrained pitch-space, especially at the lower end. Within this space, we might understand the full array of pitch material to be a sort of meta-chord

---

[45]   Dore Ashton, *Yes, but ...: A Critical Study of Philip Guston* (New York: Viking Press, 1976), 75–6.

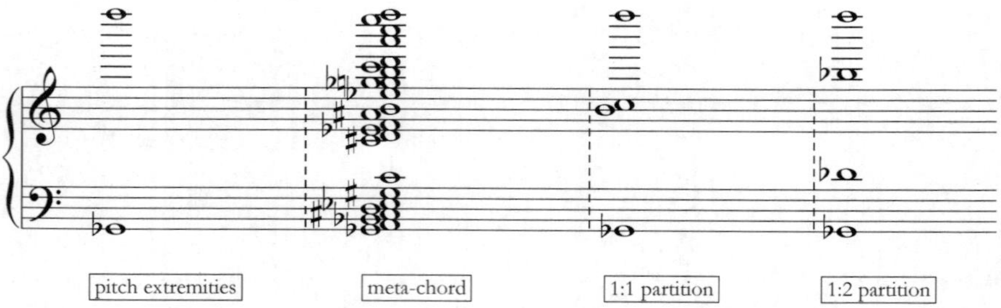

pitch extremities   meta-chord   1:1 partition   1:2 partition

Figure 4.6   Feldman, *Intermission 6.* The pitch-space and some
internal structures

– the chord consisting of all the notes actually sounded during the piece (Figure 4.6). In another sense, it is the sound we might begin to hear if the multiplication of pianos was allowed to increase from one or two to 15 or more, the theoretical white-noise of the maximum possible event-saturation. Feldman does not allow us to hear this explicitly, but it is implicit in that it forms the very 'reference of sounds' through which the performer draws 'the outline of becoming'. However free the performer might imagine themselves to be, this meta-chord is in a sense the final object of this becoming-ness, the only possible fulfilment of the outline; not just the 'reference of sounds', but the essential form and content.

There are deeper levels of organisation in terms of the partitioning of this pitch-space. This partitioning occurs through registral placement, relative proportions (in the Wolpean sense) and through context (whether notes are allowed to sound alone, as part of chords, or as octave doublings). Examining the meta-chord, we may note that there are several clusters of adjacent notes and also gaps; in other words, we are not dealing with an abstract or random cluster, but something artificially constructed. Some of these formations correspond to the divisional proportions favoured by Feldman in other contexts: there is a gap, for example close to the 1:1 division of the total range, while the two central clusters may be seen to be built upon the 1:2 and 2:1 divisions. Further, it is clear that the lower 1:2 division (D♭/C♯) was the focal point for the crucial registral plateau in the original sketch, of which a clearly audible ghost remains even in the published version of the piece. This emphasis of the 1:2 division, it turns out, is observable in each of the three pieces discussed so far in this book, along with a more subtle sensitivity (usually less audible) to the 1:1 division. Furthermore, it is important to recognise that Feldman does not emphasise both 1:2 and 2:1 division points equally, but favours one or other as the key structuring element (that which bears the main weight of the work's material). This is remarkably similar to the way in which Philip Guston's drawings and paintings of this period (1952–53) are commonly cantilevered forms built around 1:2 divisions of the canvas (as discussed in Chapter 2).

The pitch materials of the work are organised into three types of sound-event: single notes, chords (of two to four notes) and octaves. Referring to the published score, the single notes form the registral plateau at the heart of the work, the E7 which so significantly completes the aggregate, and also the explicit Wolpean proportion outlined by Events 5 and 6, of which the symmetrical division intersected in the sketch with the plateau at Event 10 (this note almost certainly intended in the original design to be the completion-note of the chromatic field, and it would have been if the E had not been omitted). The chords, with either three or four notes, are, like so much in this piece, rather restrained. There is not a clearly identifiable pattern to their disposition, and they represent a range of set-types. Nevertheless, these chords are an important part of Feldman's control of the sound of the piece; in these six instances, he has retained control over exactly which notes may be permitted to sound vertically together. The internal structures of the chords in several cases represent Wolpean proportions, albeit with varying degrees of tolerance (refer to Figure 4.7). It is consistent with Wolpe's practice for these proportions to be sometimes mathematically inexact, and in Feldman's case it seems not unlikely that they were drawn in 'by eye', as it were, rather than calculation. Notice that both the chords formed from 1:2 divisions are arrayed around the 1:1 division of the total pitch-space, and that in the sketch each marks a point of beginning, a redefinition of the pitch-space (Event 16, for example, functions as a recapitulation of the opening texture after the mid-region plateau). This adds weight to the argument that Feldman was organising his pitch material on several levels within the two-dimensional space of his defined canvas, through the disposition of individual notes and also chords. We may note here a similarity between Feldman's modelling of intersecting pitch spaces and that deployed by Varèse in the opening section of *Desèrts* (composed 1950–54), although Feldman is less concerned with a tensioned, linear unfolding of materials and neither is he thinking of an orchestrated spacial depth.

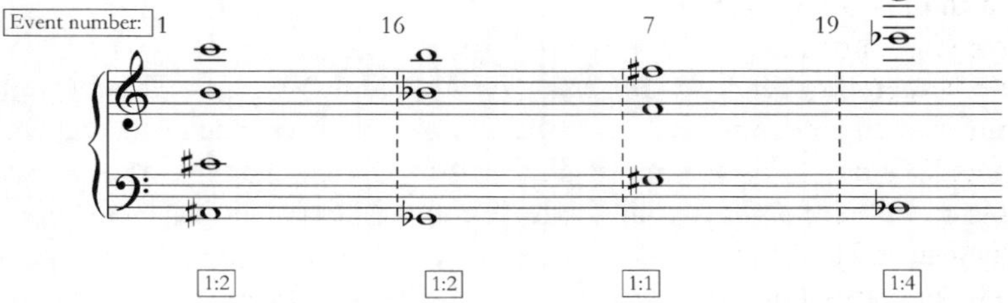

Figure 4.7   Feldman, *Intermission 6.* Some proportional subdivisions of interval (vertical space)

Similarly, in the published score he permits only seven single notes (of which two are the same pitch-class in different registers). Some pitch-classes are never permitted to sound alone, while others are never associated with a chord – the remainder seem to trace a subtle web of connections through the various forms of sonority. There are three instances of vertical octave doubling, at Events 4, 17 and 18, of which the latter two are particularly dramatic. Further, these two pitches (C, D) are neighbours to D♭/C♯, a pitch-class that is highly significant for a number of reasons. Not only is C♯ (together with C) one of the most commonly heard pitch-classes in the piece, but it is a crucial part of the registral plateau, where it functions as the defining 1:2 division of the total pitch-space. As if that were not enough, C♯/D♭ is the pitch-class added to the piece in 1963 with the supplementary Event 10, without which it would have lost its place in the hierarchy. This is further evidence that Feldman was aware of the hierarchy of weightings and also suggests that this hierarchy itself may be determined by a background design related to the proportional divisions of the pitch-space.

Finally, let us return once more to the organisation of time and durations. In his 1963 revisions, Feldman not only removed dots and stems from the notes; he added a grace-note (Event 20) and also transformed one of the existing chords into a grace-note, preceding it with a *fermata* (Event 3 in Figure 4.4). As we have already seen, the grace notes rather complicate the instruction 'hold each sound until barely audible', adding a new layer of rhythmic complexity. The two quaver rests perhaps indicate an element of silence, while the *fermata* presumably represents a prolongation of the previous sound-event beyond the point of being 'barely audible'. It is also interesting to observe that the newly added Event 20 has a *tenuto* sign. In all of these small alterations, we may sense Feldman's controlling hand; as with the revisions of pitch-material, he was giving detailed consideration to subtle elements of the organisation of time and duration even at this late stage in the composition process.

Line and Colour

On the autograph sketch for *Intermission 6*, Feldman wrote: 'This piece is just the outlines of becoming'. He wrote these words again on one of the copies made for David Tudor, so it was more than just a passing thought. It is a powerful idea, 'the outlines of becoming', which conjures up analogies with the visual arts, and abstract expressionism in particular. In the notion of becoming-ness, we may perhaps situate *Intermission 6* within the context of Harold Rosenberg's 'action painting', observing that the work takes shape in the act of performance. Significantly, however, Feldman seems to have had reservations about this idea. Discussing the concept of action painting in 1971, Feldman revealed that by this stage of his life he perceived the pre-determinate/indeterminate problem as more of a continuum than a dichotomy:

> Personally, I have never understood the term "Action Painting" as a description
> of the work of the fifties. The closest I can come to its meaning is that the painter
> tries for a less predeterminate structure. This does not mean, however, that there
> was an indeterminate intention.[46]

It is tempting to imagine the 'free' decision-making of the performer as constituting
a line, indeed a line of becoming, yet Feldman specifically uses the rather awkward
plural 'outlines' – not so much a linearity as a multiplicity of boundaries. Perhaps
his 'outlines of becoming' are in fact the work as notated, the frame within
which the performer acts – the performer's constraining canvas. I suggest that
Intermission 6 represents a compositional frame (a conceptual plane without
linearity; by analogy, the 'picture-plane') within which the performer enacts a
linearity of decision-making, progressing in time through the space defined by
Feldman's carefully manufactured, inherently coherent galaxy of possibilities.
In Varèse's terms, then, the work as notated by Feldman is form, and therefore
content. A performance enacts this form-content, constructing linearity and
narrativity through active decision. Each performance is unique, yet *Intermission
6* is always the same work, its essential formal attributes and content unchanged,
circumscribed by the 'outlines of becoming'.

It is useful, in this moment of reflection, to make reference to Deleuze and
Guattari's notion of the abstract line as a 'line of flight'.[47] More specifically, in
Deleuze and Guattari's *A Thousand Plateaus*, they suggest that 'The only way to
get outside the dualisms is to be-between, to pass between, the *intermezzo* – that is
what Virginia Woolf lived with all her energies, in all of her work, never ceasing
to become'.[48] Here, it is clear that they are discussing a progressive rather than
circumscribing kind of line, and I am struck by their use of the term 'intermezzo'
in so far as it echoes Feldman's title, *Intermission*. The idea of the intermission as
itself something that passes between dualisms gives an added drama to Feldman's
work. In this, there are implications not only of dualism, but also of an intermediate
space defined by tension and conflict (potential or actual). Deleuze and Guattari
are not speaking of a passive between-ness, but a powerfully energetic action
intensified by anxiety. The reference to Virginia Woolf in this context is salutary,
and we are reminded of Feldman's words, 'art for me is insecurity'.[49]

One might easily draw a parallel here, between the musical-aesthetic tensions
of the 1950s (Feldman's work inhabiting a space created between musical,
social, political and economic certainties) and those of the political sphere. In
particular, New York composers of this time were operating within the context of

---

[46]   Morton Feldman, 'Give My Regards to Eighth Street' [1971], in B.H. Friedman
(ed.), *Give My Regards to Eighth Street*, 99.

[47]   Gilles Deleuze and Félix Guattari, *A Thousand Plateaus: Capitalism and
Schizophrenia* [1980], trans. Brian Massumi (London: Continuum, 2004).

[48]   Ibid., 305.

[49]   Paul Sacher Foundation, Basel, Morton Feldman Collection.

a newly elected Republican government, the escalating Cold War, and the explicit appropriation of art for propaganda's sake.[50] As Pam Meecham and Julie Sheldon have noted in their essay on 'Modernism and Realism in US Art', 'The USA in the mid-1950s was a potent cocktail of power and paranoia, fuelled by fears of Communist infiltration of the body politic'.[51] In this context, Feldman's position as a *bourgeois* avant-gardist was inherently problematic, but also peculiarly safe. Nonetheless, the political, social and personal tensions that define Feldman's space of action may also be heard among the structural elements of his work – translated as tensions between composer and performer, organisation and improvisation, control and freedom, tradition and innovation, authority and disobedience.

The idea that certain kinds of artistic expression are aesthetically process-driven ('becoming'), rather than structured, is hardly new to either composition or analysis.[52] Feldman's perceived dichotomy between music composed with sound as opposed to music composed with system, as articulated in his writings of the early 1960s, was informed by an awareness of such concerns. Yet Feldman was not so naive as to imagine that the dichotomy was one of right and wrong approaches to composition. Many of the composers he castigated for being too systematic, too concerned with technique, were personal acquaintances (Cage and Babbitt) or composers he otherwise admired (Webern). In the 1967 essay 'Some Elementary Questions', Feldman attempted to explain the ambiguity of his position:

> All activity in music reflects its process. This has always been true, and it is more and more true as time goes on. Whether it is too late to change this remains yet to be seen. But the question here is not predeterminate or indeterminate. If I have a resistance to process, it is because I don't want to give up control. Control of the material is not really control. It is merely a device that brings us the psychological benefits of process – just as relinquishing control brings us nothing more than the psychological benefits of a non-systematic approach.

---

[50]   For general discussions, see Frances Stonor Saunders, *Who Paid the Piper? The CIA and the Cultural Cold War* (London: Granta, 1999); Stuart D. Hobbs, *The End of the American Avant Garde* (New York: New York University Press, 1997). For specifically music-related discussions, see also, Amy C. Beal, *New Music, New Allies: American Music in West Germany from the Zero Hour to Reunification* (Berkeley, CA: University of California Press, 2006) and Anne C. Shreffler, 'Ideologies of Serialism: Stravinsky's Threni and the Congress for Cultural Freedom', in Karol Berger and Anthony Newcomb (eds), *Music and the Aesthetics of Modernity* (Cambridge, MA: Harvard University Press, 2005), 217–45.

[51]   Pam Meecham and Julie Sheldon, *Modern Art: A Critical Introduction* (London: Routledge, 2005), 181.

[52]   Dahlhaus, for example, discussed tensions between structured and process-driven aesthetics of composition in his late essay 'Tonality: Structure or Process?'; Carl Dahlhaus, 'Tonality: Structure or Process?', in *Schoenberg and the New Music* (Cambridge: Cambridge University Press, 1987), 62–72.

In both cases, all we have gained is the intellectual comfort of having made a decision – the psychological comfort of having arrived at a point of view.[53]

In seeking to understand Feldman's procedural 'point of view', especially in terms of the 'outline of becoming' in *Intermission 6*, Deleuze's commentary on painting may have more to offer. Subsequent to *A Thousand Plateaus*, Deleuze developed his thinking in relation to abstract expressionist painting specifically, which allows us to draw closer parallels with Feldman. In his 1981 book on Francis Bacon, he wrote that abstract expressionist painting was, in his view, diagrammatic:

> Optical geometry disappears in favour of a manual line, exclusively manual. The eye has difficulty following it. The incomparable discovery of this kind of painting is that of a line (and a patch of colour) that does not form a contour, that delimits nothing, neither inside nor outside.[54]

He might almost be writing about *Intermission 6*, where the performer must choose a path, draw a line, through the prescribed pitch material. If the performer makes the moment-to-moment choices of how to proceed in the performance, without prior planning, then we may indeed see this as homologous to the 'exclusively manual line', the diagrammatic action of abstract expressionism. I am also particularly interested in the way Deleuze speaks of both a line and a 'patch of colour'. These two elements might be construed in a musical sense as (rhizomatically) homologous with the line of progressive choices made over time on the one hand, and the verticality of the sound-events along that line on the other. To speak of a 'patch of colour' or a sound-event is to imply a certain potential for surprise by virtue of the very becoming-ness of the line of action linking one event to another. As John Cage observed, 'All you can do is suddenly listen, in the same way that when you catch cold all you can do is suddenly sneeze'.[55]

I emphasise these two elements of the line and the event because this clearly coincides with the little we know of Feldman's own thinking in the 1950s: recall the diagram sketched by Feldman in his 1952 sketchbooks, with vertical and horizontal axes labelled 'time' (the horizontal) and 'timbre' (the vertical), as discussed in Chapter 1. As we have seen in earlier chapters, it is clear from this and other notes in the sketchbooks that Feldman was thinking of music as a two-dimensional form (literally a diagram, as Deleuze would say), or occupying a two-dimensional frame – like the painter's picture-plane. On the same page of his sketchbook as one of these drawings, Feldman wrote, 'I consider the basic material in a crystallised structural situation a purely sound experience divorced

---

[53]   Morton Feldman, 'Some Elementary Questions', in B.H. Friedman (ed.), *Give My Regards to Eighth Street*, 65–6.

[54]   Gilles Deleuze, *Francis Bacon: the Logic of Sensation* (London: Continuum, 2002), 74.

[55]   John Cage, 'Juilliard Lecture', in *A Year from Monday*, 100.

from harmony as well as counterpoint and melody'.[56] In these words (as noted previously) we hear a clear echo of the voice of Edgard Varèse, who was in contact with the much younger Feldman at this time, and in the diagram of timbre over time we recognise the conceptual thinking of Feldman's teacher, Stefan Wolpe. Indeed Wolpe used an almost identical diagram to illustrate his 1952 lecture 'Thoughts on Pitch and Some Considerations Connected with It'.[57] In contrast to Varèse, however (who understood music as having three or four dimensions),[58] Feldman in the 1950s seems to have been uninterested in musical form beyond these two dimensions.

This conception of music as two dimensional is also evident in Feldman's later writings. In the 1969 essay 'Between Categories', for example, he wrote:

> I'm afraid that the time has now come when I will have to tackle the problem of just what the surface aural plane of music is. Is it the contour of intervals which we follow when listening? Can it be the vertical or harmonic proliferation of sound that casts a sheen in our ears?[59]

This passage also illustrates the extent to which Feldman was concerned (at least in 1969) with the heard experience of music, the listener's perception. What is it, he asks, that dominates the aural experience – the vertical or the horizontal plane? For Feldman, seeking to position his work 'between categories', it ultimately cannot be one or the other but a crystalline growth of forms held in tension between the two.

Improvisation

To what extent is the performer's action in *Intermission 6* free or improvised? We do know from the evidence of Feldman's published writings that he did not think of his graphic scores as allowing for improvisation; rather he considered them as 'a totally abstract sonic adventure'.[60] Presumably, this would also apply to a work like *Intermission 6*. By the end of 1953, Feldman was becoming dissatisfied with graphic notation generally, as he came to realise that performers tended to

---

56   Paul Sacher Foundation, Basel, Morton Feldman Collection.

57   Stefan Wolpe, 'Thoughts on Pitch and Some Considerations Connected with It' [1952], ed. Austin Clarkson, *Perspectives of New Music*, 17/2, (1979), 28–55. This also raises the possibility that many of the annotations in Feldman's sketchbooks may be records of conversations with Varèse or Wolpe, rather than necessarily his own musings.

58   Edgard Varèse, 'New Instruments and New Music' [1936], in Elliott Schwartz and Barney Childs (eds), *Contemporary Composers on Contemporary Music*, 197.

59   Morton Feldman, 'Between Categories' [1969], in B.H. Friedman (ed.), *Give My Regards to Eighth Street*, 84.

60   Morton Feldman, 'Liner Notes' [1962], in ibid., 6.

underestimate the essentially composed nature of the pieces. Yet, as Jeremy Gilbert has pointed out in an essay concerned with the application of Deleuze's thinking to improvisation, 'All musics possess an improvisational dimension, which is to say a rhizomatic moment at which connections are made ... and at which a certain opening onto a 'cosmic' space of infinite possibility occurs'.[61]

'However', Gilbert continues, 'some forms of music-making ... would seem to foreground this moment more than others, enabling it to proliferate and self-multiply without collapsing into a mere chaos of white noise'.[62] This almost paradoxical notion of constrained improvisation is particularly relevant to discussion of *Intermission 6*, a composed work in which a space of possibilities is allowed to proliferate. Proliferation is indeed fundamental to an understanding of *Intermission 6*; surely, this is what the possibility of a second piano represents. Again, I emphasise that Feldman allows only the possibility of a second piano, but does not dictate. He was proffering an idea of proliferation, but not permission to carry it out beyond strict limits.

As noted earlier, if there were 15 or more pianos, we might actually hear the meta-chord; the 'white noise' and chromatic ground of all the notes in the piece sounded at once, an implicit sound that fundamentally defines the vertical pitch-space in which the action of *Intermission 6* takes place. In fact, we do hear the meta-chord, but not as a simultaneity of physical sound; instead, the listener apprehends it as a mental sound-image of the piece unfolded over time. As with so many aspects of music in a general sense, our understanding depends upon memory, and the human capacity to experience a musical work (indisputably taking place over a given span of time, in the formalist sense) in a non-linear way. Feldman did not need us to hear the meta-chord explicitly as a single vertical sonority; it is implicitly present, and he was too subtle a composer to allow the work to fall too far toward noise.[63] The sounds we hear in *Intermission 6* are the performer's ordering of an already carefully structured set of sound-events. This tight-rope walk along a fine line between composition and improvisation, the explicit and the implicit, between latency and action, brings to mind once again that description of the USA in the 1950s: 'a potent cocktail of power and paranoia'.[64] Here again, we may trace the outlines of Feldman's diagram; the tensioned, anxious space between dichotomies – a designed ambiguity.

---

[61]   Jeremy Gilbert, 'Becoming-Music: The Rhizomatic moment of Improvisation', in Ian Buchanan and Marcel Swiboda (eds), *Deleuze and Music* (Edinburgh: Edinburgh University Press, 2004), 135.

[62]   Ibid.

[63]   We may be reminded here of his discussion of the massive 'altered' clusters, and the need to avoid the conceptual dead-end of sounding 'all the 88 notes at one time'. Morton Feldman, *Four Lectures: New York Style* [unpublished manuscript *ca* 1967/68], Paul Sacher Foundation, Basel, Morton Feldman Collection.

[64]   Meecham and Sheldon, *Modern Art*, 181.

Richard Schechner, in his foundational work on performance theory, also wrote of this intriguing and essential tension between improvisation and structure, although he depicted it less as a tension than a sort of interconnected co-dependence, a network of 'frames' that cannot be entirely dispensed with. Schechner suggested that, although the improviser might be free of the restrictions imposed by a composer, this would in fact force them to depend ever more upon conventions.[65] This echoes Feldman's concern, as articulated in the 1960s, that if a performer made his music sound bad, it was not so much the performer's fault as the composer's own, for 'allowing their [the performer's] presence to be felt'.[66] Perhaps he was alarmed at the prospect of performers falling back upon habits and conventions when faced with a crisis of indecision. Certainly, the implication is that Feldman considered a purposeful dominance of procedures, even at the stage of performance, to be a significant responsibility for the composer.

At a fundamental level, Schechner saw this issue as part of an essential pattern of human behaviour. 'One of the qualities of play in higher primates', he observed, 'is the balance between its improvisational quality and its orderliness: in fact, play is the improvisational imposition of order'.[67] In applying this thinking to *Intermission 6*, we can see that Feldman was at this time learning ways to curtail and constrain the performer's presence, while testing the dynamic boundaries of his compositional framing devices in relation to those of performance (the necessary 'playing'). Indeed, Feldman was quite conscious of this delicate balance: 'My only argument with Cage', Feldman said in 1965, 'is with his dictum that ... "everything is music". Just as there is an implied decision in a precise and selective art, there is an equally implied decision in allowing everything to be art ... My quarrel with Cage is that he decided.'[68]

Feldman, to refer again to Deleuze and Guattari, was more concerned with steering his path between such dualities, with mapping an 'intermission'. In the same way, we may begin to understand that Feldman's music is not systematic, but neither is it unsystematic – and indeed any conception of his work in terms of such black and white dualism is destined to be fatally limited. His compositional world is one that depends upon a certain fluidity of systems, an anxiety of in-between-ness. Feldman himself wrote of these matters very precisely in 1981, with benefit of hindsight: discussing the impact of his first meeting with the painter Robert Rauschenberg in 1951, Feldman wrote that Rauschenberg:

---

[65]   Richard Schechner, *Performance Theory* (London: Routledge, 2005), 17–18. Originally published as *Essays on Performance Theory* (Ralph Pine, 1977).

[66]   Morton Feldman, 'Liner Notes' [1962], in B.H. Friedman (ed.), *Give My Regards to Eighth Street*, 6.

[67]   Schechner, *Performance Theory*, 104.

[68]   Morton Feldman, 'The Anxiety of Art', in B.H. Friedman (ed.), *Give My Regards to Eighth Street*, 29–30.

wanted "neither life nor art, but something in between". I then began to compose a music dealing precisely with "in-between-ness": creating a confusion of material and construction, and a fusion of method and application, by concentrating on how they could be directed toward "that which is difficult to categorize".[69]

Does *Intermission 6*, the work, reside in those elements that remain the same from one performance to another, or is it in the performed process of making the spontaneous line of action? It seems that the answer must necessarily be 'yes' to both understandings. The work may be understood as the enactment of a proliferation of possibilities within Feldman's given space of pitch material; it represents a chaotic space of possibility (even if the chaos is in some measure illusory) that can only be perceived and experienced in relation to Feldman's carefully constructed frame.

What began in November 1952 or 1953 as a composed and controlled musical work, somewhat nostalgically backward-looking in its reference to the old modernist 12-tone language, was subsequently broken apart by Feldman himself. Into the space created by this act of vandalism, he allows the performers to intrude – well, actually demands that the performers intrude – while giving them no acknowledged authority of creation. The work remains Feldman's alone. As already noted, *Intermission 6* represents the extreme limit of Feldman's willingness to give up certain controls: 'The question continually on my mind all these years is: to what degree does one give up control, and still keep that last vestige where one can call the work one's own?'[70] Here we have an unsettling challenge not only to conventional notions of composition, but also to conventional modes of performing and hearing. It is the performer's role to put the scattered pieces back together, but of course, the work can never be quite the same again, even though ghostly, shattered shadows of the original structures remain. One is reminded, in this context, of Rauschenberg's famous vandalisation of a De Kooning drawing, by rubbing it out.

Out of this purpose-built ruin, the work presages an uncertain post-modernism, the ever new, where the artist may approach the 'sublime',[71] (thinking perhaps of Barnett Newman),[72] through direct action – threading the piece together – not together again, but newly together – in an intense moment of anxiety, a patch of colour upon a line of becoming. One is reminded of Jean-François Lyotard's

---

[69]   Morton Feldman, 'Crippled Symmetry' [1981], in ibid., 147.

[70]   Morton Feldman, 'The Anxiety of Art' [1965], in ibid., 30.

[71]   See the discussion of the improvised sublime in relation to Deleuze and Lyotard in Jeremy Gilbert, 'Becoming-Music: The Rhizomatic moment of Improvisation', 135–6.

[72]   Barnett Newman, 'The Sublime is Now' [1948], in Ellen Landau (ed.), *Reading Abstract Expressionism: Context and Critique* (New Haven, CT: Yale University Press, 2005), 137–9. Also Philip Shaw, *The Sublime* (London: Routledge 2006), 120–30.

discussion of that aspect of the sublime that is 'terror',[73] but also of his description of certain intermission-like properties of the post-modern sublime,

> a new type of sublime, more paradoxical still than that of enthusiasm, a sublime toward which we would feel not only the irremediable gap between an Idea and what presents itself to "realise" that idea, but also the gap between the various families of phrases and their respective legitimate presentations.[74]

The Framing of Ambiguity

We have seen in this chapter that *Intermission 6* is a work that, despite first appearances, does indeed exhibit formal attributes and analysable structures in its published form. Furthermore, we find that, in consulting the sketch materials and early manuscripts, it is possible to identify organised structures of pitch-deployment and partitioning of time at the composition stage. Feldman's music may not be systematic in any totalising sense, and it is difficult to imagine any form of analysis that could adequately and comprehensively explain all aspects of his work. Nevertheless, through examination of the sketches and early manuscripts, we can identify certain kinds of structures that are the results of compositional methods and processes Feldman favoured in his practice. This rather fluid network of compositional 'frames' (to use Schechner's term) was, in a very general sense, Feldman's system.

More than this, however, these frames are in many cases homologous with the frames imposed upon the work by the field. The frames that shaped *Intermission 6* are also those that shaped Feldman's position in the field (and trajectory) in relation to the competitors who were (additionally) primary consumers of his work in this period (Cage, Wolff, Brown, Wolpe, Boulez and others). Despite the highly structured, planned, origins of the work, Feldman finally presented it in packaged, published form as a mobile score. *Intermission 6*, regardless of the methods used in its early creation (or perhaps because of them), was given a new coat of seeming-indeterminacy when taken to market (a gloss).

This cannot hide the fact, however, that the score as it existed in the 1950s was a substantially different work to that we know today as the published version. Not only did the sketch and early copies have considerably more sound-events (19 as opposed to 15, a difference of almost 20 per cent), they retained the original, composed ordering of the material on the page. For this reason, many of the internal structures of the work, as discussed in this chapter, must have been

---

[73]   Jean-François Lyotard, *The Lyotard Reader*, ed. Andrew Benjamin (Oxford: Basil Blackwell, 1989), 204.

[74]   Jean-François Lyotard, 'The Sign of History', in Derek Attridge, Geoffrey Bennington and Robert Young (eds), *Post-Structuralism and the Question of History* (Cambridge: Cambridge University Press, 1987), 178.

entirely obvious to David Tudor as he performed the piece in 1958. Tudor, so closely associated with all the composers of Feldman's circle (including, perhaps most significantly, Wolpe), would have been ideally equipped to apprehend and understand the systems, processes, methods and frames that were activated in the manufacture *Intermission 6*. It is likely that Feldman intentionally disguised the relative explicitness and simplicity of the early version of the work in making the mobile, graphic score.

If, as Feldman himself said, 'All activity in music reflects its process',[75] then all of the decisions, alterations, revisions that formed the work are integrally part of its very substance, and the composer's decision-making itself may be seen as performative. Feldman was all along, at every stage, 'playing' a work known as *Intermission 6* – but it did not always sound the way we might think it should (if our point of reference is the published score). Similarly, the work performed by Cage and Tudor in 1958 was in many respects a different piece – and yet always *Intermission 6*.

Examination of *Intermission 6* has further confirmed that Feldman was to a very great degree concerned with a 12-tone pitch-class palette. In *Intermission 6*, we find this in its most distilled form. We may also observe here methods of organisation of pitch material similar to those observed in *Intermission 5* and *Piano Piece 1952*, and also of placing the structures of sound-events in time, effectively creating proportional partitions of the time space that resemble horizontalised Wolpean proportions. In all of this, the two-dimensional model taken from Feldman's sketchbooks has facilitated constructive insight.

In this analysis, we have also seen further evidence of the connection between Feldman's work and the visual arts. This was both something that he appreciated (it was indeed one of the structuring frames of his aesthetic position) and something that we appreciate, albeit from a very different perspective in time, a different field, and indeed a different world. Here, we have seen once again the tendency to active flattening of the structures and forms beyond that called for inherently by the two-dimensional model. Furthermore, the explicit analogy, made by Feldman himself, between *Intermission 6* and notions of 'line' opens a fruitful field of analytical and philosophical investigation.

Above all, *Intermission 6* exists in a tensioned, ambiguous, in-between space. Just as Feldman's 'crystalline' sound-structures are held in place by the tensioned proportioning of vertical and horizontal (pitch and time), so is this work more broadly framed by tensions between composer and performer, concept and listener, artist and society, sound and sight, planned action and improvisation, line and space. Ultimately, this is a work that sits at the very cusp of the modern/postmodern turn, solidly founded upon the old world of European pre-war modernism yet also literally tearing modernist forms and assumptions apart.

---

[75]   Morton Feldman, 'Some Elementary Questions', in B.H. Friedman (ed.), *Give My Regards to Eighth Street*, 65–6.

Chapter 5
'Primitive Designs':[1]
Hearing and Thinking through *Intersection 3*

> In the cultist space of modern art, the grid serves not only as emblem but also myth. For like all myths, it deals with paradox or contradiction not by dissolving the paradox or resolving the contradiction, but by covering them over so that they seem (but only seem) to go away. The grid's mythic power is that it makes us able to think we are dealing with materialism (or sometimes science, or logic) while at the same time it provides us with a release into belief (or illusion, or fiction). [Rosalind Krauss][2]

Problematic Novelty

In many ways, Feldman's public career as a composer was founded upon the early attention attracted to his graph (or grid) scores of the early 1950s. These works immediately caught the attention of John Cage, and were among the first of Feldman's works to be performed, recorded, written about and published. Cage, Cowell and Wolpe spoke about these works in lectures in the 1950s and also wrote about them.[3] Several of these scores attained the dubious status of common textbook illustrations, presented by some as the first graphic scores (a debatable notion) and by others as exemplars of indeterminacy in musical composition (again, problematic), and often understood as a response to abstract expressionism (on the basis of anecdotal rather than analytical evidence). Almost every survey

---

[1]   Jan Williams and Morton Feldman, 'An Interview with Morton Feldman' [1983], in Chris Villars (ed.), *Morton Feldman Says: Selected Interviews and Lectures 1964–1987* (London: Hyphen Press, 2006), 153.

[2]   Rosalind Krauss, 'Grids', *October* 9 (Summer 1979), 54.

[3]   See for example, Henry Cowell, 'Current Chronicle', *The Musical Quarterly*, 38/1 (January 1952); Stefan Wolpe, 'On New (and not-so-new) Music in America' [Darmstadt, 1956], trans. Austin Clarkson, *Journal of Music Theory* 28/1 (1984), 1–45; and Stefan Wolpe, 'Thoughts on Pitch and some Considerations Connected with It' [1952], *Perspectives of New Music*, 17/2 (1979), 28–57 (text of a talk given at Black Mountain College, August 1952); John Cage, 'Lecture on Nothing' [1949/50], in *Silence: Lectures and Writings by John Cage* (Middletown, CT: Wesleyan University Press, 1961), 109–26; 'Lecture on Something' [1950/51], in ibid., 128–45; 'Indeterminacy', in ibid., 35–40; and 'Juilliard Lecture' [1952], in *A Year From Monday* (Middletown, CT: Wesleyan University Press, 1969), 95–111.

text on twentieth-century music from the latter half of the century contains at least one page from a Feldman grid score, most often from either the *Projection* or *Intersection* series.[4]

Despite this, the situation has changed in the twenty-first century – in recent years, enthusiasm for Feldman's music has been increasingly disassociated from the graph scores. This is partly due to an overwhelming interest in the monumental late works, but it also implicitly indicates that the graph scores are seen as less relevant to contemporary experiences of Feldman.[5] This sense is echoed also in the Feldman discography; while early LP recordings featured the grid scores quite prominently, currently available recordings on CD are dominated by later works in staff notation. To give an example from the piano works, there are notably more recordings available of late pieces such as *Palais de Mari* (16) and *For Bunita Marcus* (9), than of *Intersection 3* (six, of which two are reissues of recordings made by David Tudor).[6]

Some of these grid scores, including *Intersection 3* (1953), retain in published form Feldman's natural, poetically naive approach to this form of notation. Others, however, were published in the carefully designed, calligraphic copies made by John Cage – produced in all generosity to show Feldman how they ought to look. As Feldman said two decades later, 'He [Cage] took my early graph scores and copied them over himself, hours of careful work. Said they were too messy'.[7] Yet despite the almost childlike handwriting of Feldman's own manuscripts, we must not underestimate the seriousness of the composer's purpose, or indeed the fierce intelligence with which he explored, and ultimately abandoned, the musical possibilities of the grid notation. There are deep connections between the very nature and form of this notation and Feldman's developing musical imagination in terms of fundamental concepts and models – to such an extent that it is highly likely that the experimentation with grid notation and the development of Feldman's approaches to the deployment of musical materials (including pitch material) in a two-dimensional space (as discussed in previous chapters of this book) go hand in hand during the early 1950s. If this is the case, then we are seeing

---

[4]   For example, Paul Griffiths, *A Concise History of Avant-Garde Music* (New York: Oxford University Press, 1978), 172; Robert P. Morgan, *Twentieth-century Music: A History of Musical Style in Modern Europe and America* (New York: W. W. Norton, 1991), 365.

[5]   As an example from popular literature, Philip Clark's otherwise sensitive and measured 'primer' as published in *The Wire* and later anthologised in a book, manages to entirely avoid mention of graph notation. Philip Clark, 'Morton Feldman', in Rob Young (ed.), *The Wire Primers: A Guide to Modern Music* (London: Verso, 2009), 165–72.

[6]   Chris Villars maintains a valuable, up to date online discography at http://www.cnvill.net/mfdiscog.htm.

[7]   Morton Feldman, 'I Met Heine on the Rue Fürstenburg' [1973], in B.H. Friedman (ed.), *Give My Regards to Eighth Street: Collected Writings of Morton Feldman* (Cambridge, MA: Exact Change, 2000), 115.

the development of these concepts played out in the grid notation at the same time as it was becoming evident in the staff-notated works.

Any attempt at analysis of Feldman's grid-notated works inevitably comes up against two of the fundamental problems in Feldman studies: firstly, the issue of how exactly these works interact with notions of indeterminacy; and, secondly, how they relate to Feldman's keen interest in the visual arts. Of course, these are not only problems but also points of interest. Given that discussion of both these aspects of Feldman's work has hindered as much as aided our understanding of the music over the past six decades, however, I find it methodologically necessary to think of them as problems. We have encountered these issues in the other analyses presented in this book, but in many ways the grid scores bring such difficulties into sharp focus. In these works, we seem to be seeing a more extreme opening-up of possibilities for performance than in other works and, likewise, there appears to be a more explicit connection with the world of the visual arts.

In this chapter, following a brief discussion of existing literature regarding Feldman's grid scores, I will make some formal observations, with reference to *Intersection 3* as the primary case study, and then discuss some important aspects of the contextual analysis – bearing in mind that these are simply threads in the great web of possible analyses, isolated here for the sake of argument. *Intersection 3* has been chosen as the focus for analysis partly because it relates in time-period to the other works discussed in this book – but also because of its clarity of form and content (in this respect, it has some similarity to *Intermission 5*).

In the context of the wider argument I am making in this book, there are several aims to be addressed:

- to uncover some of the formal attributes of the work;
- to discover how these formal structures compare or contrast with those identified in the other works discussed;
- to link this formal analysis to contextual analysis, pointing to potentially fruitful lines of exploration.

Further, we may seek answers to the background questions: To what extent was *Intersection 3* 'designed' or intuitively/randomly composed? What are the implications of these findings for our general understanding of Feldman's work?

Rationalising Indeterminacy

While Cage was certainly instrumental in promoting Feldman's early work – organising performances, copying scores and so forth, his discussion of Feldman's music in lectures and writings was very narrow in focus and to a large extent represents an appropriation of Feldman's work for illustration of Cage's own developing arguments about the nature of indeterminacy in particular:

> This is a lecture on composition which is indeterminate with respect to its
> performance. The *Intersection 3* by Morton Feldman is an example. The *Music
> of Changes* is not an example.[8]

Although the subtle relation between Feldman's music and indeterminacy is
significant, it remains unhelpful to consider these works too single-mindedly from
this perspective. At the same time, however, we must recognise that, for Cage, these
works played a crucial part in his rationalising of indeterminacy. It is important to
maintain this distinction between what Cage saw as useful in Feldman's music for
his own purposes and what Feldman's work might actually represent. Aside from
his often-quoted comment that Feldman's staff-notated works are effectively the
composer performing his own grid notation, Cage's writings imply that he had
little interest in Feldman's music in more conventional forms of notation.[9]

As we shall see, there are deep connections between Feldman's various works
of this period, irrespective of notation, but the extent to which Cage actually
understood this is not certain. Certainly, Feldman's sketches from the 1950s
suggest that he may have sometimes translated sections of a piece back and forth
between staff and grid notation during the process of composition. He did this,
for example, with *Projection 4* (January 1951) and also *Marginal Intersection for
Orchestra* (July 1951), as may be seen in the surviving sketches for these works.[10]
Feldman's realisation of his own grid notation for *Projection 4*, fragmentary as it
is, does seem to be made with a concern for keeping the chromatic aggregate in
play – much as we observe in the staff-notated works. Indeed, the rather beautiful
pitch deployment of the opening section of *Projection 4*, as sketched on a staff by
Feldman, makes one wish that the composer had completed this realisation.

David Tudor's realisations and performances show a comparable approach to
the deployment of pitch materials, albeit with a tendency to cycle through the
chromatic rather more rapidly and regularly than Feldman (that is to say, Tudor
tends to set up a relatively regular rhythm of chromatic fields in comparison to
Feldman's more broadly structural approach – these, to a large extent, a result
of differences in perspective between roles of performer and composer).[11] Both
having studied with Stefan Wolpe, Feldman and Tudor had a similar appreciation
of such matters as pitch material – to such an extent that it might be argued that

---

[8]   John Cage, 'Composition as Process, II. Indeterminacy' [1958], in *Silence*, 36.

[9]   Quoted in Frank O'Hara, 'New Directions in Music: Morton Feldman' [1959], in
B.H. Friedman (ed.), *Give My Regards to Eighth Street*, 216.

[10]   Paul Sacher Foundation, Basel, Morton Feldman Collection.

[11]   With regard to Tudor's performance, this may also be a side-effect of the density
of sounding material in works such as the *Intersections* for piano; in this sense they seem
to require a comparable chromatic density. One can only imagine how Feldman might have
realised such scores, bearing in mind that he was at times quite interested in rather extreme
densities of sound (as, for example, in works like the *Vertical Thoughts* series and the
remarkable *Extensions 4* for three pianos).

works like *Intersection 2* and *Intersection 3* are not really piano pieces but rather works composed for the remarkable instrument that was Tudor himself. In fact, it was through the association with Wolpe and Feldman that Tudor and Cage were introduced to one another.[12] One of the many aspects of New York music in this period that remains to be thoroughly investigated is the influence of people like Feldman and Tudor – with the powerful figure of Wolpe in the background – on Cage, as opposed to the conventional story of his influence upon others. Feldman, significantly, seems to have approved of Tudor's methods, by which realisations of the grid score were painstakingly made in staff notation, learned and performed. All indeterminacy aside, Tudor knew how to play the right notes.

Built around reference to works like *Intersection 3*, Cage's argument was, to a very large extent, concerned with outcomes – which is to say, implications for performance. In his lectures of the 1950s,[13] he progressed from lists of attributes (aspects of the work which, in his view, were either determinate or indeterminate and to what degree) to various analogies: Feldman's score is like a camera, used by the performer to take various kinds of picture, it is also an 'intersection', apparently, because 'anyone can cross'. Repeatedly, we find Cage's cleverness with words, images and metaphors very much in evidence, but there is almost no appreciation shown of compositional process – either because Cage was not interested in this aspect of the analysis, or because Feldman was concealing the actual procedures from his older mentor. Given the way their friendship began, based upon Feldman pretending not to know how he wrote a piece, it seems probable that this disingenuity was a continuing characteristic of their complex and occasionally difficult relationship.[14] Without going into a detailed deconstruction of Cage's analysis at this point, it is reasonable to say that he inflated the significance of indeterminate aspects of Feldman's grid scores at the expense of other equally important features for his own (interesting) purposes. Cage's influence throughout

---

[12]   As Tudor recalled in a 1988 interview, 'Feldman had been a student of my composition teacher Stefan Wolpe and I had been performing Feldman's piano music and at one point John Cage needed a pianist, to perform not his own but someone else's music [Boulez, *Second Piano Sonata*] and at that point I met John and our friendship has not stopped since that time.' Teddy Hultberg and David Tudor, '"I smile when the sound is singing through the space": An Interview with David Tudor by Teddy Hultberg in Dusseldorf May 17–18 1988', http://davidtudor.org/Articles/hultberg.html.

[13]   See John Cage, 'Composition as Process, II. Indeterminacy', 36–7; John Cage, 'Juilliard Lecture', 108.

[14]   Morton Feldman, 'Liner Notes' [1962], in B.H. Friedman, (ed.), *Give My Regards to Eighth Street*, 4. See also the discussion in Chapter 1 of this book. Cage and Feldman were usually polite to each other in public, and no doubt did have a genuine regard for each other. This was strained at times, however; one spectacular misunderstanding occurred at a performance of Feldman's *Five Pianos* (under its earlier title of *Pianos and Voices*) in Berlin, 1972. Amy Beal tells a somewhat sanitised version of the incident in *New Music, New Allies: American Experimental Music in West Germany from the Zero Hour to Reunification* (Berkeley, CA: University of California Press, 2006), 236.

the later twentieth century was such that his views came to dominate discussion of Feldman's work more generally, leading to some unfortunate and misleading emphasis on indeterminacy in secondary literature.

Henry Cowell likewise, and possibly following Cage's lead, also saw Feldman's grid notation as a frame for 'improvisation': 'This is a plan for the control of improvisation and the music will of course never sound twice alike. Its success depends upon what the players contribute.'[15] While this imagined freedom granted to the performer was a major point of interest for Cage and Cowell, it was a negative feature for Boulez and Wolpe, who both found fault with the inexactness and imprecision of Feldman's notation. In Wolpe's case this was primarily a concern about the apparent laxity of pitch notation (what Ryan Vigil has sensibly described as a softening of approach rather than an abandonment of control).[16] In a lecture at Black Mountain College in 1952, Wolpe observed with some irritation that, while pitch is clearly indicated in these grid scores, it is notated only very crudely at the level of register rather than pitch-class:

> Some people think that pitch does not matter ... Or they will distinguish only high, middle, and low, and that's all what pitch there is. But why not declare the whole thing as one body, where high, middle, and low is one (three as one), and cash in the whole thing?[17]

Boulez had made similar criticism a year earlier, suggesting that the grid notation was 'Much too imprecise and too simple' and for him the problem extended also to rhythm.[18]

Feldman's own few, gnomic statements surviving from this period emphasised quite different concerns, referring neither to indeterminacy nor to painting, but to weight, balance and pulse. His earliest published words, in fact, appear quoted in Cowell's article of 1952:

> My *Projections* and *Intersections* is [*sic*] a weight either reminiscent or discovered. Weight for me does not have its source in the realm of dynamics

---

[15]   Henry Cowell, 'Current Chronicle', 133.

[16]   Ryan Vigil, 'Compositional Parameters: *Projection 4* and an Analytical Methodology for Morton Feldman's Graphic Works', *Perspectives of New Music*, 47/1 (Winter 2009), 241.

[17]   Stefan Wolpe, 'Thoughts on Pitch and Some Considerations Connected with It', 49.

[18]   Pierre Boulez, 'Letter from Pierre Boulez to John Cage: August 1951', in Jean-Jacques Nattiez and Robert Samuels (eds), *The Boulez–Cage Correspondence* (Cambridge: Cambridge University Press, 1993), 103. Cage replied, 'Feldman, who has great difficulty imagining that you do not like his work, will send you a new *Intersection* on graph for piano'. See John Cage, 'Letter from John Cage to Pierre Boulez: summer 1951', in ibid., 110.

or tensions, but rather resulting from a visual–aural response to sound as an image gone inward creating a general synthesis. Weight involves the finding of a pulse which allows for a natural fluidity. Discovered weight implies discovered balance. Discovered balance implies discovered movement from this pulse. The notation is presented graphically where each box is a clock time duration.[19]

As we shall see, the concern with weight and balance – a material interest in Varèse-like densities of sounds combined with a Wolpean appreciation of symmetry and proportion – is of crucial importance to understanding the nature of Feldman's grid scores.

In later life, Feldman noted that the grid scores in general had not worked out the way he had hoped – in so far as performers (other than Tudor) often had the impression (as did Cowell) that they could improvise, misunderstanding both the score and Feldman's intentions. In a highly suggestive statement dating from 1962, Feldman suggested that the problem was not so much a fault on the part of the performer as his own: 'because I was still involved with passages and continuity that allowed their presence to be felt'.[20] It is somewhat surprising to find Feldman thinking of these grid scores in terms of such things as 'passages and continuity', suggesting conscious organisation of material rather than intuitive, random or indeterminate procedures. Feldman's on-and-off experiments with various forms of the grid notation in the early 1950s, and again in the 1960s, indicate that, even at the time, he was ambivalent about its viability – but his self-critique later went even further, echoing both Wolpe and Boulez. In a 1983 interview, he described the notation of these early grid scores as 'very primitive', and also noted that one problem with the notation was that it was 'too easy to make wonderful designs on the page'.[21] Curiously, however, long after he had stopped publishing works in grid notation, Feldman maintained that the concept of the grid was still relevant to his composition process: 'I still use a grid. But now the grid encompasses conventional notation.'[22]

I would like to emphasise Feldman's use of the terms 'graph' or 'grid' to describe this notation. These are not graphic scores in the sense of, for example, Earle Brown's pieces of the same period or the later extravagances of Cardew and Bussotti; Feldman's notation seems not to aspire to the status of art. Instead, his pieces are literally composed on graph (or 'coordinate', as Cowell referred to it) paper,[23] within a hard-edged, squared-off set of rigid frames. The earlier

---

[19]   Quoted in Henry Cowell, 'Current Chronicle', 131.

[20]   Morton Feldman, 'Liner Notes' [1962], in B.H. Friedman (ed.), *Give My Regards to Eighth Street*, 6.

[21]   Jan Williams and Morton Feldman, 'An Interview with Morton Feldman', 153.

[22]   Ibid. Tom Hall has written in some detail on this subject, see Tom Hall, 'Notational Image, Transformation and the Grid in the Late Music of Morton Feldman', *Current Issues in Music*, 1/1 (2007), 7–24.

[23]   Henry Cowell, 'Current Chronicle', 131.

Projection pieces have a relatively open character, indeed rather more graphically pleasing, as a result of the empty squares on the grid not having boundary lines (see Figure 5.1). The later scores, like *Intersection 3* as it was published (Figure 5.2), are written with a notation that has closed in upon itself, boxed in both sound and silence entirely. We may observe then, that, as Feldman's work progresses in the early 1950s, the notation becomes effectively more restrictive and literally less open.

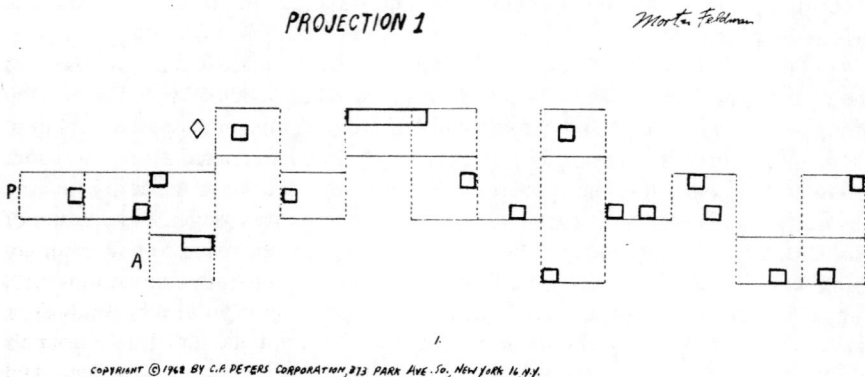

Figure 5.1   Morton Feldman, *Projection 1* (1950), p. 1

Given the nature of these grid scores, with their coordinate paper and numerical inputs, it seems only natural to consider the possibility that statistical analysis might be fruitful. John Welsh took this approach in his 1996 study of Feldman's very first grid composition, *Projection 1*, and he was able to show that the work is much more purposefully structured – designed, one might say – than was previously supposed to be the case.[24] Of particular interest, his study has shown that the work is on several levels a bi-partite structure cantilevered upon the 2:1 partition of duration. Welsh even went so far as to argue (somewhat tautologically) that 'The structure of *Projection 1* is primarily statistical in nature', adding, 'Thus, analysis of the densities of events seems to be the most effective method for discussing this piece'.[25] Through his statistical examination based upon empirical observations, Welsh showed that in composing this work

---

[24]   John Welsh. '*Projection I* (1950)', in Thomas DeLio (ed.), *The Music of Morton Feldman* (New York: Greenwood Press, 1996), 21–35.
[25]   Ibid., 24.

Feldman radically substituted timbre, density, register and silence for the more customary dominant parameter of pitch-class.[26]

A more common alternative to such empirical approaches has been to discuss the grid works in terms of visual arts, and abstract expressionism in particular. Feldman's associations with the abstract expressionist painters has a long-standing significance in the mythologies associated with the composer – yet the precise way in which these friendships and enthusiasms impacted his musical work is seldom clear. This approach was largely crystallised in the 2002 book, *The New York Schools of Music and Visual Arts*, with contributions from several notable scholars.[27] The title of the book makes explicit the myth-making agenda; there was no 'New York School of Music' in any formal, historical sense, but this book is one manifestation of a perceived need to retrospectively create such a school.[28] Having called these two schools of music and the visual arts into being, however, a natural connection between them is often taken as axiomatic.[29] Much interesting research and discussion resulted from the alignment of art and music that this volume explores, but only Stephen Johnson's contribution to the volume, an analysis of *Why Patterns?*,[30] goes substantially beyond presuppositions to make a genuinely original and important analysis of specific aspects of Feldman's interactions with painting. Most importantly, Johnson demonstrated through formal analysis a conclusive structural affinity between Feldman's later music and Jasper Johns's 'crosshatch' paintings of the 1970s. Much remains mysterious, however, and Johnson concludes of *Why Patterns?*, 'As in Johns, hidden systems abound, but the meaning of these systems is enigmatic'.[31]

Most analysis of Feldman's music has focused upon the more conventionally notated works. The reason for this is obvious: works without notated pitch-class offer little traction for conventional analytical tools. A number of researchers

---

[26]   Ibid., 35.

[27]   Steven Johnson (ed.), *The New York Schools of Music and the Visual Arts* (New York: Routledge, 2002).

[28]   The idea of a 'New York School' of composers has been around for quite some time. Feldman himself questioned this notion of schools of music and painting in a 1967 radio interview, asking rhetorically 'What do Pollock and Rothko have in common? We were all different'. Charles Shere interview (recorded Berkeley, KPFA, July 1967), http://www.archive.org/details/MortonFeldmanInterview1967.

[29]   John Holzaepfel's otherwise valuable examination of David Tudor's realisations of the *Intersection* scores, for example, assumes that Feldman's grid notation and the associated processes of composition were directly imitative of the methods and approaches of abstract expressionist painters such as Pollock. John Holzaepfel, 'Painting by Numbers: The *Intersections* of Morton Feldman and David Tudor', in Steven Johnson (ed.), *The New York Schools*, 159–72.

[30]   Steven Johnson, 'Jasper Johns and Morton Feldman: Why Patterns?', in ibid., 217–47.

[31]   Ibid., 246.

have been working on Feldman's graphic scores in recent times, however, and this growing interest in coming to grips with the formal attributes of these works suggests that the field of Feldman studies has recently reached a point where it has become possible and perhaps necessary to confront these grid scores in all seriousness. Among the several scholars working in this field, I would mention in particular Ryan Vigil, Brett Boutwell and Tom Hall. Vigil's substantial 2009 essay 'Compositional Parameters: *Projection 4* and an Analytical Methodology for Morton Feldman's Graphic Works' makes much food for thought in the contemporary context.[32] Tom Hall has made important analytical forays into one of Feldman's most puzzling works, the glittering and formidable *Intersection for Magnetic Tape*,[33] while Brett Boutwell has combined thorough historical analysis with considered musical insight in his study of the *Projection* series, providing valuable reflections on this crucial period of Feldman's work and also his relation to Cage.[34]

Form

The composition was dated April 1953 (on all surviving manuscripts), and dedicated to the pianist David Tudor. The first known public performance took place in New York in April 1954.[35] There are several sources, but no original sketch materials have been positively identified. Aside from the score published by Edition Peters in 1962 and the manuscript holograph from which it was printed, there are two early manuscript copies held by the Tudor Archive. One of these, in which the entire work is fitted onto a single page of graph paper, appears to be in Feldman's handwriting and bears his signature – and it is even possible that this is the original sketch.[36] The other is a neater copy in Tudor's hand, spaced over two pages. Additionally, there survives as part of this collection the performance realisation made by Tudor.[37] The original Edition Peters score was reprinted in the

32   Ryan Vigil, 'Compositional Parameters', 233–67.

33   Tom Hall, 'The Seduction of Graphism Alone?: The Function of Notation and Technology in the *Intersections* of Morton Feldman', [unpublished] paper presented at *Seventh International Conference on Music since 1900 and the International Conference of the Society for Music Analysis* (University of Lancaster, 2011).

34   Brett Boutwell, 'Morton Feldman's Projections: Origins, Development, and Spin', [unpublished] paper presented at *American Musicological Society Conference* (San Francisco, 2011).

35   Sebastian Claren, *Neither: Die Musik Morton Feldmans* (Hofheim: Wolke, 2000), 554.

36   The Getty Research Institute, Los Angeles, David Tudor Papers, 980039, Series 1b, Box 9, 26b.

37   Ibid.

collection of Feldman's early piano pieces issued in 2000.[38] The early manuscripts differ from the published work only in relatively minor details: the revised pagination, the '4' in *ictus* 27 which both manuscripts agree should be held across two squares instead of only one, and in that each box with a number entered in the manuscripts has a heavy line drawn around it in addition to the overall three-layered frame of the grid/staff. This last notational detail gives the early copies an effect rather like reading a computer punch-card, and it is no mere coincidence that punch-cards had become ubiquitous by the 1950s for data entry and archiving in government and industry.[39]

Given that, with such a work as *Intersection 3*, the very nature of the score and notation is of particular interest, we may begin with some superficial but significant observations:

- horizontal lines in the grid delineate three registers (high, middle and low);
- vertical lines mark time passing at the rate of metronome mark 176;
- numbers in the grid, according to Feldman's instructions, indicate 'how many keys one plays'.

Although Feldman claimed that the player is free to 'make any rhythmic entrances on or within a given situation', in practice we may observe that rhythm and durations are notated rather more precisely than this might suggest – the tempo of the work is so fast that in fact there is very little scope for flexibility in terms of either attack or duration. For this reason, David Tudor planned his performance realisation as much as possible on the beat of the *ictus* (each graph square), utilising grace notes for more complex passages;[40] there is simply no time for anything more intricate than this. As a result of this rhythmic straight-jacket, any accurate performance of *Intersection 3* is rendered immediately recognisable to someone who is familiar with the score, regardless of which precise pitches are played. From a compositional perspective, we may thus observe that the composer was clearly concerned with the placement of sounding materials in time, and that any rhythmic 'indeterminacy' in performance will be of a quite subtle and finely detailed kind.

As others have observed, Feldman did concern himself with pitch in composing the work, but at the level of register rather than pitch-class. Dynamics seem to have been irrelevant to the composition process, but like pitch-classes they are realised in performance. In contrast to Catherine Hirata and Ryan Vigil, I cannot help feeling that sonority itself was not a material of importance in the composition

---

[38]   Morton Feldman, '*Intersection 3*', in Volker Straebel (ed.), *Solo Piano Works 1950–64* (New York: Edition Peters, 2000).

[39]   See, for example, Margaret O'Neill Adams, 'Punch Card Records: Precursors of Electronic Records', *The American Archivist*, 58/2, Special Issue on Case Studies (Spring, 1995), 182–201.

[40]   See John Holzaepfel, 'Painting by Numbers', 166.

Figure 5.2   Morton Feldman, *Intersection 3*, p. 1
Copyright © 1962 by C.F. Peters Corporation. All rights reserved. Used by permission.

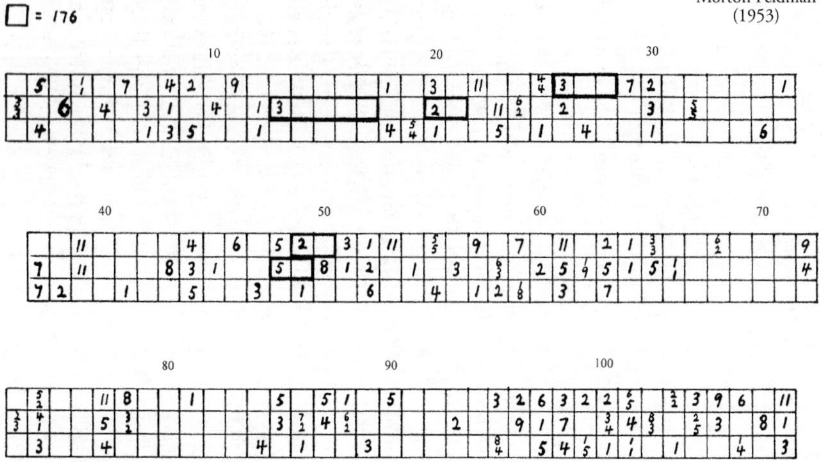

of this work, but rather that Feldman was working with rather more brutal aggregations of tones, of densities.[41] As we have already noted, Feldman himself felt that his tendency to become absorbed in designs on paper when working these grid scores was ultimately 'primitive' and problematic, perhaps partly on account of this relative brutality or crudeness of sonic deployment. On the other hand, this is also a resulting characteristic of works like *Intersection 3*, and of interest not only in terms of grid scores but also because it is an aspect of Feldman's creative personality that is often overlooked; it is seemingly at odds with the myth of his concern for the 'sound of the sounds themselves'.[42] Rather, it may be argued that, at least in these grid scores, Feldman was more concerned with an abstracted appearance of the weight of sounds, than sonority, working with numbers on paper, rather than pitch-based aural imagination in the conventional sense.

A further general but vital observation is that the notation may be easily read (and heard) as a musical score, from left to right, with two axes of pitch and time. Not only does this reflect Feldman's known preoccupation with the management of musical composition within the plane of these two axes, it also sets his grid notation firmly apart from graphic notations of other composers like Brown and Bussotti. Feldman's notation is a simple adaptation of conventional scoring, in which a double staff of 10 lines is replaced by a two-line staff (which is to say that there is a less fine-grained differentiation of pitch) and the vertical lines represent division of individual 'beats' rather than metrical bars (so, quite fine-grained rhythmic detail). Curiously, while in conventional notation, notes may stray beyond the staff on ledger lines, Feldman's primitive staff is tightly bound within its frame. Feldman's grid notation, while novel, is not as radical as it might appear at first glance; conventional staff notation is also essentially a grid, and in some respects it is more open and flexible than Feldman's closed, reduced system.

Delving a little more deeply into *Intersection 3*, we note that the numbers used to indicate the density of sounding pitches are 1–11 which, together with the empty square as 0, gives the significant number 12. Radically, the fundamental material used to compose the work is a 'chromatic' set of 12 densities, rather than 12 pitch-classes. Further investigation reveals that Feldman deploys this material in a manner directly comparable with the handling of the chromatic aggregate of pitch-classes in other works. It is a kind of translation – Feldman has mapped his pitch materials onto this scale of densities, and composes with it in much the same way as he composes with pitch-classes.

Mapping out the aggregate completions from the beginning of the work, we find that there are 16 fields (Figure 5.3). The last is seemingly incomplete (density class 10 appears to be missing); perhaps it has simply run off the canvas – incomplete closing fields are not uncommon in Feldman's other works (see

[41]   Catherine Hirata, *Analyzing the Music of Morton Feldman* (PhD Dissertation, Columbia University, 2003); Ryan Vigil, 'Compositional Parameters', 233–67.

[42]   Catherine Hirata, 'The Sounds of the Sounds Themselves: Analyzing the Early Music of Morton Feldman', *Perspectives of New Music*, 34/1 (Winter 1996), 6–27.

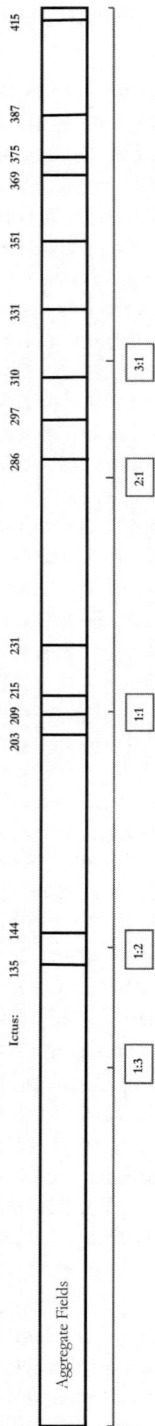

Figure 5.3   Diagram of aggregate fields in *Intersection 3*, showing primary proportions

for example *Piano Piece 1952*) – or it may have been elided with the previous field. Given that the previous-to-last field ends with 10, I would favour the elision hypothesis (this, then, is comparable to the opening field of *Piano Piece 1952*). The fields are of extremely varied length – some span more than a page of the score, and others just a few squares. Several serve explicitly as structural markers of the work's larger time-spaces. The opening field, for example (which also happens to be the longest), is completed at *ictus* 135 by density class 10. This 10 is part of an intricate structure of density classes built around the 1:2 partition of the duration of the work at *ictus* 140 (Figure 5.4); this structure is prominently audible, as a roughly symmetrical moment of density surround by much more transparent textures. As we have already seen, Feldman commonly marked major points in time by this method of building structures around or across them. Note that the second occurrence of density class 10 marks the completion of the second aggregate field (*ictus* 144).

We then find another long field extending to shortly before the 1:1 partition of the work's duration. This is followed by two shorter fields that mark out another semi-symmetrical structure built around the 1:1 partition at *ictus* 210 (Figure 5.4). These third and fourth fields are each completed by density class 10, while the fifth begins with 10.

Overall, eight of the 16 fields are completed by density class 10, and it is the (possibly) missing density class of the last field. Does this figure 10 – taking on the significance of a true figure – have any special meaning in this work? One hesitates to note a possible cabbalistic import in Feldman's recurrent numbers – too little is known about such things in Feldman's thinking, or indeed in terms of the New York of this period, to venture very far down this line of thought.[43] It is worth reminding ourselves at this point, however, of Hermann Sabbe's observation, 'Feldman does not leave anything to chance.'[44] The numbers did most likely signify something to Feldman.

It is easy to see how crucial the overall scheme of the fields is to the work's design. The 1:1 and 1:2 partitions as discussed above are very clearly delineated, while the space between the 2:1 partition and the end is filled with a more complex field of activity (Figure 5.5). Looking at this another way, we can say that in the first half of the work the first-level partitions of 1:1 and 1:2 are the primary structural features, whereas in the second half the structures move to the secondary level of partitions (i.e. partitions of partitions). As we have seen in other chapters, this kind of cantilevered, asymmetric composition is typical of Feldman – and we also see it in the paintings and drawings of his closest friend, Philip Guston. Looking at the chart of these primary and secondary partitions, we may begin to see a new

---

[43]   Of the surprisingly few investigations of such matters, one may note the discussion of Barnett Newman's interest in Kabbalah in Matthew Baigell, *Artist and Identity in Twentieth-century America* (Cambridge: Cambridge University Press, 2001), 232–42.

[44]   Herman Sabbe, 'The Feldman Paradoxes: A Deconstructionist View of Musical Aesthetics', in Thomas DeLio (ed.), *The Music of Morton Feldman*, 10.

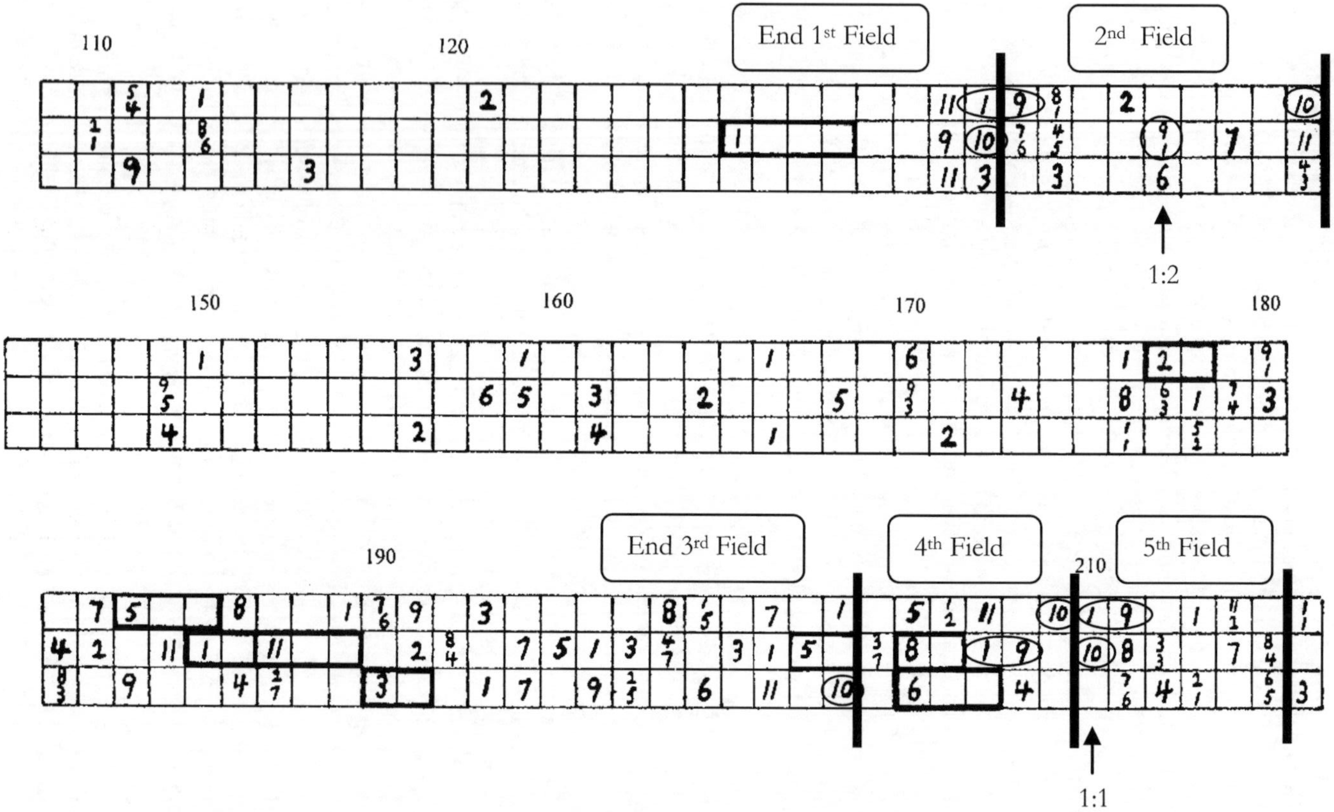

Figure 5.4   Morton Feldman, *Intersection 3*, p. 2. Aggregate fields 1–5, showing 1:2 and 1:1 partitions of the work's duration

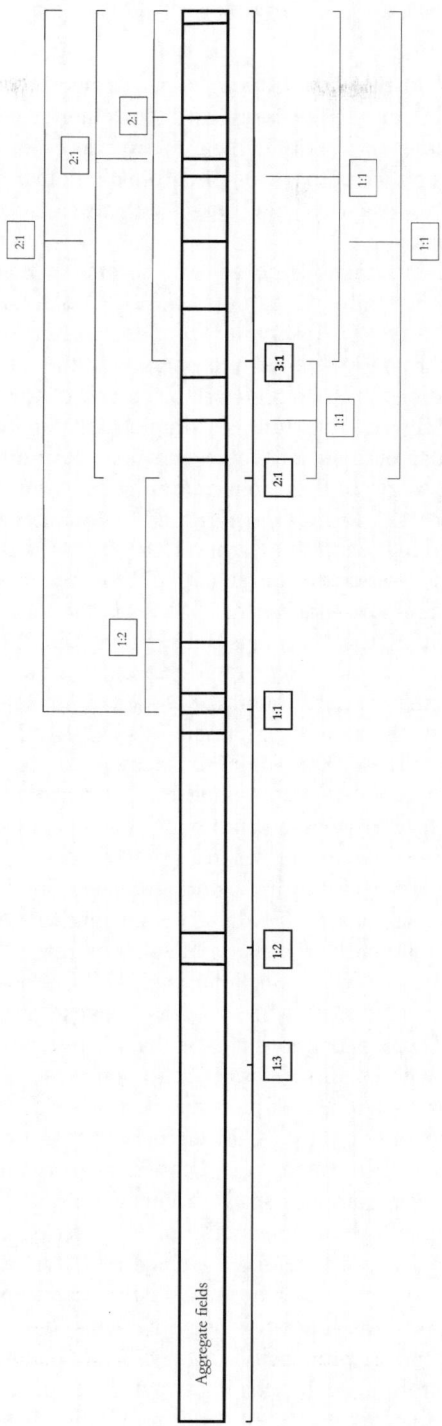

Figure 5.5   Diagram of aggregate fields in *Intersection 3*, showing primary proportions and also some secondary proportions

possibility for the origin of the title *Intersection*: from a relatively simple first half, the work unfolds through a complex network of intersecting spaces, all defined by the deployment of materials of density in the same way as Feldman defines the architecture of other works by the completion of chromatic fields. Far from being a street where 'anyone can cross' (as Cage suggested), it is a sophisticated and elegant origami-like construction.

Feldman was not thinking only of the general chromatic field of densities in composing *Intersection 3*; oddly, we can also observe his favoured set-types deployed in characteristic ways. For example, there are sections of the work in which smaller and larger chromatic sets seem to intersect, rather as if the material density is breathing in and out. In the approach to the end of the first field (*icti* 114–133, Figure 5.6) the transparent texture is a simple statement of the set 0123. Following the fiercely dense outburst of the second field built around and over *ictus* 140, the texture thins again to 0123, but in a mirrored form (*icti* 150–157). There is a clear sense that 0123 forms a background or foundation layer to this section of the piece through to the fifth field around 210–215. The 0123 chromatic set heard in icti 150–157 is also a subset of the larger chromatic unit 0123456 that fills *icti* 150–170, while the figure 9 at *ictus* 170 heralds the incursion of a new intersecting layer of material. Rather than subsiding again to the 0123 background, from this point the material layers are folded rapidly into the sustained sound mass that marks the approach to the 1:1 partition of the work at *ictus* 210.

Additionally, we find much use of such classic sets as 013. Even in the most densely weighted sections of the piece, we find these more transparent, open sets making significant appearances. The area around the 1:1 partition, for example, while dominated in one respect by massed chromatic segments (5678, 6789, etc.) is also framed by clear vertical statements of 013 at *icti* 193 and 216. The reader will easily be able to find other interesting examples; the point I wish to make here is that in this work we may observe Feldman composing with both chromatic fields and subsets of the aggregate (of densities), and as a result, displaying his usual sensitivity to certain combinations of intervals. We have already observed this in the other works discussed in this book – what makes *Intersection 3* (and by extension the other grid scores) extraordinary is that we find Feldman thinking in very abstracted terms, without pitch-class, and to some extent even without sound. Here, he is composing with densities, weights and balances, registers of sound – but perhaps more importantly, with numbers. These numbers are not deployed randomly, but are flexibly, fluently and confidently organised on macro- and micro-levels of scale in a complex array of intersecting structures. This is not only important in terms of our understanding of *Intersection 3* and the other grid scores – the fact that we can here see evidence of Feldman's thinking in such abstract terms shows that we must not underestimate the extent to which this was a part of his composition process in general. Thus, our observations of *Intersection 3* confirm Feldman's propensity for the abstract planning and design work that was necessary to formulate the existing structures of other pieces such as *Intermission 5*. Naturally, this does not preclude the possibility that at some stages

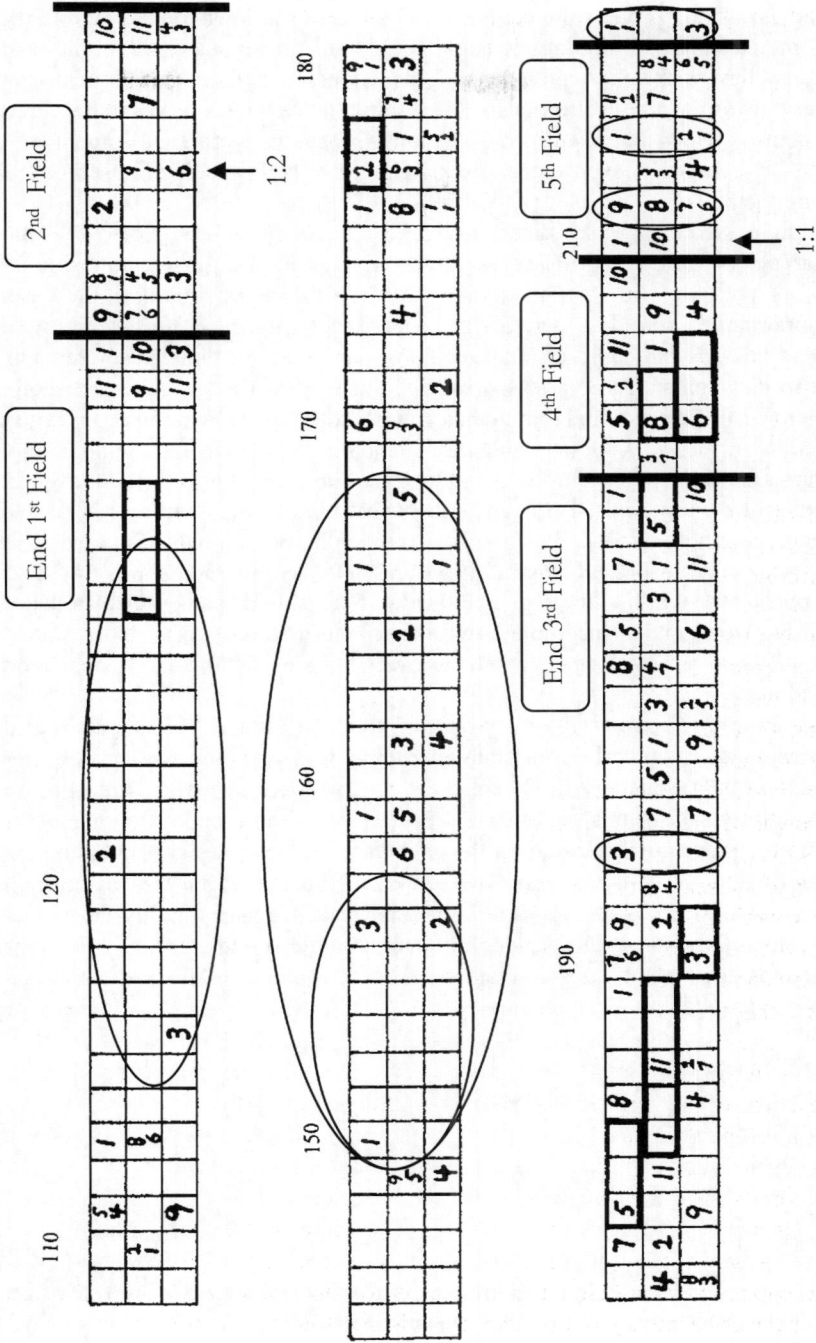

Figure 5.6   Morton Feldman, *Intersection 3*, p. 2, showing some occurrences of common set-types in this section of the work

of the composition process the composer might have sat down at the piano to try things out (testing and refining the sounds), just as at other stages he might have pinned the design sketches up on the wall (as witnessed by Christian Wolff) to get an overview of the architectural plan.[45] In a sense, this analysis serves to highlight the extent to which Feldman's compositional processes were successfully kept private; it seems that even close friends caught only isolated glimpses of his working methods.

Feldman's friend Frank O'Hara noted, in his perceptive essay of 1959, that comparison of different grid scores 'gives an idea of the great compositional flexibility possible with graph notation'.[46] While this is undoubtedly the case, it is important to note that there are also remarkable points of consistency with regard to background compositional methods – and that this consistency remains true also between staff and grid scores. Even in Feldman's very first grid score, *Projection 1* (1950), we find that he has composed the work with an aggregation of nine sonorities (10, if one includes silence): *pizzicato* (high, middle, low registers), harmonics (high, middle and low) and *arco* (high, middle and low). In deploying these materials, Feldman built one of his classic, cantilevered forms. The aggregate field of sonorities is repeated twice in the first half of the work, in time spaces of almost equal length; the second field's completion marks the exact mid-point of the work's duration. The third and final field spans the entire latter half of the work, and is incomplete (with two sonorities missing) – these almost literally erased, as the piece succumbs to overwhelming incursions of silence on the final page.

The *King of Denmark* (1964), arguably the best known of Feldman's grid scores and now standard percussion repertoire, was composed a decade after *Intersection 3*. As one would expect, it is a very different work (returning to grid notation in the 1960s, Feldman use it in a much more open, free manner – notating the piece on rather than in the grid with a variety of signs including his famous floating grace-notes, and even some staff notation), but the background compositional methods remain strikingly consistent. He uses a richly developed set of materials, notated in considerable detail: single sounds, groups of sounds sounded together or not together, clusters, glissandos and rolls. The basic material is thus an aggregate of 12 sonorities:

- silence;
- notes grouped 1–7 (and also I–VII);
- grace notes;
- clusters;
- *glissandos*;
- rolls.

---

45   David Patterson, 'Cage and Beyond: An Annotated Interview with Christian Wolff', *Perspectives of New Music*, 32/2 (Summer 1994), 72.

46   Frank O'Hara, 'New Directions in Music', 214.

Throughout the work, the number 7 functions as a special figure – not only in itself but in the combinations 4 + 3, 5 + 2 and 6 + 1. The number 6 occurs only twice, and marks out the large-scale bipartite structure of the work. Within this overall structure, there is an intricate web of intersecting and interlocking smaller structures. The four *glissandos*, for example, mark out two different spaces. The first two frame the structure that fills the third system: the 1:2 partition of the work's duration in turn divided 2:1 (echoing *Intermission 5*) – the mid-point of this internal structure marked by a prominent, single grace note in the middle register. Noting that the *glissandos* are always associated with clusters, we see that the second pair of *glissandos* frames another, more complex structure that incorporates the 1:1 partition of the work (at the 1:2 partition of this internal space) and the completion of the first aggregate field shortly after. This section ends, with *glissando*, cluster and cymbals, at *ictus* 159 – marking the golden section of the work as a whole.

Context

To summarise the analysis so far, we may identify the following points of interest:

- *Intersection 3* exhibits formal attributes that are carefully designed rather than random or intuitive.
- In so far as it is possible to compare works composed in grid notation with those in staff notation, we can see that there are remarkable structural correlations. There is clear evidence for comparable procedures employed for handling the material.
- Likewise, analogous structures may be observed in other grid scores. This is indicative of shared background composition methods.
- In *Intersection 3*, Feldman composes with densities rather than pitch-classes, engaging in a re-territorialisation of musical material – this is the most radical aspect of the work.
- The grid notation is essentially a remapping of the field of musical production on the page – but this is more subtle than radical in significance, and in some respects it is effectively concerned with restriction rather than freedom (thus literally conservative).
- There is a complex and peculiar relation between the nature of the work as it exists on the page, and the sounding work as it operates in performance.

Feldman's re-territorialisation of musical space and musical material is quite brutal, and the framing devices he imposes are rigid and highly constraining – one may argue that they are not only 'primitive' but also conservative. This is not to say that the music as it leaps off the page into the living space of performance is primitive, and indeed the internal design of the piece is a work of some intricacy, but the frame in terms of choice of fundamental material and notation rather contradicts this lively elegance. *Intersection 3* thus exhibits a very specific kind of inherent tension. We might recall once again Richard Schechner's discussion of the frames that constrain performance: he observed that, paradoxically, the more relaxed the framing device, the more conservative the performed outcome – and conversely, that radical performances are often enacted within more tightly framed spaces.[47] Feldman sensed this himself, commenting in 1980, 'I found that my most far-out notation repeated historical clichés in performance more than my precise notation'.[48] The problem was that performers (other than Tudor) tended to think they had more freedom than Feldman intended, falling back into cliché in the process as Schechner would have predicted.

Deleuze has written of the surprising 'deframing power' of Mondrian's later paintings (and it is no coincidence that Feldman was very interested in Mondrian),[49] suggesting that his abstract geometry possesses some paradoxical capability for breaking out of the framing canvas:

> In an abstraction of Mondrian's type, the painting ceases to be an organism or an isolated organization in order to become a division of its own surface, which must create its own relations with the divisions of the "room" in which it will be hung. In this sense, Mondrian's painting is not decorative but architectonic.[50]

As with Wolpe's understanding of 'proportions',[51] Feldman's partitions of conceptual spaces within *Intersection 3* (infolded) may also be understood as having the theoretical possibility, and implicit expression, of being folded-out beyond the defined boundaries of the score. In this sense, the clear, incisive lines of the internal structures of a work like *Intersection 3* are crucial to an appreciation of the work's effect. In performance, *Intersection 3* certainly seems to break away dramatically from its constraining notation; it has an inbuilt power for de-framing itself that derives partly from the punishing nature of the frame. Pitch-class, for example, is not eliminated by the notation – it escapes. Thinking of it in this way, it makes sense to interpret the final field of the work as incomplete, with the significant number 10 having escaped the canvas. In the context of this discussion,

---

[47]   Richard Schechner, *Performance Theory* (London: Routledge, 2005), 17–18. Originally published as *Essays on Performance Theory* (Ralph Pine, 1977).

[48]   Cole Gagne and Tracy Caras, 'Soundpieces Interview', in Chris Villars (ed.), *Morton Feldman Says*, 91.

[49]   Feldman wrote and spoke about Mondrian on many occasions. A few examples are: Morton Feldman, 'Some Elementary Questions' [1967], in B.H. Friedman (ed.), *Give My Regards to Eighth Street*, 66; 'Frank O'Hara: Lost Times and Future Hopes' [1972], in ibid., 106; 'After Modernism' [1967], in ibid., 72–3.

[50]   Gilles Deleuze, *Francis Bacon: the Logic of Sensation* (London: Continuum, 2002), 76.

[51]   Stefan Wolpe, 'On Proportions' [1960], trans. Matthew Greenbaum, *Perspectives of New Music*, 34/2 (Summer 1996), 132–84 (lecture given at Darmstadt, July 1960).

we can see that the ambiguity of whether the field is incomplete or elided is a key to understanding the simultaneously open and closed nature of the work, both folded in and folded out.

However, the comparison with Mondrian, while useful to a point, is also not entirely accurate; Mondrian's elaborately fluid, rectilinear constructions bear little relation to Feldman's primitive grid notation. There may well be a deeper connection at the compositional design level, where Feldman's constructions are similarly sophisticated. On the other hand, while there is a kind of flat-colour effect behind the scenes in Feldman's deployment of the chromatic field as a structural layer, the sounding surface of the music is rather more iridescent and mobile – more akin to the surface of an early 1950s Guston painting than to late Mondrian. Here, we can see that Feldman's work rather falls between the aesthetic worlds of abstraction on the one hand, and abstract expressionism on the other. It has characteristics of the former in terms of what Deleuze has described as a symbolic code ('This code is "digital", not in the sense of the manual, but in the sense of a finger that counts') and of the 'exclusively horizontal and vertical' space,[52] and of the latter in the way that it engages with the performative 'catastrophe', the violence of the 'exclusively manual space' which, to paraphrase Deleuze, subordinates the ear to the hand, imposes the hand on the ear, 'and replaces the horizon with a ground'.[53]

Feldman's sensitivity to this moment of 'catastrophe' in musical performance colours much of his work and concerned him throughout his career.[54] For Cage, as we have seen, the way in which Feldman's grid scores interacted with performers was of primary interest; Feldman, in clear contrast, rather shied away from this explicit confrontation. To some extent, this may have been a result of Cage's enthusiasm – certainly Feldman often made more-or-less polite efforts to distance himself from Cage's rather overpowering readings: 'it is the polemical work that becomes the spokesman for any age – like John Cage today, who many people feel speaks for me'.[55] (Note Feldman's peculiar syntax here, by which the polemical work was personified as a spokesman, and Cage by implication was objectified as a polemical work.)

In many ways, Feldman's 1950s works are concerned with testing boundaries (extremes rather than norms) – we have seen this with *Intermission 6* in terms of mobile scoring – and to some extent the various notational experiments of the 1950s and 1960s are a similar kind of test, a sounding of possibilities, delineating the boundaries of Feldman's space in the field of musical production. The shying

---

52   Gilles Deleuze, *Francis Bacon*, 73.

53   Ibid., 75.

54   As it does all composers, each in their own way. Deleuze argued that painting is the only art form in which the painter must 'pass through the catastrophe themselves'; painting thus represented for him a 'flight in advance', where in music, presumably, it is a flight at the point of performance. Ibid., 72.

55   Morton Feldman, 'After Modernism' [1967], 72.

away from the performative catastrophe is reflected, as the composer often noted himself, in his consistent use of relatively conventional staff notation from the late 1960s onward – but he also sought to connect this trajectory with the wider field. In an intriguing interview from 1980, he was recorded as saying that the grid notation was 'super for the time it was written', whereas 'I don't think it's now a time for performance, anyway. I think it's now a time for work and reflection',[56] and further, 'I think my tendency now [in 1980] toward longer and longer pieces is actually a tendency away from performance'.[57]

Although I have just been doing it, we need to be cautious about relating Feldman's notational experiments too closely to abstract expressionist painting, or indeed painting of any kind. This is not to say that there are not close connections between Feldman's music and the paintings of contemporary artists, but the true points of connection operate at a deep level, and this is what makes formal analysis so important for our developing understanding of the situation. Anecdotal and contextual evidence can only take us so far. The radical experiment of Feldman's grid scores is not in the grid (which, as we have seen, is mechanically not so very different from conventional notation), but in the very specific absence of notated pitch-classes. The notion of composition without pitch-class must have been quite shocking in 1950s New York, and it is not surprising that many other composers (including Feldman's own teacher and mentor Wolpe) found it alarming.

Crucially, however, the work is experienced with pitch-classes in performance – and in the most famous recordings we hear the notes carefully chosen by Tudor. Feldman has delegated the pitch-class decisions to the performer, which would perhaps be rather as if a painter had delegated the actual painting of a canvas to an assistant. There are artists who do such things, of course, but this would have been antithetical to the heroic, manual labour of abstract expressionism. For the painters of Feldman's acquaintance in the early 1950s, their work was very much concerned with a tactile, physical engagement with the canvas – as Deleuze suggests, 'the abstract expressionists in fact did nothing other than to make visible an exclusively manual space ... a violence done to the eye'.[58] There is an undercurrent of violence in much of Feldman's music, and it is perhaps most explicit in these 'boiling water'[59] pieces composed for Tudor, including *Intersection 3*. What is less clear is who the intended or actual victim of the violence was – the audience (to some extent, yes); the performer (yes, in terms of the imposed responsibility of decision-making and the physical and intellectual effort of performance); other composers (most certainly, and this may be sensed from their varied reactions); or perhaps even Feldman himself? If a Pollock painting is a violence to the eye, is this a violence to the ear? Not in quite the same way; Feldman the composer is somehow

---

56   Cole Gagne and Tracy Caras, 'Soundpieces Interview', 88–9.

57   Ibid., 91.

58   Gilles Deleuze, *Francis Bacon*, 75.

59   Morton Feldman, Letter to David Tudor (15 June 1953, typescript). The Getty Research Institute, Los Angeles, David Tudor Papers, 980039, Series IV, Box 53, 7.

withdrawn from this confrontation, detached. The confrontation seems to occur further back in the production of the work, rather more in the consideration and reflection than in the execution.

There is a sense in which Feldman is using the performer, and perhaps also the score, as a shield or buffer between himself and the audience. He has withdrawn behind a fence (the grid as wires) and thrown up a smoke-screen to cover his tracks. Cage, in this scenario, served a crucial purpose: his wilfully glib, self-serving and reductive analyses of Feldman's works were entirely predictable. It was not even necessary for Feldman to manipulate this; he simply stood by and watched. Cage's words and writings served a dual purpose for Feldman: they promoted his work effectively while providing the screen of privacy that seems to have been necessary for Feldman to occupy and maintain a position in the field. As a third benefit, this provided for Feldman something to push against at crucial moments of his subsequent career trajectory, when at times it was necessary to put some creative distance between himself and Cage. In 1987, for example, he said, 'Well, I had this out with John Cage. I said we didn't talk. John felt we did talk. But I thought when we did talk, it was just kind of creating a caste system, so to speak, of who was doing the real work.'[60]

In terms of the grid notation itself, which has so often drawn attention away from other aspects of the work, there are not many obvious, explicit parallels in the works of the artists around Feldman at this period. Somewhat later, we find a direct connection with the work of Jasper Johns, as Steven Johnson has shown in his groundbreaking analysis of *Why Patterns?*, but with painters such as Pollock, Guston and Rothko, any comparison must be to more subtle, implicit grids. This is yet another facet of Feldman's work that seems, on close examination, to be rather out of step with his supposed circle of influences in the abstract expressionist painting scene. The significant exception, however, is to be found in the black paintings of Robert Rauschenberg – like Johns, one of the younger generation of painters rather than of the older abstract expressionists. Feldman first met Rauschenberg as he was working on the famous black series:

> Rauschenberg was working on a series of black paintings. There was one big canvas I couldn't stop looking at.
>
> "Why don't you buy it?" Rauschenberg said.
>
> "What do you want for it?"
>
> "Whatever you've got in your pocket."

[60] Richard Wood Massi, 'Captain Cook's First Voyage: an Interview with Morton Feldman' [1987], in Chris Villars (ed.), *Morton Feldman Says*, p. 218.

I had sixteen dollars and some change, which he gleefully accepted. We immediately put the painting on top of the Model A, went back to "Bosa's Mansion" and hung it on the wall. That was how I acquired my first painting.[61]

The form and materials of Rauschenberg's black paintings vary; the one owned by Feldman is particularly interesting in that it is painted over sheets of paper glued to the canvas (in Feldman's description, 'a large black painting in which newspapers (also painted black) were glued to the canvas').[62] Over a large part of the painting centred on the upper left (cantilevered), the outlines of these sheets of paper clearly form a regular grid, visible through the surface of black paint.[63] The visit to Rauschenberg's studio took place in the spring of 1953; the painter had just returned from Europe.[64] It is difficult to narrow down the dates any more exactly, but the eerie synchronicity with the composition of *Intersection 3* in April 1953 is worth noting. It can surely be no accident that the two artists whose works most closely display an affinity with Feldman's grid notation, Johns and Rauschenberg, were also intimately involved with each other's lives and work over the next decade following their meeting in the winter of 1953–54.[65] Curiously, however, while Rauschenberg's work of the

---

[61]   Morton Feldman, 'Give My Regards to Eighth Street' [1971], in B.H. Friedman (ed.), *Give My Regards to Eighth Street*, 94.

[62]   Morton Feldman, 'Crippled Symmetry' [1981], in ibid., 146.

[63]   Reproductions of this painting may be found in ibid., xxii; and Seán Kissane (ed.), *Vertical Thoughts: Morton Feldman and the Visual Arts* (Dublin: Irish Museum of Modern Art, 2010), 68–9.

[64]   Sebastian Claren, 'A Feldman Chronology', in Chris Villars (ed.), *Morton Feldman Says*, 262. Feldman's chronology is inconsistent. In 1981, he suggested that the meeting at Rauschenberg's studio, where they were introduced by Cage, took place in late 1950 (Morton Feldman, 'Crippled Symmetry', 147). In 1971, however, he specifically mentioned the studio in Fulton Street that Rauschenberg took after returning from Europe in the spring of 1953 (Morton Feldman, 'Give My Regards to Eighth Street', 94). The date of 1950 seems too early, as many sources report that Cage and Rauschenberg first met in May/June 1951 (see, for example, Peter Gena, 'Cage and Rauschenberg: Purposeful Purposelessness meets Found Order' [1992], http://www.petergena.com/cageMCA.html), although it is surprising that they had not met earlier at Black Mountain College. As further evidence for the later date of 1953, we note that Rauschenberg completed a set of black paintings in 1952, and a further series in 1953 on his return from Europe. The picture once owned by Feldman is generally thought to be one of these latter (see Seán Kissane (ed.), *Vertical Thoughts*, 68–9).

[65]   In a late interview, Feldman made some interesting comments about the complex nature of social and professional interactions between gay and straight artists, composers and writers in 1950s New York. Richard Wood Massi, 'Captain Cook's First Voyage', pp. 218–20.

early 1950s engaged Feldman's creative imagination, it was not until the late 1970s that he began to pay serious attention to the painting of Johns.[66]

I hesitate to suggest that that there might be a direct influence in play, that these artists and their works made any direct impact upon Feldman's composition. Rather, I prefer to think of it in terms of a structural homology, a deep and important affinity between creative works that was, in such cases as the black painting and *Intersection 3*, of startling synchronicity. The composer himself, however, had no such hesitation about describing his perception of the long-lasting influence of this particular painting on his musical thinking:

> I'm looking at it now (thirty years later) as I write this. After living with this painting and studying it intensely now and then, I picked up an attitude about making something that was absolutely unique to me ... I then began to compose a music dealing precisely with "in-between-ness": creating a confusion of material and construction, and a fusion of method and application, by concentrating on how they could be directed toward "that which is difficult to categorize".[67]

In this relation between the black painting and a work like *Intersection 3* (not to mention all of Feldman's subsequent work), we can see that the composer's deepest affinity in the realm of painting is not with the older generation of abstract expressionists, with their anxious dogmatism, but rather with the younger artists like Rauschenberg and Johns. This is not to dismiss the close personal friendships with people such as Guston, but to distinguish between personal affinities and those that exist between creative works. Deleuze's penetrating analysis of the art field in this period remains useful, as he argues that it was necessary for an artist like Francis Bacon (as presumably also for Rauschenberg) to negotiate a third path between abstraction (as represented by Mondrian) on the one hand, and Abstract Expressionism (exemplified by Pollock) on the other; for Deleuze this is a path that necessitates limitation and control – neither the abstract diagram nor the 'violent methods' of abstract expressionism may be allowed to run free. This is 'a third path, which is neither optical like abstract painting, nor manual like action painting'.[68]

The musical implications of this painterly homology are obvious. Feldman had to find a path 'between categories', with the old modernist abstraction on the one hand (exemplified by the Webern/Mondrian legacy) and the also aging legacy of surreal experimentalism (Duchamp/Cage) on the other.[69] Of course these are not such easy binary oppositions as Deleuze implied; and indeed significant

---

[66] More on this in Steven Johnson (ed.), 'Jasper Johns and Morton Feldman: Why Patterns?', 218.

[67] Morton Feldman, 'Crippled Symmetry', 147.

[68] Gilles Deleuze, *Francis Bacon*, 77.

[69] See also Olivia Mattis, 'Varèse and Dada', in James Leggio (ed.), *Music and Modern Art* (New York: Routledge, 2002), 129–62.

figures like Wolpe, with his links to both Dadaism and Webern embodied complex artistic lineages. For Feldman, it was necessary to find a way to control the mixed inheritance of transcendental diagram and eruptive catastrophe. *Intersection 3* was one iteration of this larger, ongoing project.

While discussion of Feldman's work in the context of painting seems logical on account of his own personal interests and friendships, it is also useful to consider affinities with architecture of the early 1950s. In particular, there is a strong resonance between Feldman's grid notation and the iconic design of steel-framed, glass-encased skyscrapers of the period. Built in 1952, George Bunshaft's seminal Lever House on Park Avenue is an elegantly proportioned rectangle with a non-load-bearing curtain wall of glittering stainless steel and glass wrapped around it like graph paper. Structurally, the building was the first of its kind in New York, and much copied; Feldman must surely have been aware of it. Slightly later, but equally iconic, is Ludwig Mies van der Rohe's Seagram Building (designed in collaboration with Philip Johnson), just across the avenue from Lever House. Built between 1954 and 1958, it is widely considered to be a key masterpiece of the International Style, pioneering further technical innovations – and again we find the building clad in a lustrous grid, in this case of bronze and glass; beautifully dark. As with the paintings discussed above, I do not think it is possible or desirable to argue for a direct influence from one type of work on another; it is clear, however, that a remarkable and timely homology may be observed.

This homology extends beyond the grid, the facing curtain-wall, to a deeper structural and aesthetic level – but it is perhaps in the relation between surface and internal structures that we find the closest affinity with Feldman's grid music. For Mies van der Rohe, this relation between structure and surface was a crucial aspect of the style:

> Skyscrapers reveal their bold structural pattern during construction. Only then does the gigantic steel web seem impressive. When the outer walls are put in place, the structural system, which is the basis of all artistic design, is hidden by a chaos of meaningless and trivial forms.[70]

As a piece of musical architecture, *Intersection 3* is a formidable piece of work. Unlike the paintings of Feldman's friends in New York, or the famous 1950s New York City buildings of George Bunshaft and Ludwig Mies van der Rohe, however, I suggest that it has never been fully appreciated or understood. To some degree, this is both a virtue and a handicap of music as an artform; while the 'gigantic steel web' of a skyscraper is essentially a public performance (a theatre of engineering) documented with plans and photographs, the composer's structural work is private and often undocumented. This natural tendency of music towards

---

[70]   Quoted in Philip Johnson, *Mies van der Rohe* (New York: Museum of Modern Art, 1978), 187. Original source is Ludwig Mies van der Rohe, 'Hochhausprojekt für Bahnhof Friedrichstrasse in Berlin', *Frühlicht*, 1 (1922), 122–4.

concealment is exaggerated in a work like *Intersection 3*, where the fashionable and interesting surface – in this sense, grid notation (as Feldman admitted, very much of its time)[71] and seeming indeterminacy (reflecting the outside world rather like Rauschenberg's black or white paintings)[72] – effectively hinders apprehension of internal structures. Whereas the internal structure and engineering design of the Seagram Building is a matter of public record, with much information online and in architectural text-books, the concrete-clad steel core of *Intersection 3* is only apprehended through retrospective analysis. Once again, and at the risk of sounding didactic, I stress the importance of formal analysis for the contemporary study of music. Without this, we can only speak of surfaces, and if, as van der Rohe suggested, the real innovative beauty of the Seagram Building was in its inner structure (hidden from view since 1958), then there is a real likelihood that we have been missing the point of *Intersection 3* for the past 60 years.

Distinction has been made in architectural criticism and theory between the work of the 'artist' architects like Mies van der Rohe, Johnson and Bunshaft on the one hand, and commercial work on the other. Yet this also allows for such works as the Seagram Building to be seen as casting a symbolic 'veneer' of a European-derived modernist aesthetic over post-war US corporate triumphalism.[73] Even admirers of such buildings as Lever House and the Seagram Building noted concerns; the repetition of rectilinear forms had several drawbacks. As Paul Rudolph noted in 1958 (writing of the Seagram Building), 'it depends upon a very finite formalism for success, any deviation from the regularity will draw the eye and defeat the purpose'.[74] This very regularity, and the proliferation of commercial derivatives of the artist-architect's works, had by the end of the 1950s led to a sense that the style had already become tedious: 'the curtain wall has now reached its end as a transparent and reflective membrane in which surface rhythms have become a yawning bore'.[75] In such a context it makes perfect sense that Feldman's rectilinear grid had already disappeared from view after November 1953 with the completion of *Intersection 4* for cello. Like the Seagram Building, the splendour of *Intersection 3* could not bear frequent repetition.

Further, broken spaces (such as that created by the Seagram Building, set back from Park Avenue behind its grand plaza like 'a very nice Victorian lady with her

---

[71]   Cole Gagne and Tracy Caras, 'Soundpieces Interview', 88–9.

[72]   'one sees behind the canvas the wall to which it is committed; the reflective surfaces changing what is seen by means of what is happening; lights going on and off; and the radios. The white paintings were airports for the lights, shadows, and particles.' John Cage, 'On Robert Rauschenberg, artist, and his work', in *Silence*, 102.

[73]   Reinhold Martin, 'Atrocities. Or, Curtain Wall as Mass Medium', *Perspecta* 32 (2001), 66–75.

[74]   Paul Rudolph, 'To Enrich Our Architecture', *Journal of Architectural Education*, 13/1 (Spring, 1958), 10.

[75]   Albert Bush-Brown, 'The Architectural Polemic', *The Journal of Aesthetics and Art Criticism*, 18/2 (December 1959), 151.

best foot forward and great bustles bringing up the rear'),[76] while admirable as a deviation from the norm, also had the longer-term effect of destroying the larger-scale architecture of the avenue itself. The problem was not the Seagram design, but repetition of the design. This concern with street-scapes and city planning was very much a point of discussion in the 1950s, as the US embarked upon a monumental effort of highway building. Architects and architectural theorists became increasingly alarmed by the overwhelming tendency towards highway strips, 'America is witnessing a deadly struggle between a new highway culture, the culture of the strip, and a new and potentially brilliant urbanity ... The strip seems to me to be winning all the skirmishes; and I do not see how anyone can be very confident of the outcome of this aesthetic Armageddon'.[77] The whole situation of the post-war urban environment was now seen as part of the larger problem of political and aesthetic competition with the Soviet Union. John Ely Burchard made this explicit when writing in 1958, 'I think we may find a way to a good democratic taste and do a good deal to dismiss public ignorance and apathy. On all these counts even now and in the area of architecture at least our competitors in Moscow are not to be mentioned in the same breath.'[78]

None of this makes much sense without the backdrop of US politics in the period, and beyond that the wider Cold War, and likewise I do not think it is possible or desirable to separate the analysis of *Intersection 3* from the background of US politics in 1953. The brilliance, innovation and excitement of the 1950s was heavily larded with darkness and cynicism. Even the relative post-war prosperity was not unalloyed, with the US economy technically in recession during 1953–54 and again in 1957–58. Once the general public's paranoias and fears were made manifest in the Eisenhower government from 1953, such anxieties began to be enacted in security legislation. From October of 1953, Eisenhower and his government were increasingly explicit and belligerent in their advocacy for nuclear weapons, seeing them as 'as available for use as other munitions'.[79] At the same time as signing the agreements to end the Korean War in mid-1953, the US was engineering a *coup d'état* in Iran that would in August replace democratic government with the Shah's dictatorship. In the arts, this was the beginning of an escalation of the persecution of public figures deemed to be politically suspect (this often became mixed up with anti-Semitism, amongst other things) at the same time that American art and music were being exported to the world as a

---

[76]   Paul Rudolph, 'To Enrich Our Architecture', 10.

[77]   John Ely Burchard, 'The Meaning of Architecture', *The Review of Politics*, 20/3 (July 1958), 371–2.

[78]   Ibid., 371.

[79]   United States National Security Council document NSC 162/2 (30 October 1953). The document is accessible online, http://www.fas.org/irp/offdocs/nsc-hst/nsc-162-2.pdf.

weapon in the cultural Cold War.[80] Perhaps this goes some way to explaining the uneasy contradictions between Feldman's cruel, boxed-in notation of tightened frames, and the extraordinary energy of *Intersection 3* in performance. No doubt the changing structures of the political field through the early 1950s also had a bearing on the increasingly closed nature of Feldman's grid notation as it developed through this period, and perhaps also on the relative strength and clarity of the music's structural design. Adorno might have put this more strongly: perhaps the structure of Feldman's music of the 1950s was the structure of US politics.[81]

Speaking of Adorno, we are reminded inevitably of his famous suggestion (in an essay written in 1951) that: 'Cultural criticism finds itself faced with the final stage of the dialectic of culture and barbarism. To write poetry after Auschwitz is barbaric.'[82] In closing, I suggest that one useful way to understand the sounding wonder and notated horror of Feldman's *Intersection 3* is as part of a collective response to the holocaust – and that this intersects with the anxieties and contradictions of 1950s American politics. Feldman's notation is a grid of wires, a fence, a line that artificially separates; it constrains and punishes. We recall the flattened, ghostly faces of the holocaust survivors, pressed against the line of wire at Auschwitz – violently flattened, like the last fading figures in Guston's paintings of the late 1940s, passing away into an abstraction of smoke and ashes. This might seem an unnecessarily grim way of hearing Feldman's music, but I think that it is important to recognise these darker shadows – and as with the paintings of his friends, or the buildings of Bunshaft and Mies van der Rohe, that there is much more in play than simply a beautiful, glittering surface. Lynne Cooke, reviewing an exhibition of Rauschenberg's work from the early 1950s, wrote that

> Judiciously selected, the exhibition includes small groups of each type of work, with the exception of the mostly destroyed fetishes. Larger groups of the black paintings would perhaps have made for a more charged ambience, giving weight to the darker mood that is otherwise barely perceptible. Overall, this turbulent period in Rauschenberg's art deserves a more exacting scrutiny.[83]

---

[80]   For general discussions, see Frances Stonor Saunders, *Who Paid the Piper? The CIA and the Cultural Cold War* (London: Granta, 1999); Stuart D. Hobbs, *The End of the American Avant Garde* (New York: New York University Press, 1997).

[81]   Such radical conflation is most evident in relation to Adorno's thinking about sonata form. See the discussion in Robert W. Witkin, *Adorno on Music* (London: Routledge, 1998), 28–49.

[82]   Theodor Adorno, 'Cultural Criticism and Society' [1951], in *Prisms*, trans. Samuel and Sherry Weber (Cambridge, MA: MIT Press, 1983), 34.

[83]   Lynne Cooke, 'Robert Rauschenberg: The Early 1950s. San Francisco, MoMA', *The Burlington Magazine*, 134/1070 (May 1992), 336.

This is equally true of Feldman's music of the period, and all the more so when we think of that large, black Rauschenberg looming over Feldman's living room. There is so much we do not know and do not yet understand about Feldman's music, but some of it might be read, however indistinctly, in the darkly reflective surfaces of works like *Intersection 3*. Ultimately, of course, what we see might be shadowed by our own reflection – an attribute of Rauschenberg's paintings that Cage famously pointed out ('The white paintings caught whatever fell on them')[84] – but that is also in the very nature of analysis.

Dore Ashton, not only an important art critic but also a close friend to both Guston and Feldman, has reminisced,

> And I have one more thought: Morty's Jewishness. By that, I mean his propensity for thinking, as we Jews often do, on the one hand, and on the other. Such habits are far from Hegelian certitudes, and leave us open, painfully open, to the velleities of life. And above all, of art.

> On some level, some dreadfully deep level, Morty's *oeuvre* ... is the *oeuvre* of a wandering Jew.[85]

Feldman was very reluctant to speak about a sense of Jewishness in his music ('I must say you did bring up something that I particularly don't want to talk about publicly'), but he did speak about mourning ('my music is mourning, I just don't know what to say. I said just earlier, that perhaps just mourning').[86] Like the paintings of Guston and Rothko in this period, Feldman's work is a lament – perhaps also an offering, a sacrifice. *Intersection 3*, which Feldman described as part of an effort to write music like boiling water, is a powerful and challenging memorial to lost worlds as much as it is innovative. Ambiguously radical, and anxiously nostalgic, it represents an illusory, re-territorialised modernism in a post-war age where, as Feldman himself noted, music was delusion and hypocrisy, without any 'moral basis': 'to some degree I do believe for example ... that after Hitler perhaps there should no longer be art'.[87] Yet for all that, there's something beautiful alive in that unforgiving, cold frame; and we can still hear it, even now.

---

[84]   John Cage, *Silence*, 108.

[85]   Dore Ashton, 'No Way To be Mortified', in Seàn Kissane (ed.), *Vertical Thoughts*, 85.

[86]   Heinz-Klaus Metzger and Morton Feldman, 'Prolog: Über Jiddishkeit', in Walter Zimmermann (ed.), *Morton Feldman Essays* (Kerpen: Beginner Press, 1985), 7.

[87]   Ibid.

Chapter 6
Playing Feldman

Beautiful Designs

Structures of both pitch and of time in Morton Feldman's music of the early 1950s were designed and composed in identifiable ways. This has been conclusively demonstrated in each of the four analyses with regard to several levels of pitch organisation (or, in the case of *Intersection 3*, the reterritorialised mapping of pitch onto density), the time-architecture of the four works and also in terms of interactions between these structures of pitch/density and of time. The analysis has also revealed particular aspects of this organisation that are common to all four works: the fundamental 12-tone ground (or equivalent in terms of density), the proportional partitioning of time to generate both form and rhythm, the organised deployment of abstracted pitch-classes within the frame of time-structures, and also a handling of vertical space according to structuring proportions similar to those applied to the time-frame. Reinforcing the importance of the vertical space, we have observed Feldman's use of 'Wolpean' intervallic proportions as the registral surface-level deployment of pitch-classes.

To what extent may the conclusions drawn from these four studies be extrapolated to develop understanding of Feldman's work as a whole? That such distinctive commonalities have been found here between superficially dissimilar works does suggest that wider application may indeed be possible, taking into consideration other works in various forms (such as ensemble and orchestral), and from a wider period of Feldman's career. Let there be no doubt, however, that the Feldman who composed each of the works discussed here was a sophisticated, informed composer who, on his own account, resisted giving up control of musical processes and materials.[1] Stephen Johnson has pointed out that, in contrast to Cage (and indeed paraphrasing him), Feldman 'had something to say and says it'.[2] Feldman scholars, I am convinced, need no longer defend this position. Rather, the next questions to resolve are: What was Feldman saying? How did he say it? What does it mean? In this book, I have sought to contribute to the discussion of these questions on the basis of empirical examination of particular works.

---

[1]   Morton Feldman, 'Some Elementary Questions', in B.H. Friedman (ed.), *Give My Regards to Eighth Street: Collected Writings of Morton Feldman* (Cambridge, MA: Exact Change, 2000), 65.

[2]   Steven Johnson, 'Jasper Johns and Morton Feldman: *Why Patterns?*', in Steven Johnson (ed.), *The New York Schools of Music and the Visual Arts* (New York, London: Routledge, 2002), 219.

Over the past half-century, many have heard Feldman's music of the 1950s as expressive of indeterminacy, freedom and chance, or of a near-mystical, intuitive pursuit of beauty. As Jonathan Kramer wrote, Feldman 'simply put down one beautiful sound after another'.[3] Although I hear the music differently, this is not suggest that the way in which such (informed) listeners have heard Feldman's work (and discussed it) is incorrect; the situation is more complex than a simple right or wrong apprehension of the work. Cage, for example, heard what he heard in Feldman's music for very interesting reasons, and this is a whole study unto itself. The contribution that we in musicology may make is to investigate more closely, to study the widest possible range of source materials, and at the very least to argue the case for an ever more intelligent listening. In one not-so-subtle subtext, this book represents an argument for close reading and close listening as the crucial underpinnings of analytical method – hence the primary focus on only a few works.

On the basis of the analyses presented in this book, I suggest that, while this music may certainly be beautiful, and may indeed involve (constrained) elements of indeterminacy, these are only fragments of a more complex understanding. The opening chord of *Intermission 5*, for example, is not without beauty (especially in its long decay of harmonic resonance, shaped by subsequent notes), but it is also shocking and certainly impolite. Likewise, *Intermission 6* makes explicit use of a certain kind of indeterminacy in performance to generate the ordering of its sounding events – but those very sounds are so carefully chosen and the whole procedure so carefully framed, that the performer's decision-making has a relatively minor effect upon the outcome.

One of the fundamental problems is that the musical 'work' itself is notoriously elusive. I argued in introducing this book that the primary source materials are the nearest evidence we have for the existence of the work and the nature of its formal properties: scores, recordings, performances and closely associated writings. Each of these in turn is manifold, and since none of them entirely agree, none can be said to embody the work absolutely. None of the works discussed here is represented by anything so convenient as a single definitive score, and this is not unusual in musicology. Likewise, there are many ways of hearing this music, and the analysis presented in this book offers just one perspective, determined by the space of possibilities opened by my informed but necessarily personal hearing and reading of the materials – and as such it represents an early twenty-first-century perspective.

One cannot know, ultimately, what Feldman was thinking as he composed, and such speculation is not my aim in this book. We may, however, trace certain courses of action, and examine the evidence for those actions, framed by the wider mechanisms of the field. In following the trail of his sketches and manuscripts we may reconstruct patterns of decision-making to a limited extent. What those decisions mean is no longer for Feldman to say, but entirely our responsibility.

---

3   Quoted in ibid., 217.

Transformations

In the four works discussed here, structural organisation has been revealed through several methods of analysis. One of these involves the detailed study of the marks upon the page, most especially with regard to Feldman's manuscripts. The examination of primary sources has revealed, among other things, that Feldman did rework and revise his pieces after the initial sketch was made, often several times and sometimes drastically. This study has thus uncovered hitherto 'lost' parts of these works, like the dismembered first movement of *Piano Piece 1952* and the deleted 'moments' of *Intermission 6*. Without doubt, Feldman had his own reasons for making such changes – this does not render the material any less interesting and, in particular, it is in this investigative space that aspects of Feldman's decision-making reveal themselves.

One important stage of Feldman's composition process is what I think of as a moment of ambiguation. In both *Piano Piece 1952* and *Intermission 6*, crucial and dramatic decisions were made that partially conceal the fundamental structures of the works; in the former, one half of an explicit, planned dialectic was deleted while in the other the composed material was torn up and redistributed in dismembered form on the page. By the early 1960s when these pieces were prepared for publication, Feldman apparently felt that it was necessary to conceal certain aspects of the ideology and construction of his early 1950s works. Harold Rosenberg coined the phrase 'discipline of vagueness' to describe a certain aspect of New York painting of the early 1950s.[4] In the case of Feldman, and what I propose as a moment of ambiguation ('moment', because an element of compositional process), we are perhaps witnessing literally the reverse: a vagueing of discipline.

It is evident from my choice of words (dismembered, deleted, torn) that I consider some of these creative decisions to represent, in some sense, acts of implicit violence. There is, in such radical retooling of the structuring mechanisms and drastic modification of design, an aspect of creative vandalism. This is not to suggest that I consider the initial sketches to be superior to later forms of the work (or indeed vice versa – they are of equal interest), simply that we should recognise this destructive element as characteristic of Feldman's compositional practice at certain moments. Such vandalism, revisionism, dismembering – or whatever we wish to call it – is integral to the very substance of two of the four case studies discussed.

Richard Schechner has written of 'deconstruction/reconstruction' processes as they affect performance.[5] Specifically, he argues that

---

[4]   Harold Rosenberg, 'The American Action Painters', in Ellen Landau (ed.), *Reading Abstract Expressionism: Context and Critique* (New Haven, CT: Yale University Press, 2005), 194.

[5]   Richard Schechner, *Performance Theory* (London: Routledge, 2003), 321 (2nd edn, 1988).

> The external artwork – the performance the spectators see – is the visible
> result of a trialog among: 1) the conventions or givens of a genre, 2) the
> stretching, distorting, or innovation of new conventions, and 3) brain-centred
> psychophysical transformations of self.[6]

There is much that might be discussed in relation to these three ideas, but
what interests me here is this: that in this view we may understand Feldman's
compositional processes, in so far as we observe them in analysis, as performative.
In composing his initial sketch, Feldman was enacting certain conventions
of genre and also establishing conventions of design for that particular work.
Making revisions, at later stages, Feldman was not only stretching, distorting and
redesigning those 'conventional' structures, but implementing new ones – and
the significance of these lies at least partly in their relationships, the network of
frames.[7]

In examining the rare recordings of Feldman performing, in conjunction
with those of his close colleague and favoured interpreter (at least of the period
in question) David Tudor, we have observed further fascinating complications.
Neither of them, for example, played *Intermission 5* as it is notated in the published
score we know today. This is particularly interesting in so far as Feldman's own
recording post-dates publication by more than a decade – so this may hardly be
considered an early draft version. On this evidence, we may argue that as late as
the mid-1970s the work was undergoing further distortion and deformation. This
is a very important point even in a more general sense, because indeed none of
these works sounds today as they did in the 1950s. Each has taken a trajectory
of its own, changing its form, sound and meaning. Even if it were possible to
generate literally the sounds that, for example, Berio heard at a performance of
Piano Piece 1952 in 1952,[8] we in the twenty-first century cannot hear what he
heard. We have only small clues as to what the work may have meant to him, and
how it sounded to his ears.

Music is not, of course, necessarily heard; it may be seen, felt and
imagined. The kinetic sensation of playing Feldman's music does suggest
that he composed using the piano itself as a tool in many instances. The very
mechanics of the human body's interaction with the keyboard is one of the
structuring frames of *Piano Piece 1952*, with its design concept based upon
the alternation of hands, and there are aspects of keyboard ergonomics clearly
evident in all four works discussed. Many years later, Feldman would lecture

---

[6]   Ibid.

[7]   Ibid., 14–18.

[8]   Christian Wolff, 'The Sound Doesn't Look Back (1995): On Morton Feldman's
Piano Piece 1952', http://www.cnvill.net/mfwolff2.htm#wolff5. Originally published in
Christian Wolff, *Cues: Writings and Conversations* (Köln: MusikTexte, 1998), 370–78.

younger composers 'Know thy instrument! You can't orchestrate unless you know thy instrument. Know thy instrument!'[9]

More than this, however, the works are to a large extent mental apprehensions (I hesitate to use the word 'images', although this would not necessarily be inappropriate). It is in the space of one's own mind that the musical work is experienced and takes form and meaning upon itself. I can 'hear' *Intermission 6* now, as I write these words, but the only sound in the room is that of the office air-conditioning. The piece in my aural imagination sounds like the published score, the sketch, and the Tudor manuscript somehow all at once. I can, of course, 'tune in' to any one of these, but the others always hover in the wings. I argue for a 'listening' that is as broadly informed as possible: the work we apprehend is ineffably complex to the point of seeming incommunicable, yet we do 'hear' it. Presented in this book are only a few aspects of my hearing of these four works, translated to a literary form and framed by a secondary literature produced by other 'listeners'.

The 'work' is perhaps an interface between us and an 'other' – or, just as likely, between us and a mirror. Yet, to pursue this conceit, it is a mirror that was made by a certain skilled craftsman, and his created work (as form and structure) frames, shapes and colours our view of the reflection. In this, perhaps, we touch upon the third part of Schechner's triadic model of performance: the 'brain-centred psychophysical transformations of self'.[10] The meaning of the work may be a reflection of our own mind, but the mirror is nonetheless structured and framed by the maker. The reflection of ourselves in the perceived work is not truly us, any more than the work is absolutely Feldman's – somewhere in the relational matrix between, perhaps, is the music.

Materials and Methods

What are the forms and structures that we may identify in these works as having been 'manufactured' by Feldman, in the conventional understanding? Firstly, each of these works (even, surprisingly, *Intersection 3*) has been shown to be fundamentally concerned with the manipulation of the total chromatic, and sub-sets drawn from it; the music is not serial but nevertheless structured entirely out of a 12-tone sensibility. Even in his grid scores he was unable to give this up, translating the principles to another set of materials. This overwhelming sensitivity to the circulation and completion of the 12-tone aggregate, and to the relations between the total aggregate and particular subsets, may also be heard in Feldman's late works. Listen, for example, to the impeccably staged, gradual unfolding of the chromatic field in the first six pages of *For Bunita Marcus* (1985).

---

[9]   Morton Feldman, 'XXX Anecdotes & Drawings', in Walter Zimmermann (ed.), *Morton Feldman Essays* (Kerpen: Beginner Press, 1985), 194.

[10]   Richard Schechner, *Performance Theory*, 321.

In such instances, it is as though we are hearing the structures of *Intermission 5* reversed: rather than drawing a pitch-class set (and motif) out of the ground of the total chromatic, *For Bunita Marcus* begins with a small pitch-class set (clarified by repetition) around which Feldman gradually conjures the field. In case there should be any doubt of Feldman's design, he recapitulates the opening set once the field is complete. Thus, we may also observe that, in the late works, the small repetition-sets may be explicitly motivic and at the same time used for structural purposes as fragments unhinged from the chromatic field.

Despite their great differences (most particularly of scale), such clear material and procedural connections between Feldman's early and late works are distinctly audible. In 1984, Feldman himself spoke explicitly about the importance of the chromatic field, the motif and the relation between the two on one of the very rare occasions when his technical observations were recorded:

> I'm trying to balance, a kind of coexistence between the chromatic field and those notes selected from the chromatic field that are not in the chromatic series. And so I'm involved like a painter, involved with gradations within the chromatic world. And the reason I do this is to have the ear make these trips. Back and forth, and it gets more saturated. But I work very much like a painter, insofar as I'm watching the phenomena and I'm thickening and I'm thinning and I'm working in that way and just watching what it needs. I mean, I have the skill to hear it.[11]

A moment later Feldman added,

> So essentially I am working with three notes and of course we have to use the other notes. But the other notes are like shadows of the basic notes. So then all I have to decide is where I'm going to start on the three notes, chromatic, you know.[12]

These, I would suggest, are the most important sentences in all of Feldman's recorded words. While we must remain alert to the fact that he was here speaking more than 30 years after first sketching the compositions discussed in this book, the correspondence between these statements and the basic structures observed in the 1950s work is extraordinary. Within a two-dimensional conception of musical structure ('I work very much like a painter'), Feldman spoke of constructing a work out of the binary relation between the chromatic field and a smaller set partitioned from it. This is absolutely fundamental to the understanding of Feldman's work developed in this book, and offers a coherent way of explaining Feldman's use of motif, and also of the more subtle weighting of the aggregate field. Always, the field follows the chosen set like a shadow – indeed, 'we have to use the other

---

[11]   Morton Feldman, 'XXX Anecdotes & Drawings', 183–4.

[12]   Ibid., 184–5.

notes'. Here the underlying principles of Feldman's musical language are exposed more clearly than in any other of his public statements. It is easy to understand, in this context, how Feldman's musical language could so comfortably accommodate occasionally explicit 12-tone rows;[13] and, perhaps more importantly, why various kinds of matrix chart became useful for the composer in managing the pitch materials of the late works (as seen in the substantial surviving sketch materials).

Furthermore, the three-note set of which Feldman spoke was not any kind of set but a chromatic set – illustrated on a blackboard during the lecture quoted above.[14] We have seen in the analyses of this book that chromatic sets (more usually of four pitch-classes) are crucially important in each of the four works studied. See, for example, the closing section of *Intermission 5* and the opening chord (as sketched) of *Intermission 6*. The three-note set Feldman used to illustrate the lecture is identical to that which opens *For Bunita Marcus* (C♯, D, E♭). More strikingly, the slow, impeccably staged conjuring of the chromatic field in *For Bunita Marcus* takes place according to an ordered design (new pitch-classes introduced are chromatically adjacent to the expanding set of those previously heard). In Chapter 4, a similar procedure was observed in the opening section of *Intermission 6*, as it was originally sketched – the field was expanded by adding notes chromatically adjacent to a previously established chromatic set. There are clear points of procedural continuity between even these two very different works, composed 30 years apart. Thus, we may observe that, in the late works (as with the 1950s pieces), the small repetition-sets and the process of aggregate completions are integral to the structural design.

As the chromatic field is truly the ground of Feldman's work, so the partitioning of the pitch-class content of the total chromatic into smaller, organised sets is both the mid-level structure and in many cases the very surface of the music (as, for example, in the closing section of *Intermission 5*), just as the planned partitioning of time serves to structure both form and rhythm/duration. In detailing the observable partitions of time in the four analyses, it has become evident that Feldman favoured a few simple proportions in determining the placement of significant structures; most particularly, we find in each work crucial proportions of 1:1, 1:2 and 1:3, often on several levels of activity (subdivisions of divisions).

Further to this, I have shown that the vertical partitioning of the pitch-space was developed with a sensitivity to very similar proportions. Thus we may make sense of Feldman's understanding of musical materials as 'crystalline' forms, shaped and held in place by the conceptual axes of pitch over time. In this proportional structuring of interlocking formations, we have observed clear echoes of Wolpe's and Varèse's thinking, crucially suggesting that Feldman's technical apparatus may also have been more closely related to theirs than Cage's.

---

[13] See Chapter 2, footnote 57 for more information.

[14] Morton Feldman, 'XXX Anecdotes & Drawings', 185.

Intermission: Feldman and Varèse

On 28 December 1966, John Cage and Morton Feldman were on the radio in New York, having a conversation:

> Feldman: "Well, don't you think that, for example, like Varèse was to us here in New York, perhaps, what Webern was to them in Europe?"

> Cage: "... he could have been, but I don't think he was for the reason that we didn't know how he did what he was doing."[15]

I cannot help but wonder, what if Feldman *did* know what Varèse was doing? The evidence for direct contact between Varèse and Feldman is mostly in Feldman's own writings, lectures and interviews. (Varèse, as far as I know, never wrote or spoke of Feldman directly in any way that has been passed down to us.) Reading through Feldman's writings, lectures and interviews, we find that Varèse is one of the composers mentioned most often (perhaps out-done only by John Cage), and over the full period of Feldman's working life. Feldman's very first published essay, in fact, was about Varèse, and he was still talking about the man and his music in 1987, the year of his death. I note this, because other figures come and go from Feldman's field of interest. Even Cage, it is fair to say, was not always someone Feldman represented as being of current musical interest; he often appears in Feldman's writings and lectures rather as a supporting character in stories of Feldman's own early life. Further to this, I note that Feldman was consistently admiring of Varèse – which again is not really true of any other composer mentioned in his writings.

Feldman tells us that he met Varèse shortly after finishing high-school, sometime in the late 1940s. Their first meeting seems to have been at the home of Stefan Wolpe.[16] Wolpe and Varèse knew each other well, and according to Feldman, were close friends.[17] Frustratingly, despite claiming to have met with Varèse on an almost weekly basis, Feldman does not give much indication of exactly what it was they talked about.[18] However, this is not so unusual – the same

---

[15]   Morton Feldman and John Cage, *Radio Happenings: Conversations – Gespräche*, trans. Gisela Gronemeyer (Köln: MusikTexte, 1993), 99.

[16]   Austin Clarkson, 'Conversation about Stefan Wolpe: 13 November 1980', in Chris Villars, *Morton Feldman Says: Selected Interviews and Lectures 1964–1987* (London: Hyphen Press, 2006), 107.

[17]   Ibid.

[18]   Morton Feldman, 'Darmstadt Lecture, July 1984', in Chris Villars, *Morton Feldman Says*, 196. There is unfortunately little corroborating evidence for these weekly meetings. The Paul Sacher Stiftung holds a series of Varèse's diaries for the period of the late 1940s and early 1950s (they are perhaps better described as appointment-books than diaries) – but they contain no mention of Feldman. On the other hand, the two men must certainly have

might be said to some extent of his reminiscences of his teachers, Riegger and Wolpe. So we are left with mere fragments of corroborating evidence for meetings between Feldman and Varèse: the art critic Dore Ashton, for example, tells us that Feldman sometimes took Varèse to visit the studio of his friend Philip Guston in the early 1950s.[19]

Turning our attention from the personal contact, what did Feldman have to say about Varèse's music? Here is a sample from 1958:

> Sound is all our dreams of music. Noise is music's dreams of us. And those moments when one loses control, and the sound like crystals forms its own planes, and with a thrust there is no sound, no tone, no sentiment, nothing left but the significance of our first breath – such is the music of Varèse. He alone has given us this elegance, this physical reality.[20]

There are two things I want to draw out of this quote – in particular, there is the emphasis on sonority, and indeed thinking beyond sonority. This was a lifelong preoccupation for Feldman, and runs as a strong current through all his writings. Secondly, I note the use of the word 'crystals'. Of course, this has a strong resonance for a great deal of 12-tone music in the period after the war – particularly for those composers interested in Webern, as Feldman certainly was. More importantly, though, for the present study, it is a term Feldman uses with reference to his own work. As early as 1952, as we noted in Chapter 1, he had written in a sketchbook: 'music exists as crystalline formations in a two dimensional space'.[21]

This is a crucial point of contact between Varèse's and Feldman's musical thinking: both spoke about their music in terms of crystalline formations, and formations operating on interactive, intersecting planes. Yet whereas Varèse used to speak of three or four dimensions of music space (Milton Babbitt went further to make five),[22] Feldman admits only two: pitch over time. (Recall that in Feldman's sketchbooks he tends to treat 'pitch' and 'timbre' as interchangeable terms.) So, while inheriting the pre-war modernist language of musical space and geometry, Feldman adopted a post-war abstract expressionist approach to the picture plane – he took the older model and squashed it flat.

---

seen each other around town – on at least some occasions they were at the same parties, or attending the same new-music events, mixing very much in the same circles. So, while there was certainly direct contact between the two composers, the true nature and extent of communication is rather harder to establish.

[19]   Dore Ashton, *Yes, but ...: A Critical Study of Philip Guston* (New York: Viking Press, 1976), 95.

[20]   Morton Feldman, 'Sound, Noise, Varèse, Boulez', in B.H. Friedman (ed.), *Give My Regards to Eighth Street*, 2.

[21]   Paul Sacher Foundation, Basel, Morton Feldman Collection.

[22]   Milton Babbitt, 'Who Cares if You Listen?', *High Fidelity*, 8 (February 1958), 38–40.

In 1986, only a year before his death, Feldman wrote, 'I want to thank Edgard Varèse for the insight on how to separate skills from models and aesthetics.'[23] Feldman had a lifelong suspicion of pure technique for its own sake, and it is striking that he attributed this to Varèse's influence. Feldman's position is most markedly observed in his frequent denunciations of those composers he considered to have abandoned the intensity of detailed decision-making to a controlling system. This is not to say that he was not interested in technical matters – he retained a lifelong interest in serial technique, for example, although the true extent of his applied use of serial procedures has only become clear since his death, with the access we now have to his sketches.

There are certainly many aspects of Feldman's music that point to influences from Varèse. On a superficial level, many titles of his works reflect Varèsian preoccupations: there are *Projections*, *Intersections*, *Durations*, and so on. More importantly, we may note a similar concern with symmetry and balance – but then this was also of prime importance to Wolpe, so not necessarily attributable to Varèse directly. Yet what of the deeper technical processes and structures of the music itself? Is there any evidence that Feldman may have cracked the code of Varèse's work, and if so how did this affect his own music?

One of Varèse's works seems to have had a special significance for Feldman. This is *Déserts*, composed in the period 1950–54. I am sure that it is no coincidence that this is exactly the period when Feldman was (apparently) seeing Varèse often. Of course, Feldman often mentioned other Varèse works, but I think it is notable that *Déserts* is a work he gave analytical lectures about later in life, and that he would use in classes with his composition students.[24]

A single page of analytical notes on *Déserts* has recently been identified among Feldman's papers in Basel. The page in question is associated with sketches for his orchestral work *The Turfan Fragments*, composed in 1980.[25] In this analysis, Feldman was taking apart the opening pages of *Déserts*, looking specifically at the unfolding of the total chromatic. He did not find 12-tone rows, but a remarkably regular rate of aggregate completion. Furthermore, he discovered some interesting patterns in these chromatic cycles that show that Varèse was not only working with a highly developed sensitivity to the rate of aggregate deployment and also aggregate completion – but also that these aspects of the pitch material were carefully and consciously managed. The pitch-classes are not strictly ordered in the manner of a row, but certainly subsets of the aggregate recur in the manner of motivic cells. Most striking is this: that in each cycle (or 'set' as Feldman described them, somewhat inappropriately) the pitch-classes appear in different registers to those of the previous cycle – with the dramatic exception of the last note in each,

[23]   Morton Feldman, 'I want to Thank' [1986], in B.H. Friedman (ed.), *Give My Regards to Eighth Street*, 202.

[24]   See for example, Sebastian Claren, 'A Feldman Chronology', in Chris Villars, *Morton Feldman Says*, 272.

[25]   Paul Sacher Foundation, Basel, Morton Feldman Collection.

which repeats the register of its appearance in the previous cycle. Feldman called this a 'cadence'.

Feldman's analysis of this opening section of *Déserts* reveals a deep structure of regular aggregate completions – a rhythmic breathing in and out of the chromatic field. Each concludes with a phrase-ending formula – Feldman's use of the term cadence is here not inappropriate – which links a particular pitch event back to the preceding phrase. The pitch material of the work unfolds, in this view, rather like a chain of interlocked fields of activity. Examples of the carefully structured deployment of pitch materials over time abound in Feldman's later music, as in the earlier works discussed in this book. We may refer, to give one such example, to the opening pages of *The Turfan Fragments* (1980) itself. Here, Feldman fills 10 pages with a four-note chromatic set, introducing the completion of the total chromatic abruptly at rehearsal mark 15, the 1:5 partition of the works' real-time duration.

As well as organising the unfolding of the 12-tone aggregate over determined time spans, Feldman's late works also show a careful control of fixed and movable registers, and while never exactly the same as what Varèse did in *Déserts*, the underlying principles are comparable. Here then, I would argue, we are beginning to see the 'models and aesthetics' for which Feldman thanked Varèse.[26] While specifics of the musical language, and details of technique, may vary from piece to piece, one aesthetic principle remains constant: it consists of a highly developed and sensitive approach to the deployment of the 12-tone aggregate over time.[27]

Of course, Feldman's analysis accounted for only two of Varèse's three or four musical dimensions – there is much going on in *Déserts* that seems not to interest Feldman. Feldman's musical aesthetic, then, may be seen as a radically compressed variant of Varèse's: the model is stripped bare, pared back to what Feldman saw as the fundamental materials of music – pitch and time.

We have observed the same manner of controlled deployment of chromatic fields over carefully designed time-spaces in Feldman's pieces dating from around 1951–52, while the traditional myths tell us that this is the period when Feldman fell completely under the spell of Cage. More importantly, I would argue, he was working in the shadow of Varèse. Thinking back to that radio conversation with Cage in 1966, I would suggest that Feldman did most certainly know what Varèse was doing in his work of the early 1950s, and he knew about it at the time. On the basis of musical evidence alone, I think we can safely conjecture that Feldman

[26] Morton Feldman, 'I want to Thank', 202.

[27] In the recently revealed sketches for *Déserts*, we find pages of serial matrices. Although there is little evidence of this material in the finished form of the work, we can see that Varèse and Feldman were both interested in the potential of serial techniques for generating material at a certain stage of the composition process. Denise von Glahn, 'The Conceptual Origins of *Déserts*', in Felix Meyer and Heidy Zimmermann (eds), *Edgard Varèse: Composer Sound Sculptor Visionary* (Woodbridge: The Boydell Press, 2006), 304.

was indeed talking to Varèse at this period, and that their conversations must have included detailed discussion of Varèse's compositional procedures.

This examination of the relation between these two composers is not only valuable for our understanding of Feldman's music; we also learn something about Varèse. When Feldman talked about Varèse, or analysed his music, he was trying to tell us how he heard Varèse. He was trying to tell us about the things in Varèse's music that he thought were most important, giving us the clues that he thought we needed. This is not to say that Feldman's analysis as it survives is in any way ideal or complete – but it does point us forward from Cage's position of wilful ignorance. For Cage, Varèse was rather irrelevant because he did not understand (or chose not to understand) how the music was made. For Feldman, it was of crucial and lifelong importance – and he did, at the very least, try to understand.

Public and Private Spaces

In addressing the subsidiary theme of Feldman's place in the field of cultural production as it was in New York of the early 1950s, it is apparent that a full analysis is much beyond the scope of the present study. Nevertheless, the reader will be aware that I have in this book sketched what might be understood as a preliminary outline of such an investigation. Central to this is a revisionist approach to the understanding of Feldman's immediate circle. John Cage, for example, while clearly a powerful figure in Feldman's life and with a certain influence over Feldman's career trajectory, exerted much less direct influence over Feldman's work than has been commonly supposed. In contrast, analysis of Feldman's 1952 works shows explicit structural, technical and aesthetic connection with the work of Riegger, Varèse, and Stefan Wolpe in particular. Wolpe's description of the basic procedures of 12-tone composition, as we saw in Chapter 2, bears a close likeness to the actual structures observed in the works analysed here:

> Every pitch constellation smaller than the all-chromatic circuit is either a delay in completing the whole, or is an autonomous fragment which can exist outside the total circuit. It may be first unhinged as a part of the total circuit, later hinged back.[28]

In my general appreciation of Feldman as fundamentally a 12-tone composer, I am also suggesting that, on this ground alone, his work is more closely allied with other 12-tone composers (whether serial or not) than with the more radical experimentalists of the 1950s and 1960s. His long-lasting respect for Babbitt as

---

[28]   Stefan Wolpe, 'Thinking Twice' [1959], in Elliott Schwartz and Barney Childs (eds), *Contemporary Composers On Contemporary Music* (New York: Holt, Rinehart and Winston, 1967), 287.

a composer is just one manifestation of this subtle affinity.[29] Certainly, in 1950 Feldman had anticipated that Babbitt would understand his early work for string quartet, only showing the work to Cage when this failed (and then with a less-than-honest obfuscation regarding how it was made).[30] In such events, and more importantly, Feldman's telling of such stories, we may begin to map the positions available to Feldman in the field, and the positions he would eventually take, together with the linking trajectories. Among Feldman's personal papers are numerous notes for classes and seminars at SUNY Buffalo; among the composers whose works Feldman discussed analytically were Webern and Babbitt.[31]

As an aside to this argument concerning the importance of 12-tone serialism in Feldman's aesthetic and intellectual milieu, it is interesting to note that as early as 1948 the critic Clement Greenberg had drawn parallels between the 'polyphonic' aspect of Schoenberg's 12-tone music and Jackson Pollock's all-over paintings.[32] This correlation between the deployment of an intricate 'chromatic field' and abstract expressionist painting was reiterated in 1959, by the poet Frank O'Hara, in an essay on Feldman's music. O'Hara was well aware of Feldman's antipathy toward serial systems (as he noted in the same essay), but nonetheless made this perceptive comparison: 'we find that making the analogy between certain allover paintings of Jackson Pollock and the serial technique of Webern clarifies the one by means of the other'.[33] Although he tactfully stops short of directly linking Feldman to either Pollock (who had recently died) or Webern, it is nonetheless clear that O'Hara had divined the essentially 12-tone flavour of Feldman's musical language.

In terms of musical materials and compositional procedure, I propose that among the experimental composers of 1950s New York, Feldman was as much a conservative modernist as radical experimentalist. This is manifest in many ways, perhaps most obviously in his use of conventional instruments and his resistance to experimental playing techniques such as Cagean preparation or Cowell's playing inside the piano. Similarly, while he may have 'invented' the graphic score for his generation of composers, his use of it as a notational vehicle was almost

---

[29] For one excellent example of Feldman's admiration for Babbitt's music, refer to the interview conducted by Charles Shere for radio KPFA. Charles Shere and Morton Feldman, *Interview with Morton Feldman, July 1967*, http://radiom.org/detail. php?omid=C.1967.07.01.

[30] Morton Feldman, 'Liner Notes' [1962], in B.H. Friedman (ed.), *Give My Regards to Eighth Street*, 4.

[31] Paul Sacher Foundation, Basel, Morton Feldman Collection.

[32] Clement Greenberg, 'The Crisis of the Easel Picture' [1948], in *Art and Culture: Critical Essays* (Boston, MA: Beacon Press, 1965), 156–7. For discussion of this in relation to Feldman, see Ulrike Rausch, *Grenzgänge: Musik und Bildende Kunst im New York der 50er Jahre* (Saarbrücken: Pfau-Verlag, 1999), 42–3.

[33] Frank O'Hara, 'New Directions in Music: Morton Feldman', in B.H. Friedman (ed.), *Give My Regards to Eighth Street*, 211.

perversely restricted and conservative when compared with those who took up the idea subsequently (Brown, Bussotti and Cardew, for example).

In his valuable study of Francis Bacon, Deleuze considers three essential 'invisible' forces in Bacon's work: isolation, deformation and dissipation.[34] These three forces are in striking parallel to the forces I have argued are at work in Feldman's music, and Deleuze's theoretical basis for the reading of such forces is apposite, reminding us also of Bourdieu:

> Since the visible movements of the figures are subordinated to the invisible forces exerted upon them, we can go behind the movements to these forces, and make an empirical list of the forces.[35]

Such 'visible' elements of Feldman's work may be similarly understood to reveal the activity of deeper forces. In this way, the formal attributes of Feldman's music may be understood to have implications beyond the works themselves, and to relate (either homological or rhizomatically) to broader structures of the musical, social, economic and political. In the course of analytical discussions, I have shown that it is both fruitful and appropriate to read Feldman's structures as active rather than passive, designed rather than indeterminate; the space in which he acts is both tensioned and ambiguous and Feldman's own activity is structured by this space. The definition of this space is the creative 'insecurity' (to use Feldman's own word) that is so important to my understanding of his work. We have also seen that it was Feldman's understanding of art that it should in some way stand apart from everyday life and society – the 'intermission' was not an empty space but rather a space of action, framed by oppositions.[36] This has far-reaching political and social ramifications, and is perhaps also related to Feldman's later annoyance with popular music in public spaces, which he felt interfered with the work of an artist 'deep in thought', invading his private creative space.[37] Feldman's deep thought is not democratic, nor is it anarchic in the sense that perhaps certain aspects of Wolpe's or Cage's thinking might be understood; it is the romantic deep thought of the artist as philosopher-aristocrat. As Feldman ironically observed, Wolpe's 'man in the street' turned out to be Jackson Pollock.[38]

---

[34]   Gilles Deleuze, *Francis Bacon: The Logic of Sensation* [1981], trans. Daniel W. Smith (London: Continuum, 2003), 44–5.

[35]   Ibid., 44.

[36]   Similarly, Feldman once explained that the title *Intersection*, derived from the idea that musical materials might be placed anywhere in the middle of the time span, and not just worked from beginning to end. The beginning and the end remain, however, the defining frame, and the piece exists 'between a green light and a red light'. Morton Feldman, 'XXX Anecdotes & Drawings', 158.

[37]   Morton Feldman and John Cage, *Radio Happenings: Conversations – Gespräche*, trans. Gisela Gronemeyer (Köln: MusikTexte, 1993), 17.

[38]   Morton Feldman, 'XXX Anecdotes & Drawings', 186.

Feldman was interested in a Nietzschean artistic 'distinction', and in the effort to sustain musical thought as an individual exercise of will.[39] Yet occasionally he would allow others to interfere, to a very limited degree, with the internal structures of his works. Crucially, however, Feldman was best satisfied when it was David Tudor as performer who did the interfering – never the audience, and not just any performer.[40] Even this seeming indeterminacy was not everyone's freedom (in a democratic sense), but a carefully defined space in which a specialist performer who understood the essential properties of Feldman's music might be allowed a certain discretion: Feldman trusted Tudor to choose the right notes. Rather than exercising their own will freely, the performer is able to act only within parameters defined by the composer – the performer's decision-making is in fact manipulated by Feldman and thus constitutes part of his instrument.

Clearly, there was an important social aspect to Feldman's music production of the 1950s. There was not much of an audience for his work at this time, beyond a circle of friends, and friends of friends – just as David Tudor was the trusted, authoritative performer, this was music dependent upon a close (arguably even closed) social space. Artists like Rauschenberg and Guston were not merely friends but an important part of Feldman's audience. Robert Rauschenberg invited Feldman to perform a recital of his own compositions at the opening of the exhibition of 'Red Paintings' at the Charles Egan Gallery, in 1955[41] – an action that has several levels of significance, not least of which is that of patronage. The complicated web of connections between Feldman and the world of the visual arts was not only philosophical and aesthetic, but structural and (to an extent) economic.[42]

Feldman's work, then, resonates within a space defined by powerful forces, tensions and ambiguities. Many of these may be seen to be part of the wider tensions of the time, in terms of society and politics. One example is in the curious tension, also evident with the abstract expressionists, of the emphasis on the 'now moment' of artistic expression, while at the same time seeming to champion a

[39] Stuart Morgan, 'Pie-Slicing and Small Moves: Morton Feldman in Conversation with Stuart Morgan' [1977], in Chris Villars (ed.), *Morton Feldman Says*, 84.

[40] In this sense it is interesting to compare Feldman's discussion of the problems of graphic scores in performance with the 1953 letter written to David Tudor. Morton Feldman, 'Liner Notes', in B.H. Friedman (ed.), *Give My Regards to Eighth Street*, 6; The Getty Research Institute, Los Angeles, David Tudor Papers, 980039, Box 53, f., http://www.getty.edu/research/conducting_research/digitized_collections/davidtudor/zoom/zoom_grl_tudor33l.html (letter written by Morton Feldman to David Tudor, 1953).

[41] Sebastian Claren, *Neither: Die Musik Morton Feldmans* (Hofheim: Wolke, 2000), 530.

[42] Reciprocally, Feldman bought paintings from several artist-friends in the early 1950s (Rauschenberg, Guston) and was also given a Pollock drawing in return for composing music for the Hans Namuth film. See B.H. Friedman, 'Morton Feldman: Painting Sounds', in B.H. Friedman (ed.), *Give My Regards to Eighth Street*, xii.

utopian modernist past. In this also are strong resonances of a European/American tension that is not resolved but integral to the work as a structural ambiguity. Yet, within this creatively energised and active space (between oppositions of past/ present, European/American, conservative/radical, modernist/post-modernist), Feldman seems to have taken a position of relative balance, and one senses that the ambiguity in his work is in some ways a protective device, and his 'intermezzo' (to use Deleuze and Guatarri's word) a safe-zone constructed between confrontational forces.

His is a 12-tone music without (for the most part) noticeable ordered rows, it is experimental yet built from conventional sounds, ideologically presenting itself in the now moment of the 1950s ('the sound doesn't look back', said Christian Wolff)[43] yet inescapably not simply the 'sound of the sound itself'.[44] The analysis presented in this book has shown that Feldman would sometimes go to extreme lengths to maintain the ambiguity of his work, deleting the explicitly gestural first part of *Piano Piece 1952*, and utterly dis-articulating *Intermission 6*. This is indeed a matter of covering tracks, concealing structural underpinnings, censoring elements of a dialectic. Through this vandalism of his own pieces, Feldman worked to create and maintain the protective zone of in-betweenness. In Bourdieu's model, such actions are never merely personal intent, but reflect aspects of the nature of Feldman's position in the field, and the structure of the field.

We may begin to recognise just how perceptive was Wolpe's critique of the emphatic vagueness of Feldman's 1950s work, and of the crucial importance of this calculated ambiguity: 'He [Feldman] is interested in surfaces that are as spare as possible and in the remnants of shapes that are barely heard at a distance. Can I express this more precisely? No!'[45] Spare and barely heard Feldman's figures may be, but to Wolpe's ears these were not necessarily passive or pleasant, but rather a 'diabolical test of beauty';[46] they are akin to the steamrollered ghosts of Auschwitz in Ashton's haunted, nightmarish understanding of Guston's paintings.

This brings us to one of the most significant aspects of this research: the discovery of Feldman's two-dimensional model of musical structure as expressed in his early 1950s sketchbooks. This simple diagrammatic model has offered significant insight into the structures of Feldman's music and, more importantly than anything it might suggest to us about Feldman's intentions, this offers a way of modelling the analysis of his work in a manner that is consistent with the views expressed in his writings and interviews. This enables us, in a sense, to triangulate the analysis of Feldman's music with the analysis of his words, and also the paintings of friends and colleagues like Guston. Here, for the first time, we

---

[43]   Christian Wolff, 'The Sound Doesn't Look Back', 370–78.

[44]   Catherine Hirata, *Analyzing the Music of Morton Feldman* (PhD Dissertation, Columbia University, 2003), 32–3.

[45]   Stefan Wolpe, 'On New (And Not-so-New) Music in America' [1956], ed. Austin Clarkson, *Journal of Music Theory*, 1/28 (Spring 1984), 25.

[46]   Ibid.

have a conceptual mechanism for the formal, structural comparison of music and painting; the pitch- and time-axes of Feldman's model were designed for the very purpose of describing a conceptual, two-dimensional musical canvas. With benefit of hindsight and with the results of analysis in hand, we can now appreciate more clearly what Feldman was trying to tell us about his work in this rare moment of plain speaking:

> The new painting made me desirous of a sound world more direct, more immediate, more physical than anything that had existed before. To me my score is my canvas, my space. What I do is try to sensitize this area – this time-space. The reality of clock-time comes later in performance, but not in the making of the composition. In the making of a composition the time is frozen. The time structure is more or less in vision before I begin. I know I need eight or ten minutes as an artist needs five yards of canvas.[47]

Despite this, however, it must be admitted that direct comparison between art forms of a very different substance should be developed cautiously. To this end, I have in this book concentrated upon a few aspects of the works discussed that seemed to lend themselves most directly to such analysis. If the notion of 'quietness' in Feldman's music, for example, is taken to refer to something other than just dynamic level, then we may perhaps draw a connection to the relatively muted colour of Guston's early 1950s palette. Certainly, Guston's work is not entirely without strong colouring, any more than Feldman's is without loud sounds, yet a certain tendency may be identified.

Similarly, the notion of 'flatness' in abstract expressionist paintings, and of the flattened picture-plane, is a more complex subject than it sounds. There are, nonetheless, direct echoes of this in Feldman's conceptual modelling ('space is an illusion'),[48] and this enables us to begin observing correlations between his work and that of the painters. Importantly, this notion of flatness has a complex theoretical and philosophical framework in terms of art history, and is strongly associated with the formalist criticism of Clement Greenberg. At the same time, we have seen that other critics of abstract expressionist painting read the flatness as having very specific contextual and historical meanings. Dore Ashton, as we have seen, wrote in some detail of the flat picture-plane in Guston's work as emblematic of the holocaust, and of her belief that it expressed Guston's thinking on this subject.

The point here is not that this is necessarily true in any absolute sense, but that it offers an insight, at once contextual and structural, into the thinking of several of Feldman's closest friends, and their understanding of certain works. Feldman did not often speak of such matters as the holocaust, yet it is inconceivable that a

---

[47] Quoted in Joseph Machlis, *Introduction to Contemporary Music: a Guide to the Understanding of 20th Century Music* (London: J.M. Dent and Son, 1963), 633–4.

[48] Sketchbook annotation. Paul Sacher Foundation, Basel, Morton Feldman Collection.

subject so important to his own family and so many of his friends and colleagues had no impact upon his work, even tangentially. As late as 1959, Feldman's friend Mark Rothko refused to have his work exhibited in Germany unless it took the form of a memorial – in which case he offered to paint it without a fee.[49] (As an alternative to the other labels we give to Feldman's music – experimental, atonal, New York School, post-modern and so forth – a strong case may be made for reading and hearing Feldman as primarily a post-holocaust composer.)

It is problematic, even using Feldman's model, to draw direct connections between the finer details of Feldman's musical organisation and equivalent structures in the painting of his colleagues. I have, however, shown that parallels may be drawn at a macro-structure level between the strong, simple proportions of Feldman's partitioning of musical space and the manner in which both Guston and Franz Kline partitioned the canvas at this period. In support of this analysis, we may note that Feldman himself claimed that both these painters understood colour to be an 'intrusion', and that the formal, structural elements of their work were of primary concern.[50] By establishing that there is indeed a homology on this level between the music and the painting, I aim to pave the way for future studies to explore the cross-artform analysis in greater depth and detail. Finally, I suggest that two concepts are essential to an understanding of Feldman's early 1950s work: his interest in 'symmetry and design', and the relation between 'colour' and form (sound-events placed in time).

A Beginning

This book contributes to the ongoing exploration of Feldman's work through a close examination of four pieces from a crucial period of Feldman's career, a mere moment upon the trajectory of his life's work. The incorporation of early drafts, sketches and other manuscripts, together with primary source documents and recordings, is a unique aspect of this study in the arena of Feldman studies, in terms of both content and methodology – and the examination of this material has brought many new insights. There are still those who doubt the relevance of sketch studies, but I would argue that, as the study of such materials has so clearly the capability to deeply affect the ways in which we read, perform, listen and (to echo Dora Hanninen) think the music, any argument in favour of ignoring them must be noted with a certain scepticism.

As explained in the introductory chapter, the scope of this work is deliberately narrow in terms of time-period and works analysed. My approach is based upon a determination to work from particulars, and each chapter follows this pattern; wider philosophical or aesthetic discussions grow out of the effort to apprehend

---

[49]   Dore Ashton, *About Rothko* [1983] (Cambridge, MA: Da Capo Press, 2003), 178.

[50]   Morton Feldman, 'A Compositional Problem', in B.H. Friedman (ed.), *Give My Regards to Eighth Street*, 110.

specific aspects of particular works. I have noted at several points in this study that it should be considered as preliminary, and in writing this closing chapter I cannot help but think of the closing words of Catherine Hirata's dissertation, 'As I said a moment ago, it's a beginning'.[51] Hirata and I have this in common (and not only this): the certain knowledge that there is still so much work to do; that we understand so little about Feldman's music.

I would argue further that, as long as this remains the case, we cannot claim to understand the field in which he worked, and thus our understandings of Cage, of Boulez, of Guston, of Stockhausen (and the list spirals outwards into the haze of a conceptual horizon) all require constant reassessment. Even this is not the end of the matter, for if our understanding of the structures and mechanisms of the field of cultural production (which in Bourdieu's terms defined the space and structures of Feldman's work) are so desperately limited, so too is our understanding of the wider contingent fields of social, political and economic forces. At this point, musicology (in the broader sense that includes music analysis) at its most particular, with uniquely privileged source materials, may be shown to have the capacity to make an essential contribution to the wider humanities. Given the necessary nature of this book, as a beginning rather than a comprehensive study, I have endeavoured at certain points to indicate areas of study that may be fruitfully investigated in future research. I revisit these here in order to close with an outward-looking stance, as we turn from the particularities of the present study to the wider, general field – but also as a final framing of the content and structure of this present work.

Firstly, I would suggest that the relations between Feldman's works and those of his immediate circle of so-called 'New York School'[52] composers (Cage, Brown, Wolff and Tudor, in particular) have been shown here to be more complex than many earlier studies allow. I think that this area demands further analysis on two levels: that of the comparative analysis of works, and that of the analysis of the social, economic and political relations between the persons. A great deal of what we think we know about these people and their works, especially in relation to the 1950s period, is on close examination shown to be largely anecdotal or even mythological. Ongoing archival work to complement the stories with documentation is crucial, not least in the not-so-simple matter of establishing a working chronology.

This present research has also produced many significant indicators that relations between people to some extent on the margins of the supposed inner circle of New York School composers (I am thinking here, with respect to the 1950s, of Wolpe, Varèse, Babbitt, Riegger, Boulez and Stockhausen) are of great importance in understanding Feldman and, more importantly, understanding his work. This has been noted in passing by previous writers (Christopher Hasty, for

---

[51]   Catherine Hirata, *Analyzing the Music of Morton Feldman*, 272.

[52]   This label, although in common usage, is unwieldy and problematic – I have generally avoided it for these reasons.

example, has noted that 'Morton Feldman, in his own particular way, followed Wolpe's example quite beautifully'),[53] but I would argue for a broad-based and rigorous effort to unravel this network of creative agents and works. Furthermore, the names I have suggested above are the obvious ones – the people we already know to be significant. I am more than a little concerned by the thought that there might be other, equally significant agents in this field whose names, for one reason or another, we do not associate with Feldman, or have forgotten altogether. Where, for example, were the women? This is no idle rhetorical question, but something that should be a real concern; why does it seem that there were no Elaine de Koonings, Lee Krasners or Helen Frankenthalers in the musical field? Were they truly absent (if so, how and why?), or is there a crippling blind-spot in our analytical equipment?

In this book, I have frequently drawn attention to certain aspects of the explicit relationship between Feldman's music and that of Wolpe and Varèse. It is clear, however, that much more research and analysis needs to be done on this subject to clarify the connections in more detail, and to identify more specifically the tensions in this relationship, as evident in the work. This is a project that may be carried out in several directions, but I would suggest that serious examination of Feldman's 1940s music (for example the startling *Illusions* of 1948), composed under Wolpe's direct influence, should be one of the priorities of Feldman research.

Equally important is the continuing investigation of Feldman's relations with the world of the visual arts (as has been noted by many previous writers, most significantly Johnson, Bernard, Rausch, Claren and Borio). I propose that, while the ongoing documentation of personal, aesthetic and philosophical connections is vital, we must just as urgently work to document and theorise the structural homologies between Feldman's work and that of the visual artists close to him in the field of cultural production. While Feldman's connections with the world of painting have been much discussed (perhaps even too much), I suggest that the potential homologies with the work of the New York poets of the 1950s are also a fruitful but neglected field of investigation. John Ashbery, for example, cultivated an interest in contemporary music,[54] while Frank O'Hara was (unlikely as it seems) a friend of Feldman's and among the more perceptive of his early

---

[53]   The quotation in context reads, 'The quality of Wolpe's music I will draw attention to here is the vividness or particularity of its detail – the creation of luminous moments alive with individual, particular character. Such particularity is by no means Wolpe's alone, but I think Wolpe cultivated this quality with an intensity and consistency rare among his contemporaries. (In this regard, Morton Feldman, in his own particular way, followed Wolpe's example quite beautifully.)' Christopher Hasty, 'Broken Sequences: Fragmentation, Abundance, Beauty', *Perspectives of New Music*, 40/2 (Summer 2002), 157.

[54]   Geoff Ward, *Statutes of Liberty: The New York School of Poets*, 2nd edn (Basingstoke: Palgrave, 2001), 112.

critics.[55] Indeed, O'Hara and Feldman seem to have taken a keen interest in each other's work, to the extent that it may, in future studies, be necessary to investigate their relationship as a foil to that of Feldman and Guston. As with the visual arts, the key question in terms of musicology is whether, in addition to the personal connections, there are homologies at a structural level between the works. Given the tension between 'accident and design' that was such a key aspect of O'Hara's work,[56] we may expect that there may indeed be deep connections between his and Feldman's respective works, yet to be revealed by analysis. In this respect, my analysis of *Intermission 6* might serve as a starting point.

Operating behind all the surface activity of painting, music and writing are the complex forces of two fields of power: the economic and the political. Future studies must eventually examine closely the economics of musical production in 1950s New York. Bluntly, who actually paid the bills? Why? To a large extent, Feldman's career trajectory may be mapped by documenting the financial apparatus supporting his work in the public arena, moving from the support of individual friends like Cage, Tudor and Rauschenberg to a greater dependence upon institutional grants, teaching salaries and funded commissions. Two crucial junctures in this regard require close attention: the circumstances and effects of the publishing contract with Peters (1962), and Feldman's appointment to a professorial chair at SUNY Buffalo (1972). The documentation and analysis of these should not be considered as simply biographical or contextual but, as I argued in the introductory chapter, aspects of the analysis of the work itself. Feldman understood the political implications of his changing position in the field with surprising clarity and prescience, writing in the late 1960s,

> It's not that easy for me to talk to young composers or young painters and give them a sermon about the world. But this particular sermon is part of the lesson. The fact that people like me are now being quietly kicked "upstairs" makes this sermon doubly necessary. It wouldn't be long before I'll be up there so high in the establishment – that no matter how loud I shout – you'll not hear my voice at all.[57]

Bourdieu has described this 'trajectory leading from the avant-garde to consecration' as one of the obvious mechanisms of the field of cultural production, a symptom of the relatively non-commercial cultural producer 'growing old' in

[55] O'Hara, Frank. 'New Directions in Music: Morton Feldman' [1959], in B.H. Friedman (ed.), *Give My Regards to Eighth Street*, 211–17.

[56] Geoff Ward, *Statutes of Liberty: the New York School of Poets*, 36–82.

[57] Morton Feldman, *Four Lectures: New York Style* (unpublished manuscript *ca* 1967/68), Paul Sacher Foundation, Basel, Morton Feldman Collection.

the field.[58] Feldman was keenly aware that his generation of (supposed) avant-garde radicals was rapidly becoming the institutional establishment, and while passages like that quoted above indicate that he understood the process, there is little evidence that he did not welcome it. One further point must be raised on this subject: that the field of direct and indirect US government patronage of the arts (and the political implications of this in the cold war context) has been the subject of several studies.[59] There is much yet to discover in this area, however, and close study of this in relation to the musical field of the 1950s and 1960s will no doubt continue to be revealing in terms of undercurrents of finance, power, patronage and politics.[60]

Hearing, Thinking, Playing

I hear the four case studies presented here as abstract works, yet inhabited by the ghosts of nearly recognisable figures, 'shadows' that flicker in the corners of our ears, and the backs of our minds. I do hear each of these pieces as beautiful in a general sense, but it is a beauty alloyed with loss and sadness, anxiety and insecurity. At times, the music does seem to float away from conventional foundations … and yet the quality of floatingness seems to me to be made possible by the inherent tensions of Feldman's conceptual structures. This designed tension, architecturally, is what keeps his 'buildings' from falling to the ground. 'Without the system', he said, 'it falls on the floor'.[61] Like Feldman's birds, these sounds are never truly free:

> Artists talk a lot about freedom. So, recalling the expression "free as a bird,"
> Morton Feldman went to a park one day and spent some time watching our

---

[58] Pierre Bourdieu, 'The Production of Belief' [1977], in Randal Johnson (ed.), *The Field Of Cultural Production: Essays on Art and Literature* (New York: Columbia University Press, 1993), 104.

[59] Frances Stonor Saunders, *Who Paid the Piper? The CIA and the Cultural Cold War* (London: Granta, 1999); Stuart D. Hobbs, *The End of the American Avant Garde* (New York: New York University Press, 1997).

[60] Some work has been done in this area, for example Amy Beal, *New Music, New Allies: American Music in West Germany from the Zero Hour to Reunification* (Berkeley, CA: University of California Press, 2006); and also Anne C. Shreffler, 'Ideologies of Serialism: Stravinsky's *Threni* and the Congress for Cultural Freedom', in Karol Berger and Anthony Newcomb (eds), *Music and the Aesthetics of Modernity* (Cambridge, MA: Harvard University Press, 2005).

[61] Morton Feldman, 'The Future of Local Music' [1984], in B.H. Friedman (ed.), *Give My Regards to Eighth Street*, 183.

feathered friends. When he came back, he said, "You know? They're not free: they're fighting over bits of food".[62]

A kind of flatness is apparent in Feldman's work, but it is a flatness akin to the richly textured, many-figured flatness of a Pollock painting. Furthermore, I prefer to think of Feldman's music as flattened rather than flat, because I understand it as the product of a significant process of flattening (a 'resultant', as Varèse would have said).[63] Is the music quiet? Often, yes – however it is not simply a quietness of loud or soft, but something more sophisticated. It is a quietness of speaking in measured tones, of keeping one's temper under control (or in the vivid case of *Intermission 5*, bringing it under control). In some works, like *Intersection 3*, the music boils (to use Feldman's own metaphor) but never boils over – it is constrained by a strong and beautiful structural design.

Despite their wonders, Feldman's gloriously vast late works are both literally and conceptually painful, and the early music is not so dissimilar as the outward surfaces might suggest. *Piano Piece 1952* might be relatively short, but it has a similar sensation of subtle violence: it is slow, and it is quiet, but once the piece is commenced we (performer and listener alike) are snared in a grimly beautiful trap of Feldman's devising, and we are at his mercy, waiting (patiently or impatiently) for the mechanism to be released at the end.

Not everyone will hear this music in quite the way I do, and neither should they. I do hope, however, that this research contributes to the complication of Feldman's work, because music is complicated and, paradoxically, the most significant elucidation will always be that which adds to the complexity of our understanding. As the American modernist poet Wallace Stevens observed, at a time when Feldman was still a child, 'Everything is complicated; if that were not so, life and poetry and everything else would be a bore'.[64]

Writing of the explorer and adventurer Henry Morton Stanley, Jason Roberts recently noted that 'it is impossible to view [him] plain. One must filter his image through two distorting prisms, that of his era and that of our own.'[65] I wonder if it is possible to translate this historian's cliché to a sound-based analogy, better suited to our discussion of Feldman? I imagine the sound of Feldman's music distorted, compressed and translated through one of those 'telephones' of tin-cans and string that children used to play with, in the days before MP3 players. Actually, a chain of

[62]   John Cage, 'Indeterminacy' [1959], in *Silence: Lectures and Writings by John Cage* (Middletown, CT: Wesleyan University Press, 1961), 265.

[63]   Edgard Varèse, 'Rhythm, Form, Content' [1959], in Elliott Schwartz and Barney Childs (eds), *Contemporary Composers on Contemporary Music*, 203.

[64]   Wallace Stevens (Letter, 19 December 1935), in Holly Stevens (ed.), *Letters of Wallace Stevens* (New York: A.A. Knopf, 1966), 303.

[65]   Jason Roberts, 'The Great Opportunist: Don't Presume you Know the Strange Truth about Henry Morton Stanley', *The Washington Post* (23 December 2007), http://www.washingtonpost.com/wp-dyn/content/article/2007/12/21/AR2007122100158_pf.html.

two of them, like the two prisms: one representing the 1950s and one the present. This analogy highlights the fact that, while the sounds reach us only through the dual distorting frames and mediating forces of Feldman's own time and ours, we can hear something – and that is the wonder of it, ultimately.

Dora Hanninen asked, 'What is it about Feldman's music? If we can hear it, can we find ways to "think it"?'[66] I would answer with words borrowed from John Cage (who, despite my efforts to prise open a space between his views and the works discussed here, must be acknowledged as a wise musician):

> the music is difficuLt
> > to Play
> > > wE must work at it[67]

Cage was here writing in memory of Wolpe, but the words apply equally well to Feldman's music. I like to think that Cage meant the sense of 'play' to include more than the obvious, but including, as I have in this book, the 'play' of composition, of performance, of listening, of analysis, of Hanninen's thinking. In this broad sense, the play of music is fundamental to human experience and, as Schechner observed, represents a process by which order is improvised.[68]

---

[66]   Dora Hanninen, 'Feldman, Analysis, Experience', *Twentieth-century Music*, 1/2 (2004), 250.

[67]   John Cage, 'In Memoriam S.W.', in *M: Writings '67–'72* (Middletown, CT: Wesleyan University Press, 1973).

[68]   Richard Schechner, *Performance Theory*, 104.

Bibliography

Manuscript Sources

Music Library, University at Buffalo, The State University of New York Buffalo, C.F. Peters Collection of Morton Feldman Manuscripts, 1961–69, Mus. Arc. 2.4, Box 1, 16 (manuscript master copy of *Intersection 6*, made for publication, 1962).

Music Library, University at Buffalo, The State University of New York Buffalo, C.F. Peters Collection of Morton Feldman Manuscripts, 1961–69, Mus. Arc. 2.4, Box 1, 27 (manuscript master copy of *Piano Piece 1952*, made for publication, 1962).

Music Library, University at Buffalo, The State University of New York Buffalo, C.F. Peters Collection of Morton Feldman Manuscripts, 1961–69, Mus. Arc. 2.4, Box 1, 34 (manuscript master copy of *Intermission 6*, made for publication, 1962).

Music Library, University at Buffalo, The State University of New York Buffalo, C.F. Peters Collection of Morton Feldman Manuscripts, 1961–69, Mus. Arc. 2.4, Box 1, 41 (manuscript master copy of *Intermission 5* made for publication, 1962).

Paul Sacher Foundation, Basel, Morton Feldman Collection. The collection includes sketch materials and early drafts of almost all works of the 1950s period, correspondence and other personal papers.

The Getty Research Institute, Los Angeles, David Tudor Papers, 980039, Series Ib, Box 9, 24 (an early manuscript copy of *Intermission 5*).

The Getty Research Institute, Los Angeles, David Tudor Papers, 980039, Series Ib, Box 9, 26b (two early manuscripts of *Intersection 3*, and Tudor's realisation).

The Getty Research Institute, Los Angeles, David Tudor Papers, 980039, Series Ib, Box 186, 4 (two early manuscripts of *Intermission 6*).

The Getty Research Institute, Los Angeles, David Tudor Papers, 980039, Series Ib, Box 186, 6 (early copy of *Piano Piece 1952*).

The Getty Research Institute, Los Angeles, David Tudor Papers, 980039, Series IV, Box 53, 7 (letter written by Morton Feldman to David Tudor, 1953), http://www.getty.edu/research/conducting_research/digitized_collections/davidtudor/zoom/zoom_grl_tudor33l.html.

The Getty Research Institute, Los Angeles, David Tudor Papers, 980039, Series VIa, Box 70 (program note for a recital given by David Tudor at the University of Illinois on 22 March 1953), also at http://www.cnvill.net/mftitles.htm.

The Getty Research Institute, Los Angeles, David Tudor Papers, 980039, Series
VIa, Box 70 (concert program, Tudor's first performance of Boulez's *2nd
Piano Sonata*, 17 December 1950), http://www.getty.edu/research/conducting_
research/digitized_collections/davidtudor/zoom/zoom_grl_tudor27l.html.

Published Sources

Adams, Margaret O'Neill, 'Punch Card Records: Precursors of Electronic
Records', *The American Archivist*, 58/2, Special Issue on Case Studies (Spring,
1995), 182–201.
Adorno, Theodor, 'Cultural Criticism and Society' [1951], trans. Samuel and
Sherry Weber, in *Prisms* (Cambridge, MA: MIT Press, 1983).
Ames, Paula, 'Piano (1977)', in Thomas DeLio (ed.), *The Music of Morton
Feldman* (Westport, CT: Greenwood Press, 1996), 99–143.
Ashton, Dore, 'New York: Feldman's Music', *Canadian Art*, 21 (January 1964),
48.
Ashton, Dore, *Yes, but ...: A Critical Study of Philip Guston* (New York: Viking
Press, 1976).
Ashton, Dore, *About Rothko* [1983] (Cambridge, MA: Da Capo Press, 2003)
Ashton, Dore, 'Stefan Wolpe – Man of Temperament', in Austin Clarkson (ed.),
On the Music of Stefan Wolpe: Essays and Recollections (Hillsdale, NY:
Pendragon Press, 2003).
Ashton, Dore, 'No Way To be Mortified', in Seàn Kissane (ed.), *Vertical Thoughts:
Morton Feldman and the Visual Arts* (Dublin: Irish Museum of Modern Art,
2010).
Babbitt, Milton, *Recollections of Stefan Wolpe*, http://www.wolpe.org/page1/
page10/page10.html#Milton%20Babbitt.
Babbitt, Milton, *Words about Music*, ed. Stephen Dembski and Joseph N. Strauss
(Madison, WI: University of Wisconsin Press, 1987).
Baigell, Matthew, *Artist and Identity in Twentieth-century America* (Cambridge:
Cambridge University Press, 2001), 232–42.
Baldridge, Wilson. 'Morton Feldman: One Whose Reality is Acoustic',
Perspectives of New Music, 21/1–2 (1982/83), 112–13.
Barras, Vincent, 'Une interprétation de la musique de Morton Feldman', *Dissonanz
– Dissonance*, 25 (1990), 11–15.
Beal, Amy, '"Time Canvases": Morton Feldman and the Painters of the New York
School', in James Leggio (ed.), *Music and Modern Art* (London: Routledge,
2001).
Beal, Amy, *New Music, New Allies: American Music in West Germany from the
Zero Hour to Reunification* (Berkeley, CA: University of California Press,
2006).

Beckett, Alan, '*International Times* Interview' [1966], in Chris Villars (ed.), *Morton Feldman Says: Selected Interviews and Lectures 1964–1987* (London: Hyphen Press, 2006).

Behrman, David, 'What Indeterminate Notation Determines', in Benjamin Boretz and Edward T. Cone (eds), *Perspectives on Notation and Performance* (New York: W.W. Norton, 1976), 74–89.

Berger, Karol, 'Time's Arrow and the Advent of Musical Modernity', in Karol Berger and Anthony Newcomb (eds), *Music and the Aesthetics of Modernity: Essays* (Cambridge, MA: Harvard University Press, 2005).

Berger, Karol and Anthony Newcomb (eds), *Music and the Aesthetics of Modernity: Essays* (Cambridge, MA: Harvard University Press, 2005)

Bernard, Jonathan, 'Feldman's Painters', in Steven Johnson (ed.), *The New York Schools of Music and the Visual Arts* (New York: Routledge, 2002).

Bernstein, David W., 'Cage and High Modernism', in David Nicholls (ed.), *The Cambridge Companion to John Cage* (Cambridge: Cambridge University Press, 2002), 204–5.

Bohlman, Philip, 'Ontologies of Music', in Nicholas Cook and Mark Everist (eds), *Rethinking Music* (Oxford: Oxford University Press, 1999).

Borio, Gianmario, 'Morton Feldman e l'Espressionismo astratto: La costruzione di tempo e suono nelle miniature pianistiche degli anni Cinquanta e Sessanta', in *Itinerari della musica americana* (Lucca: Una Cosa Rara, 1996), 119–34, http://www.cnvill.demon.co.uk/mfborio.htm.

Böttinger, Peter, 'Das exakte Ungefähre: Ein analytischer Versuch über *Instruments I* (1974) von Morton Feldman', *Musik-Konzepte*, 48/49 (Munich: Edition Text + Kritik, 1986), 105–14.

Boulez, Pierre, 'Letter from Pierre Boulez to John Cage: May 1950', in *The Boulez–Cage Correspondence*, ed. Jean-Jacques Nattiez, trans. and ed. Robert Samuels (Cambridge: Cambridge University Press, 1993).

Boulez, Pierre, 'Letter from Pierre Boulez to John Cage: August 1951', in *The Boulez–Cage Correspondence*, ed. Jean-Jacques Nattiez, trans. and ed. Robert Samuels (Cambridge: Cambridge University Press, 1993).

Boulez, Pierre, 'Morton Feldman's Projections: Origins, Development, and Spin' (unpublished) paper presented at *American Musicological Society Conference* (San Francisco, CA, 2011).

Bourdieu, Pierre, 'Field of Power, Literary Field and Habitus' [1986], in Randal Johnson (ed.), *The Field Of Cultural Production: Essays on Art and Literature* (New York: Columbia University Press, 1993).

Bourdieu, Pierre, 'Principles for a Sociology of Cultural Works' [1986], in Randal Johnson (ed.), *The Field Of Cultural Production: Essays on Art and Literature* (New York: Columbia University Press, 1993).

Bourdieu, Pierre, 'The Field of Cultural Production, or: The Economic World Reversed' [1983], in Randal Johnson (ed.), *The Field Of Cultural Production: Essays on Art and Literature* (New York: Columbia University Press, 1993).

Bourdieu, Pierre, 'The Production of Belief' [1977], in Randal Johnson (ed.), *The Field Of Cultural Production: Essays on Art and Literature* (New York: Columbia University Press, 1993).

Boutwell, Brett, *A Static Sublime: Morton Feldman and the Visual 1950–1970* (PhD Dissertation, University of Illinois, 2006).

Bredekamp, Horst, 'John Cage and the Principle of Chance', in Karol Berger and Anthony Newcomb (eds), *Music and the Aesthetics of Modernity* (Cambridge, MA: Harvard University Press, 2005).

Burchard, John Ely, 'The Meaning of Architecture', *The Review of Politics*, 20/3 (July 1958), 358–72.

Bush-Brown, Albert, 'The Architectural Polemic', *The Journal of Aesthetics and Art Criticism*, 18/2 (December 1959), 143–58.

Cage, John, 'Composition as Process' [three lectures given at Darmstadt, 1958], in *Silence: Lectures and Writings by John Cage* (Middletown, CT: Wesleyan University Press, 1961).

Cage, John, 'Indeterminacy', in *Silence: Lectures and Writings by John Cage* (Middletown, CT: Wesleyan University Press, 1961).

Cage, John, 'Lecture on Nothing' [1949/50], in *Silence: Lectures and Writings by John Cage* (Middletown, CT: Wesleyan University Press, 1961).

Cage, John, 'Lecture on Something' [1950/51], in *Silence: Lectures and Writings by John Cage* (Middletown, CT: Wesleyan University Press, 1961).

Cage, John, *Silence: Lectures and Writings by John Cage* (Middletown, CT: Wesleyan University Press, 1961).

Cage, John, 'On Robert Rauschenberg, artist, and his work', in *Silence: Lectures and Writings* (London: Marion Boyars, 1968).

Cage, John, 'Juilliard Lecture' [1952], in *A Year From Monday* (Middletown, CT: Wesleyan University Press, 1969).

Cage, John, 'In Memoriam S.W.', in *M: Writings '67–'72* (Middletown, CT: Wesleyan University Press, 1973).

Cage, John, 'Letter from John Cage to Pierre Boulez: summer 1951', in *The Boulez–Cage Correspondence*, ed. Jean-Jacques Nattiez, trans. and ed. Robert Samuels (Cambridge: Cambridge University Press, 1993).

Cage, John and Morton Feldman. *Radio Happenings: Conversations – Gespräche*, trans. Gisela Gronemeyer (Köln: MusikTexte, 1993).

Carter, Elliott, *Recollections of Stefan Wolpe*, http://www.wolpe.org/page1/page10/page10.html#Elliott%20Carter.

Charlton, David and Jolyon Laycock, 'An Interview with Morton Feldman' [1966], in Chris Villars (ed.), *Morton Feldman Says: Selected Interviews and Lectures 1964–1987* (London: Hyphen Press, 2006).

Claren, Sebastian, *Neither: Die Musik Morton Feldmans* (Hofheim: Wolke, 2000).

Claren, Sebastian, 'A Feldman Chronology', in Chris Villars (ed.), *Morton Feldman Says: Selected Interviews and Lectures 1964–1987* (London: Hyphen Press, 2006).

Clark, Philip, 'Morton Feldman', in Rob Young (ed.), *The Wire Primers: A Guide to Modern Music* (London: Verso: 2009), 165–72.

Clarkson, Austin, 'Stefan Wolpe and Abstract Expressionism', in Steven Johnson (ed.), *The New York Schools of Music and Visual Arts* (New York: Routledge, 2002).

Clarkson, Austin (ed.), *On the Music of Stefan Wolpe: Essays and Recollections* (Hillsdale, NY: Pendragon Press, 2003).

Clarkson, Austin, 'Conversation about Stefan Wolpe: 13 November 1980', in Chris Villars (ed.), *Morton Feldman Says: Selected Interviews and Lectures 1964–1987* (London: Hyphen Press, 2006).

Cooke, Lynne, 'Robert Rauschenberg: The Early 1950s. San Francisco, MoMA', in *The Burlington Magazine*, 134/1070 (May 1992), 336.

Cowell, Henry, 'Current Chronicle', *The Musical Quarterly*, 38/1 (January 1952), 123–36.

Cowell, Henry, 'Wallingford Riegger: *String Quartet No. 1*, Op. 30' [review], *Notes*, 2nd Series, 3/4 (June 1947), 358–9.

Dabrovski, Magdalena, *The Drawings of Philip Guston* (New York: The Museum of Modern Art, New York, 1988).

Dahlhaus, Carl, 'Tonality: Structure or Process?', in *Schoenberg and the New Music*, trans. Derrick Puffett and Alfred Clayton (Cambridge: Cambridge University Press, 1987).

DeLio, Thomas, 'Toward an Art of Imminence: Morton Feldman's *Durations III*, No. 3', *Interface*, 12/3 (1983), 465–80. Reprinted in Thomas DeLio, *Circumscribing the Open Universe* (Lanham, MD: University Press of America, 1983), 29–47.

DeLio, Thomas, '*Last Pieces* #3 (1959)', in Thomas DeLio (ed.), *The Music of Morton Feldman* (Westport, CT: Greenwood Press, 1996).

DeLio, Thomas (ed.), *The Music of Morton Feldman* (Westport, CT: Greenwood Press, 1996).

Deleuze, Gilles, *Francis Bacon: the Logic of Sensation* (London: Continuum, 2002).

Deleuze, Gilles and Félix Guattari, *A Thousand Plateaus: Capitalism and Schizophrenia* [1980], trans. Brian Massumi (London: Continuum, 2004).

De Visscher, Éric, 'Surfaces de temps. À propos de Morton Feldman', in Fabien Lévy (ed.), *Les écritures du temps (musique, rythme, etc.)* (Paris: L'Harmattan [Les cahiers de l'Ircam], 2001), 141–53.

Dickinson, Peter, 'Feldman Explains Himself During His First Visit to Europe in 1966', in Chris Villars (ed.), *Morton Feldman Says: Selected Interviews and Lectures 1964–1987* (London: Hyphen Press, 2006).

Dohoney, Ryan W., '"Allying necessity with unpredictability": Morton Feldman's Early Music and Ideologies of Abstraction', paper presented at the *Annual Meeting of the American Musicological Society*, Quebec City (Canada), 1–4 November 2007.

Dorian, Frederick, 'Wallingford Riegger: *Symphony No. 3* for orchestra' [review], *Notes*, 2nd Series, 4/6 (September 1949), 637–8.

Dufallo, Richard, *Trackings: Composers Speak with Richard Dufallo* (New York: Oxford University Press, 1989).

Erdmann, Martin, 'Zusammenhang und Losigkeit: Zu Morton Feldmans Kompositionen zwischen 1950 und 1956', *Musik-Konzepte*, 48/49 (Munich: Edition Text + Kritik, 1986), 67–94.

Feldman, Barbara Monk, 'Music and the Picture Plane: Poussin's *Pyramus and Thisbe* and Morton Feldman's *For Philip Guston*', *Res: Journal of Anthropology and Aesthetics*, 32 (Autumn 1997).

Feldman, Morton, '*Illusions*' [*ca* 1948], *New Music. A Quarterly of Modern Composition*, 23/4 (October 1951).

Feldman, Morton, *Intermission 5* (New York: Edition Peters, 1962).

Feldman, Morton, *Intersection 3* (New York: Edition Peters, 1962).

Feldman, Morton, *Piano Piece 1952* (New York: Edition Peters, 1962).

Feldman, Morton, *Intermission 6* (New York: Edition Peters, 1963).

Feldman, Morton, '*Marginal Intersection* (1951), *Intersection 2* (1951), *Intermission 6*', *Kulchur*, 3/11 (Autumn 1963).

Feldman, Morton, 'XXX Anecdotes & Drawings', in Walter Zimmermann (ed.), *Morton Feldman Essays* (Kerpen: Beginner Press, 1985) [transcribed by Gerhard Westerrath from a seminar given in Frankfurt, 1984; trans. Hanfried Blume].

Feldman, Morton, 'A Compositional Problem' [1972], in B.H. Friedman (ed.), *Give My Regards to Eighth Street: Collected Writings of Morton Feldman* (Cambridge, MA: Exact Change, 2000).

Feldman, Morton, 'A Life Without Bach and Beethoven' [1964], in B.H. Friedman (ed.), *Give My Regards to Eighth Street: Collected Writings of Morton Feldman* (Cambridge, MA: Exact Change, 2000).

Feldman, Morton, 'After Modernism' [1967], in B.H. Friedman (ed.), *Give My Regards to Eighth Street: Collected Writings of Morton Feldman* (Cambridge, MA: Exact Change, 2000).

Feldman, Morton, 'Between Categories' [1969], in B.H. Friedman (ed.), *Give My Regards to Eighth Street: Collected Writings of Morton Feldman* (Cambridge, MA: Exact Change, 2000).

Feldman, Morton, 'Conversations Without Stravinsky' [1967], in B.H. Friedman (ed.), *Give My Regards to Eighth Street: Collected Writings of Morton Feldman* (Cambridge, MA: Exact Change, 2000).

Feldman, Morton, 'Crippled Symmetry' [1981], in B.H. Friedman (ed.), *Give My Regards to Eighth Street: Collected Writings of Morton Feldman* (Cambridge, MA: Exact Change, 2000).

Feldman, Morton, 'Frank O'Hara: Lost Times and Future Hopes' [1972], in B.H. Friedman (ed.), *Give My Regards to Eighth Street: Collected Writings of Morton Feldman* (Cambridge, MA: Exact Change, 2000).

Feldman, Morton, 'Give My Regards to Eighth Street' [1971], in B.H. Friedman (ed.), *Give My Regards to Eighth Street: Collected Writings of Morton Feldman* (Cambridge, MA: Exact Change, 2000).

Feldman, Morton, 'I met Heine on the Rue Fürstenberg' [1973], in B.H. Friedman (ed.), *Give My Regards to Eighth Street: Collected Writings of Morton Feldman* (Cambridge, MA: Exact Change, 2000).

Feldman, Morton, 'I Want to Thank' [1986], in B.H. Friedman (ed.), *Give My Regards to Eighth Street: Collected Writings of Morton Feldman* (Cambridge, MA: Exact Change, 2000).

Feldman, Morton, '*Intermission 5*', in Volker Straebel (ed.), *Solo Piano Works 1950–64* (New York: Edition Peters, 2000), 3–4.

Feldman, Morton, '*Intermission 6*', in Volker Straebel (ed.), *Solo Piano Works 1950–64* (New York: Edition Peters, 2000), 5.

Feldman, Morton, '*Intersection 3*', in Volker Straebel (ed.), *Solo Piano Works 1950–64* (New York: Edition Peters, 2000).

Feldman, Morton, 'Liner Notes' [1962], in B.H. Friedman (ed.), *Give My Regards to Eighth Street: Collected Writings of Morton Feldman* (Cambridge, MA: Exact Change, 2000).

Feldman, Morton, 'More Light' [1982], in B.H. Friedman (ed.), *Give My Regards to Eighth Street: Collected Writings of Morton Feldman* (Cambridge, MA: Exact Change, 2000).

Feldman, Morton, 'Mr. Schuller's History Lesson' [1963], in B.H. Friedman (ed.), *Give My Regards to Eighth Street: Collected Writings of Morton Feldman* (Cambridge, MA: Exact Change, 2000).

Feldman, Morton, '*Piano Piece 1952*', in Volker Straebel (ed.), *Solo Piano Works 1950–64* (New York: Edition Peters, 2000), 6–7.

Feldman, Morton, 'Some Elementary Questions', in B.H. Friedman (ed.), *Give My Regards to Eighth Street: Collected Writings of Morton Feldman* (Cambridge, MA: Exact Change, 2000).

Feldman, Morton, 'Sound, Noise, Varèse, Boulez' [1958], in B.H. Friedman (ed.), *Give My Regards to Eighth Street: Collected Writings of Morton Feldman* (Cambridge, MA: Exact Change, 2000).

Feldman, Morton, 'The Anxiety of Art' [1965], in B.H. Friedman (ed.), *Give My Regards to Eighth Street: Collected Writings of Morton Feldman* (Cambridge, MA: Exact Change, 2000).

Feldman, Morton, 'The Future of Local Music' [1984], transcribed by Gerhard Westerrath in B.H. Friedman (ed.), *Give My Regards to Eighth Street: Collected Writings of Morton Feldman* (Cambridge, MA: Exact Change, 2000).

Feldman, Morton, 'Darmstadt Lecture' [1984], in Chris Villars (ed.), *Morton Feldman Says: Selected Interviews and Lectures 1964–1987* (London: Hyphen Press, 2006).

Feldman, Morton, 'Johannesburg Lecture 2: Feldman on Feldman', transcribed by Rüdiger Meyer in Chris Villars (ed.), *Morton Feldman Says: Selected Interviews and Lectures 1964–1987* (London: Hyphen Press, 2006).

Feldman, Morton, 'Toronto Lecture: April 17th 1982', transcribed by Linda Catlin Smith, in Chris Villars (ed.), *Morton Feldman Says: Selected Interviews and Lectures 1964–1987* (London: Hyphen Press, 2006).

Feldman, Morton and Iannis Xenakis, 'A Conversation on Music', *Res*, 15 (Spring 1988), 177–81. Reprinted in a German translation as, 'wie eine Ausdünnung der Musik durch Terpentin. Morton Feldman und Iannis Xenakis im Gespräch', *MusikTexte*, 52 (January 1994), 43–6.

Feldman, Morton and John Cage, *Radio Happenings: Conversations – Gespräche*, trans. Gisela Gronemeyer (Köln: MusikTexte, 1993).

Franke, Daniël, 'Analytische Contemplation des Feldmanschen Klavierstückes "For Bunita Marcus"', *Musik-Konzepte*, 48/49 (Munich: Edition Text + Kritik, 1986), 135–47.

Friedman, B.H, 'Morton Feldman: Painting Sounds', in B.H. Friedman (ed.), *Give My Regards to Eighth Street: Collected Writings of Morton Feldman* (Boston, MA: Exact Change, 2000), xi–xxx.

Gagne, Cole and Tracy Caras, 'Soundpieces Interview', in Chris Villars (ed.), *Morton Feldman Says: Selected Interviews and Lectures 1964–1987* (London: Hyphen Press, 2006).

Gareau, Philip, *La musique de Morton Feldman ou le temps en liberté* (Paris: L'Harmattan, 2006).

Gaugh, Harry F., *Franz Kline* (New York: Abbeville Press, 1985).

Gena, Peter, 'Cage and Rauschenberg: Purposeful Purposelessness meets Found Order' [1992], http://www.petergena.com/cageMCA.html.

Gilbert, Jeremy, 'Becoming-Music: The Rhizomatic Moment of Improvisation', in Ian Buchanan and Marcel Swiboda (eds), *Deleuze and Music* (Edinburgh: Edinburgh University Press, 2004).

Glahn, Denise von, 'The Conceptual Origins of *Déserts*', in Felix Meyer and Heidy Zimmermann (eds), *Edgard Varèse: Composer Sound Sculptor Visionary* (Woodbridge: The Boydell Press, 2006).

Goldstein, Louis, 'Morton Feldman and the Shape of Time', in James R. Heintze and Michael Saffle (eds), *Perspectives on American Music Since 1950* (New York: Garland, 1999).

Greenbaum, Matthew, 'The Proportions of *Density 21.5*: Wolpean Symmetries in the Music of Edgard Varese', in Austin Clarkson (ed.), *On the Music of Stefan Wolpe: Essays and Recollections* (Hillsdale, NY: Pendragon Press, 2003).

Greenberg, Clement, 'The Crisis of the Easel Picture' [1948], in *Art and Culture: Critical Essays* (Boston, MA: Beacon Press, 1965).

Greenberg, Clement, '"American-Type" Painting' [1955], in Ellen Landau (ed.), *Reading Abstract Expressionism: Context and Critique* (New Haven, CT: Yale University Press, 2005).

Gresser, Clemens, 'Earle Brown's 'Creative Ambiguity' and Ideas of Co-creatorship in Selected Works', *Contemporary Music Review*, 26/3–4 (June 2007), 377–94.

Griffiths, Dai, 'Review of Anne Shreffler, *Webern and the Lyric Impulse* (Oxford, 1994)', *Music Analysis*, 16/1 (1997), 144–54.

Griffiths, Paul, *A Concise History of Avant-Garde Music* (New York: Oxford University Press, 1978).

Griffiths, Paul, *Modern Music and After: Directions since 1945* (New York: Oxford University Press, 1995).

Griffiths, Paul, 'Morton Feldman: Shimmering Orchestral Tapestries', *New York Times* (31 January 1999).

Gronemeyer, Gisela, 'Momente von grosser Schönheit. Zu Morton Feldmans neuem Stück *Crippled Symmetry*', *MusikTexte*, 4 (April 1984), 5–9.

Guck, Marion, 'Analytical Fictions', in *Music Theory Spectrum*, 16/2 (Autumn 1994), 217–30.

Hall, Patricia and Friedemann Sallis (eds), *A Handbook to Twentieth-century Musical Sketches* (Cambridge: Cambridge University Press, 2004).

Hall, Tom, 'Notational Image, Transformation and the Grid in the Late Music of Morton Feldman', *Current Issues in Music*, 1/1 (2007), 7–24.

Hall, Tom, 'The Seduction of Graphism Alone?: The Function of Notation and Technology in the *Intersections* of Morton Feldman' (unpublished) paper presented at *Seventh International Conference on Music since 1900 and the International Conference of the Society for Music Analysis* (University of Lancaster, 2011).

Hamman, Michael, 'Three Clarinets, Cello, and Piano (1971)', in Thomas DeLio (ed.), *The Music of Morton Feldman* (Westport, CT: Greenwood Press, 1996).

Hanninen, Dora, 'Feldman, Analysis, Experience', *Twentieth-century Music*, 1/2 (2004), 225–51.

Hasty, Christopher, 'Segmentation and Process in Post-tonal music', *Music Theory Spectrum*, 3 (Spring 1981), 54–73.

Hasty, Christopher, 'Broken Sequences: Fragmentation, Abundance, Beauty', *Perspectives of New Music*, 40/2 (Summer 2002).

Hasty, Christopher, *Meter as Rhythm* (New York: Oxford University Press, 1997).

Hess, Thomas, 'Mondrian and New York Painting', in *Six Painters* (Houston, TX: University of St. Thomas, 1967).

Hirata, Catherine, *Analyzing the Music of Morton Feldman* (PhD Dissertation, Columbia University, 2003).

Hirata, Catherine, 'The Sounds of the Sounds Themselves: Analysing the Early Music of Morton Feldman', *Perspectives of New Music*, 34/1 (1996), 6–22.

Hobbs, Stuart D., *The End of the American Avant Garde* (New York: New York University Press, 1997).

Holzaepfel, John, *David Tudor and the Performance of American Experimental Music, 1950–1959* (PhD Dissertation, City University of New York, 1994).

Holzaepfel, John, 'Reminiscences of a Twentieth-century Pianist: An Interview with David Tudor', *Musical Quarterly*, 78/3 (Autumn 1994), 626–36.

Holzaepfel, John, 'Painting by Numbers: The *Intersections* of Morton Feldman and David Tudor', in Steven Johnson (ed.), *The New York Schools of Music and Visual Arts* (New York: Routledge, 2002), 159–72.

Howat, Roy, *Debussy in Proportion: A Musical Analysis* (Cambridge: Cambridge University Press, 1983).

H.T., 'Hisses, Applause for Webern Opus', *New York Times* (27 January 1950), 4–5.

Hultberg, Teddy and David Tudor, '"I smile when the sound is singing through the space": An Interview with David Tudor by Teddy Hultberg in Dusseldorf May 17–18 1988', http://davidtudor.org/Articles/hultberg.html.

Jameson, Frederic, *Postmodernism, or, The Cultural Logic of Late Capitalism* (London: Verso, 1991).

Janello, Mark, *The Edge of Intelligibility: Late Works of Morton Feldman* (PhD Dissertation, University of Michigan, 2001).

Jewitt, Clement, 'Music at the Bauhaus, 1919–1933', *Tempo*, New Series, 213 (July 2000), 5–11.

Johnson, Philip, *Mies van der Rohe* (New York: Museum of Modern Art, 1978).

Johnson, Steven, *'Rothko Chapel* and Rothko's Chapel', *Perspectives of New Music*, 32/2 (1994), 6–53.

Johnson, Steven, 'Jasper Johns and Morton Feldman: Why Patterns?', in Steven Johnson (ed.), *The New York Schools of Music and the Visual Arts* (New York: Routledge, 2002).

Johnson, Steven (ed.), *The New York Schools of Music and the Visual Arts* (New York: Routledge, 2002).

Josek, Suzanne, *The New York School. Earle Brown, John Cage, Morton Feldman, Christian Wolff* (Saarbrücken: Pfau Verlag, 1998).

Kissane, Seán (ed.), *Vertical Thoughts: Morton Feldman and the Visual Arts* (Dublin: Irish Museum of Modern Art, 2010).

Kohn, Andrew, *The Development of Stefan Wolpe's Compositional Style 1948–1963 and the Role of Other Arts, with 'Never Any Jam Today' (Original Composition)* (PhD Dissertation, University of Pittsburgh, 1995).

Krauss, Rosalind, 'Grids', *October* 9 (Summer 1979), 50–64.

Landau, Ellen, 'Abstract Expressionism: Changing Methodologies for Interpreting Meaning', in Ellen Landau (ed.), *Reading Abstract Expressionism: Context and Critique* (New Haven, CT: Yale University Press, 2005).

Lyotard, Jean-François, 'The Sign of History', in Derek Attridge, Geoffrey Bennington and Robert Young (eds), *Post-Structuralism and the Question of History* (Cambridge: Cambridge University Press, 1987).

Lyotard, Jean-François, *The Lyotard Reader*, ed. Andrew Benjamin (Oxford: Basil Blackwell, 1989).

Machlis, Joseph, *Introduction to Contemporary Music: A Guide to the Understanding of 20th Century Music* (London: J.M. Dent and Son, 1963).

Mahnkopf, Claus-Steffen (ed.), *Mythos Cage* (Hofheim: Wolke, 1999).

Massi, Richard Wood, 'Captain Cook's First Voyage: an Interview with Morton Feldman' [1987], in Chris Villars (ed.), *Morton Feldman Says: Selected Interviews and Lectures 1964–1987* (London: Hyphen Press, 2006).

Martin, Reinhold, 'Atrocities. Or, Curtain Wall as Mass Medium', *Perspecta*, 32 (2001), 66–75.

Mattis, Olivia, 'Morton Feldman: Music for the Film *Jackson Pollock* (1951)', in Felix Meyer (ed.), *Settling New Scores: Music Manuscripts from the Paul Sacher Foundation* (Mainz: Schott, 1998), 165–7.

Mattis, Olivia, 'Varèse and Dada', in James Leggio (ed.), *Music and Modern Art* (New York: Routledge, 2002), 129–62.

Meecham, Pam and Julie Sheldon, *Modern Art: A Critical Introduction*, 2nd edn (London: Routledge, 2005).

Mellers, Wilfrid, *Caliban Reborn: Renewal in Twentieth Century Music* (New York: Harper and Row, 1967).

Mellers, Wilfrid, 'Panic or Paradise: Abstract Expressionism and the Music of Morton Feldman', *Modern Painters*, 12/2 (Summer 1999), 68–73.

Metzger, Heinz-Klaus. 'Prolog: Über Jiddishkeit', in Walter Zimmermann (ed.), *Morton Feldman Essays* (Kerpen: Beginner Press, 1985).

Mies van der Rohe, Ludwig, 'Hochhausprojekt für Bahnhof Friedrichstrasse in Berlin', *Frühlicht*, 1 (1922), 122–4.

Miles, Stephen, 'Critical Musicology and the Problem of Mediation', *Notes*, 2nd Series, 53/3 (March 1997), 722–50.

Moelants, Dirk, 'What is Slow? – Timing Strategies in the Performance of Feldman's *Last Pieces*', in H. Lappalainen (ed.), *Proceedings of the VII International Symposium on Systematic and Comparative Musicology – III International Conference on Cognitive Musicology* (Jyväskylä: University of Jyväskylä, 2001), 121–8.

Mörchen, Raoul, 'Music as a Musical Process. Morton Feldmans *Palais de Mar*', *MusikTexte*, 66 (November 1996), 53–62.

Mörchen, Raoul, 'Welt ohne Namen. Die abstrakte Musik Morton Feldmans', *MusikTexte*, 66 (November 1996), 31–3.

Morgan, Robert P., *Twentieth-century Music: A History of Musical Style in Modern Europe and America* (New York: W. W. Norton, 1991).

Morgan, Stuart, 'Pie-slicing and Small Moves: Morton Feldman in Conversation with Stuart Morgan' [1977], in Chris Villars (ed.), *Morton Feldman Says: Selected Interviews and Lectures 1964–1987* (London: Hyphen Press, 2006).

Newman, Barnett, 'The Sublime is Now' [1948], in Ellen Landau (ed.), *Reading Abstract Expressionism: Context and Critique* (New Haven, CT: Yale University Press, 2005).

Nicholls, David, 'The Music of Morton Feldman [review]', *Music and Letters*, 78/4 (November 1997), 631.

Nicholls, David, 'Getting Rid of the Glue: The Music of the New York School', in Steven Johnson (ed.), *The New York Schools of Music and Visual Arts* (New York: Routledge, 2002).

O'Doherty, Brian, 'Feldman Throws a Switch between Sight and Sound', *New York Times* (2 February 1964), 11.

O'Hara, Frank, 'New Directions in Music: Morton Feldman' [1959], in B.H. Friedman (ed.), *Give My Regards to Eighth Street: Collected Writings of Morton Feldman* (Cambridge, MA: Exact Change, 2000).

Osmond-Smith, David, *Berio* (Oxford: Oxford University Press, 1991).

Paccione, Molly and Paul Paccione, 'Did Modernism Fail Morton Feldman?', *ex tempore: A Journal of Compositional and Theoretical Research in Music*, 6/1 (Spring 1990), 73–84; revised and reprinted in *Contemporary Music Forum: Proceedings of the Bowling Green State University New Music and Art Festival*, Vol. 2 (1990), 1–11.

Patterson, David, 'Cage and Beyond: An Annotated Interview with Christian Wolff', in *Perspectives of New Music*, 32/2 (Summer 1994), 54–87.

Rausch, Ulrike, *Grenzgänge: Musik und Bildende Kunst im New York der 50er Jahre* (Saarbrücken: Pfau-Verlag, 1999).

Reich, Steve, *Writings on Music, 1965–2000*, ed. Paul Hillier (Oxford: Oxford University Press, 2002).

Riegger, Wallingford, *New and Old: Twelve Pieces for Piano* (London: Boosey and Hawkes, 1944).

Roberts, Jason, 'The Great Opportunist: Don't Presume you know the Strange Truth about Henry Morton Stanley', *The Washington Post* (23 December, 2007), http://www.washingtonpost.com/wp-dyn/content/article/2007/12/21/AR2007122100158_pf.html.

Rosenberg, Harold, 'The American Action Painters' [1952], in Ellen Landau (ed.), *Reading Abstract Expressionism: Context and Critique* (New Haven, CT: Yale University Press, 2005).

Rothko, Mark, 'The Romantics Were Prompted' [1947/48], in Ellen Landau (ed.), *Reading Abstract Expressionism: Context and Critique* (New Haven, CT: Yale University Press, 2005).

Rudolph, Paul, 'To Enrich Our Architecture', *Journal of Architectural Education*, 13/1 (Spring, 1958), 9–12.

Sabbe, Herman, 'The Feldman Paradoxes: A Deconstructionist View of Musical Aesthetics', in Thomas DeLio (ed.), *The Music of Morton Feldman* (Westport, CT: Greenwood Press, 1996).

Sallis, Friedemann and Patricia Hall, 'Introduction', in Patricia Hall and Friedemann Sallis (eds), *A Handbook to Twentieth-century Musical Sketches* (Cambridge: Cambridge University Press, 2004).

Saltzman, Lisa, 'Reconsidering the Stain: On Gender, Identity, and New York School Painting', in Ellen Landau (ed.), *Reading Abstract Expressionism: Context and Critique* (New Haven, CT: Yale University Press, 2005).

Saunders, Frances Stonor, *Who Paid the Piper? The CIA and the Cultural Cold War* (London: Granta, 1999).

Saxer, Marion, *Between Categories: Studien zum Komponieren Morton Feldmans von 1951 bis 1977* (Saarbrücken: Pfau-Verlag, 1998).

Schechner, Richard, *Performance Theory* (London: Routledge, 2005). Originally published as *Essays on Performance Theory* (Ralph Pine, 1977).

Shaw, Philip, *The Sublime* (London: Routledge 2006).

Shreffler, Anne C., *Webern and the Lyric Impulse: Songs and Fragments on Poems of Georg Trakl* (Oxford: Oxford University Press, 1994).

Shreffler, Anne C., 'Ideologies of Serialism: Stravinsky's *Threni* and the Congress for Cultural Freedom', in Karol Berger and Anthony Newcomb (eds), *Music and the Aesthetics of Modernity* (Cambridge, MA: Harvard University Press, 2005).

Skempton, Howard, 'Feldman's B Flat', *KunstMusik*, 1 (Autumn 2003).

Stiles, Kristine, 'Performance', in Robert Nelson and Richard Shiff (eds), *Critical Terms for Arts Theory* (Chicago, IL: The University of Chicago Press, 2003).

Stevens, Wallace (letter, 19 December 1935), in Holly Stevens (ed.), *Letters of Wallace Stevens* (New York: A.A. Knopf, 1966).

Straebel, Volker, 'Notes on the Edition', in Volker Straebel (ed.), *Morton Feldman: Solo Piano Works 1950–64* (New York: Edition Peters, 2000), 59 [unnumbered].

Taruskin, Richard, 'Tradition and Authority', *Early Music*, 20/2 (May 1992), 311–25.

Taruskin, Richard, *Text and Act: Essays on Music and Performance* (Oxford: Oxford University Press, 1995).

Tomlinson, Gary, 'The Web of Culture: A Context for Musicology', *Nineteenth Century Music*, 7/3 (April 1984), 350–62.

Undreiner, Paul Stephen, *Pitch Structure in Morton Feldman's Compositions of 1952* (PhD Dissertation, State University of New Jersey, 2009).

Varèse, Edgard, 'The Liberation of Sound', in Elliott Schwartz and Barney Childs (eds), *Contemporary Composers On Contemporary Music* (New York: Holt, Rinehart and Winston, 1967).

Varèse, Edgard, 'New Instruments and New Music', in Elliott Schwartz and Barney Childs (eds), *Contemporary Composers on Contemporary Music* (New York: Holt, Rinehart and Winston, 1967).

Varèse, Edgard, 'Rhythm, Form, Content' [1959], in Elliott Schwartz and Barney Childs (eds), *Contemporary Composers on Contemporary Music* (New York: Holt, Rinehart and Winston, 1967).

Vigil, Ryan, 'Compositional Parameters: *Projection 4* and an Analytical Methodology for Morton Feldman's Graphic Works', *Perspectives of New Music*, 47/1 (Winter 2009), 233–67.

Villars, Chris, *Morton Feldman: Discography*, http://www.cnvill.net/mfdiscog. htm.

Walser, Robert. 'Popular Music Analysis: Ten Apothegms and Four Instances', in Allan F. Moore (ed.), *Analyzing Popular Music* (Cambridge: Cambridge University Press, 2003).

Ward, Geoff, *Statutes of Liberty: The New York School of Poets*, 2nd edn (Basingstoke: Palgrave, 2001).

Warnaby, John, 'Morton Feldman on CD', *Tempo: A Quarterly Review of Modern Music*, 207 (December 1998), 39–43.

Welsh, John, '*Projection I* (1950)', in Thomas DeLio (ed.), *The Music of Morton Feldman* (New York: Greenwood Press, 1996), 21–35.

Williams, Jan and Morton Feldman, 'An Interview with Morton Feldman' [1983], in Chris Villars (ed.), *Morton Feldman Says: Selected Interviews and Lectures 1964–1987* (London: Hyphen Press, 2006).

Wimsatt, W. and M. Beardsley, 'The Intentional Fallacy' [1954], in *The Verbal Icon: Studies in the Meaning of Poetry* (London: Methuen, 1970).

Witkin, Robert W., *Adorno on Music* (London: Routledge, 1998).

Wolff, Christian, 'The Sound Doesn't Look Back (1995): On Morton Feldman's *Piano Piece 1952*', http://www.cnvill.net/mfwolff2.htm#wolff5. Originally published in Christian Wolff, *Cues: Writings and Conversations* (Köln: MusikTexte, 1998), 370–78.

Wolpe, Stefan, 'Thinking Twice' [1959], in Elliott Schwartz and Barney Childs (eds), *Contemporary Composers on Contemporary Music* (New York: Holt, Rinehart and Winston, 1967).

Wolpe, Stefan, 'Thoughts on Pitch and Some Considerations Connected with It', Austin Clarkson (ed.), *Perspectives of New Music*, 17/2 (1979), 28–57. [Text of a talk given at Black Mountain College, August 1952.]

Wolpe, Stefan, 'On New (and not-so-new) Music in America' [Darmstadt, 1956], trans. Austin Clarkson, *Journal of Music Theory*, 28/1 (1984), 1–45.

Wolpe, Stefan, 'On Proportions' [1960], trans. Matthew Greenbaum, *Perspectives of New Music*, 34/2 (Summer 1996), 132–84. [Lecture given at Darmstadt, July 1960.]

Xenakis, Iannis and Morton Feldman. 'A Conversation on Music', *Res*, 15 (Spring 1988), 177–81. Reprinted in a German translation as, 'wie eine Ausdünnung der Musik durch Terpentin. Morton Feldman und Iannis Xenakis im Gespräch', *MusikTexte*, 52 (January 1994), 43–6.

Zimmermann, Walter, *Desert Plants: Conversations with 23 American Musicians* (Vancouver: Aesthetic Research Center Publications, 1976).

Zimmermann, Walter (ed.), *Morton Feldman Essays* (Kerpen: Beginner Press, 1985).

Zimmermann, Walter, 'Personism als das Abstrakte in der Musik von Morton Feldman', in Elisabeth Schmierer, Susanne Fontaine, Werner Grünzweig und Matthias Brzoska (eds), *Töne–Farben–Formen: über Musik und die bildenden Künste* (Laaber Verlag, *ca* 1995).

Index